U0638718

苏蕾 著

The
Pulitzer
Prizes

普利策新闻奖案例库及话语分析

长春出版社
国家一级出版社
全国百佳图书出版单位

图书在版编目(CIP)数据

普利策新闻奖案例库及话语分析 / 苏蕾著. —长春:
长春出版社,2020.11
ISBN 978-7-5445-6070-2

Ⅰ.①普… Ⅱ.①苏… Ⅲ.①新闻语言–研究 Ⅳ.
①G210

中国版本图书馆 CIP 数据核字(2020)第194340号

普利策新闻奖案例库及话语分析

著　者:苏 蕾	
责任编辑:孙振波	
封面设计:宁荣刚	

出版发行 长春出版社	总编室电话:0431-88563443
地　址:吉林省长春市建设街 1377 号	发行部电话:0431-88561180
邮　编:130061	
网　址:www.cccbs.net	
制　版:荣辉图文	
印　刷:三河市华东印刷有限公司	
经　销:新华书店	

开　本:710 毫米×1000 毫米　1/16	
字　数:210 千字	
印　张:13.25	
版　次:2020 年 11 月第 1 版	
印　次:2020 年 11 月第 1 次印刷	
定　价:48.00 元	

版权所有　盗版必究

如有印装质量问题,请与印厂联系调换　　　　　　　　　　印厂电话:13933936006

Contents

目 录

第一章　普利策及普利策新闻奖

第一节　普利策小传①

原谅我这一生不羁放纵爱自由

约瑟夫·普利策，生于 1847 年。

这一年，是清朝第八位皇帝爱新觉罗·旻宁在位的第 27 年，这位皇帝特别勤劳，然而勤政图治却鲜有作为，是他一生的写照。在他任上，古老而尊贵的中华民族签下了第一个耻辱的不平等条约——中英《南京条约》，不仅向英国赔款 2100 万银圆，而且把香港岛割了出去。大清帝国与世界的差距正越拉越大。

这一年，大发明家爱迪生诞生在美国俄亥俄州一个小镇——米兰。没有爱迪生，我们就享受不到电灯、电影和唱片。

一个月后，发明电话的贝尔也出生了。

在中国，一位传奇的武术大师黄飞鸿来到人间。

这一年，夏洛蒂和艾米莉姐妹分别出版了《简·爱》和《呼啸山庄》，两位在文学史上的杰出成就也顺带把妹妹的作品《阿格尼斯·格雷》带进圣殿。

在这些天才人物出生的时候，不会有人知道后来的他们是怎样影响着世界。他们和其他刚出生的小孩子一样，柔弱而依赖于父母的照顾。

---

① 《普利策小传》这一章内容首发在作者的公众号"白石读书"。

普利策出生在匈牙利一个叫毛科的小镇子，位于毛罗什河畔，临近罗马尼亚边境，面积是西安的 1/44，人口到现在才不到 30000 人，是西安市人口的 1/345。

毛科没有雾霾，温暖宜人，那里的洋葱很有名气。

普利策的父亲是一个谷物商人，他有犹太人的血统，但已经融入匈牙利的主体民族——马扎尔人。有一只匈牙利球队的名字就叫"神奇的马扎尔人"（Mighty Magyars）。马扎尔这个词有点像"龙的传人"之于中国，也就是匈牙利的另一个称谓。[①]

普利策的母亲是个德国人，并且是一个虔诚的罗马天主教徒。

普利策有一个弟弟，叫艾尔伯特。母亲希望他成为神职人员，但是这个目标没有实现。

普利策是在布达佩斯的私立学校完成学业的，并且老普利策为他请了家庭教师。

看起来，普利策出生在一个中产以上的家庭，这个家庭富有、保守、有宗教信仰，舍得在教育上花钱，但是隐隐感觉有一点刻板。

普利策后来靠着下棋推开新世界的一扇门，原生家庭是起了作用的，他会说德语、法语，喜欢文学和音乐，中上层社会的社交就是他可以亲眼看见的。

一个人的成功和后天的教育密不可分，然而，决定一个人从小镇毛科起步，投身到新大陆美国广阔天地的，绝不仅仅是教育一个环节，这其中天赋的个性起着更为关键的作用。正是在这一点上，完全有理由认为，1847 年诞生在小镇毛科的那个柔弱的婴孩，注定是不平凡的。

在设立普利策奖的遗嘱中，普利策说："我相信自我奋斗的人。"卓越，是普利策奖颁奖词中的一个词，这个发着光的字眼，只属于那些每年从全美所有媒体中被选拔出来的最优秀的记者。跨过这个字眼，这些获奖者留下另外两位不幸的入围者，走入了新闻的名人堂，这样的景象从 1917 年到现在已经超过了 100 年。

[①]《普利策小传》参考了 Seymour Topping 撰写的普利策传记，网址是：https://www.pulitzer.org/page/biography-joseph-pulitzer.

普利策 1847 年出生，1911 年去世。普利策奖 1917 年第一次颁发，每年的 4 月，我们翘首以待新的获奖者出现。

出生在小镇毛科的普利策，从未停止奋斗。

31 岁开创《圣路易斯邮报》

2019 年 4 月 15 下午，三点刚过，《圣路易斯邮报》的办公室，迎来了一个振奋人心的好消息。该报的托尼·曼森哲，一位资深的专栏作家，获得了 2019 年普利策新闻评论奖。

这不是《圣路易斯邮报》第一次获得普利策奖了，是第十九次。尽管如此，大家还是张大了嘴巴，激动地拥抱托尼。而托尼看起来，就像是个得了 100 分的孩子，陶醉在获奖的喜悦中。

《圣路易斯邮报》是美国中西部第五大报纸，是美国第二十六大报纸。这家报纸最初的老板正是约瑟夫·普利策。

1878 年，31 岁的约瑟夫·普利策，风华正茂，在一次公开拍卖会上，他花了 2500 美元，买下了破产的《圣路易斯快报》，此后不久，《圣路易斯邮报》诞生。

《圣路易斯邮报》使普利策跻身圣路易斯市富豪之列，这只花了两年时间。此时，邮报的发行量是 9000 份，与现在童大焕这样的公号大 V 动辄 10 万＋的阅读量相比，我们不由感叹新闻媒体经历了沧海桑田的变化。

普利策去世后，《圣路易斯邮报》由小约瑟夫·普利策接管。他是普利策最看不上的孩子，因此只得到遗产的 10％。然而普利策看走了眼，小约瑟夫可能是最靠谱的那一个，他勤勤恳恳，干得很不错。

2004 年 1 月 13 日，《圣路易斯邮报》迎来了 125 周年的纪念版，列举了在新闻事业上的辉煌成绩。其中 1939 年对圣路易斯市雾霾的报道，格外引人注意。这篇报道忠实记录了"好山好水好寂寞"的美国，大约在 20 世纪三四十年代，也就是距离现在八九十年前，被空气污染深深困扰着。邮报发布的一张照片上，一个男子在街上抽烟，大白天，路灯亮着，烟幕弥漫。目前，我国雾霾问题也是一个很大的公共问题。柴静在

2015年发布了《穹顶之下》，对雾霾问题做了反思，然而结局不同的是：邮报因报道该市的空气污染而再次获得了普利策奖。

普利策通过普利策奖的设立，给新闻界带来一种传统，一种标杆，这个传统和标杆鼓励着记者和专栏作家们为了社会的良性发展而努力。

除了新闻报道，《圣路易斯邮报》也以言论版出名，特别是言论版上的社论性漫画，那是它的强项。所以托尼·曼森哲能够获奖，也和邮报的氛围分不开。

托尼·曼森哲也是普利策喜欢的那类记者，刨根问底，锲而不舍。我们从托尼作品中报道的一个故事可以看出。有一个叫布兰森的女士，一辈子活得凄苦，年轻时嫁了人，又离了婚。她唯一的儿子有几个月交给父亲抚养，却没有给抚养费，为此，布兰森被起诉。时隔多年，陈年旧案被一个叫桑德拉的女法官翻了出来，赡养费和诉讼费加到一块要5000美金。布兰森无力支付，于是被送进监狱。到了监狱，吃吃喝喝睡睡，都要产生费用，布兰森只能眼看着账单越堆越高。布兰森从此就得上了密苏里州的流行病：犯小罪—进监狱—吃账单，不得翻身。

这样的故事，正是普利策奖所喜欢的——为穷人发声，保护社会基本价值，揭露腐败。

2005年1月31日，迈克尔·普利策把连同邮报在内的普利策公司卖给了另一个传媒大亨达文波特李家族，卖了14.6亿美元。普利策为这个家族带来了巨大财富，却无法扭转《圣路易斯邮报》易主的命运。"王师北定中原日，家祭无忘告乃翁。"然而子孙的事情，谁也做不了主。

17 岁没有小清新

资料没有显示青少年时期的普利策经历过什么，只知道他父亲去世之后，家道中落，母亲改嫁，普利策和继父的关系以及他对家庭氛围的不满，迫使他想要离开。

17岁的普利策已经长到1.87米，他看起来又高又瘦，也有些笨拙。他郁郁寡欢，并且想到了参军。他是个行动派，因此他尝试了很多，比如奥地利军队，在墨西哥服役的拿破仑外籍军团，在印度服役的英国军队，这些尝试都被断然拒绝。原因是他的视力很弱，身体单薄，并不适合当一名军人。

但是，很快好运降临。普利策在德国汉堡，遇到了美国前来欧洲招兵的人，这些人承诺只要愿意为美国联邦军队打仗，就可以获得一笔奖金。普利策签了合同，很快前往波士顿。

当招兵船快要到达波士顿港口的时候，普利策却跳了船，趁着夜色靠游泳上了岸。原因说法不一，有的资料说，是因为他知道了一个黑幕，招兵的人私吞了大部分募兵资金，这让普利策气愤不已，决定拿着奖金逃离。另一种说法是，普利策根本就是一个有着双重标准的人，他对别人要求很高，轮到自己，就可以离经叛道。总之，这个细节，是仁者见仁，智者见智。因此，有人看出了他的勇敢，有人看出了他的低道德水准。

让我们回到事实。事实是普利策作了逃兵，并且私吞了招募金，违反了契约。不论出于什么原因，事实就是事实。后来，普利策参加了林肯骑兵，这说明他还是想要当兵的，这个让他离开家庭的初衷还是实现了。所以更可能的原因是，普利策不满意先前招募军的一些做法，让他选择了身体和道义都要面临危险的跳船逃离行为。普利策一生都有及时止损的能力，这也使得他摆脱不了道义上被诟病的困境。

由于美国内战已近尾声，所以普利策并没有参加什么实质性的战斗。战争结束后，他来到了圣路易斯市。和移居美国的第一代移民必须承认"洗盘子可以获得面包"一样，年轻的普利策也放下了他欧洲富人的生活标准，甚至在骡马店做过一段时间赶骡子的工作，此外他也搬过行李，做过招待。但是，他知道这不会永远属于他，他利用一切业余时间，把自己泡在图书馆里，刻苦学习英语和法律。

在图书馆的棋室里，普利策迎来了生命中的贵人。

贵人是一家德语日报《西方邮报》的编辑，常来棋室下棋，年轻的普利策时不时几句评价，让他们注意到这个年轻人并非凡人。于是，一个录用通知就这样拿到了。这个时候的普利策只有 21 岁。

这里有必要啰嗦一下贵人，这个人就是埃米尔·普里托里乌斯。他在图书馆下棋的时候，注意到了普利策的才艺和勤奋，在他的邀请下，普利策成了一名初级记者。没有证据证明埃米尔的合伙人卡尔·舒尔茨也在棋室下棋，但是当普利策来到《西方邮报》的时候，舒尔茨给了他很多庇护。卡尔·舒尔茨在美国政治历史中扮演着非常重要的角色。他曾经在美国参议院中代表密苏里州，是美国第 13 任内政部长，短暂担任过美国驻西班牙大使，并在美国内战中担任过将军。对普利策来说，这的确是一个非常重要的政治人脉。

1867 年受聘成为记者，1872 年普利策成了《西方邮报》的股东之一，他也在圣路易斯市的新闻圈子里获得了一个名声：记者中的战斗机。事实上，这个时候，当年推他上马的贵人，已经发现离不开普利策了，普利策成为挽救他们濒临破产的救命稻草。然而到了 1873 年，普利策选择了离开，他把股份卖给了两位贵人：普里托里乌斯和舒尔茨，这再一次体现了他对新闻事业的理解绝不仅仅只是做一个刀笔吏，买进卖出这样的媒介投资行为，在他一生中发生过很多次。

中国有句古话，叫"千里马常有，而伯乐不常有"。事实上千里马也不常有。普利策这匹千里马，从此要踏上改变美国新闻界的征途。

总之，普利策靠着行动力、止损力、生存力、学习力、比 996 更狠的工作力，为自己在新大陆赢得了一个先机，也告别了自己郁郁寡欢的 17 岁。

娶了杰弗逊总统的表妹

1878 年的普利策，真可谓春风得意马蹄疾，一日看尽长安花。

这一年，他和凯特·戴维斯小姐（1853—1927）结婚，不久他又成了《圣路易斯邮报》的老板。

戴维斯小姐美丽、优雅，是华盛顿社交界的明星。这种美丽、优雅一直保持到她 1927 年去世，人们称赞她在老年时，依然是居住在法国尼斯和多维尔的那些豪门贵妇中的佼佼者。

戴维斯小姐的父亲是乔治城的一名法官，也有说是煤炭商人。她的家庭已经摆脱了早期移民者的那种艰辛，有着稳定的新教信仰生活，衣食无忧。而最引人注意的是，她是杰斐逊·戴维斯的表妹。

杰斐逊·戴维斯是美国人的英雄,今天很多地方都建有戴维斯雕像。在密西西比州、亚拉巴马州、佛罗里达州,还设有戴维斯的纪念日。他是美国内战时期,南方联盟国唯一的总统,是让林肯万分头疼的人物,战功赫赫,信念笃定。他的葬礼据说是南方最大规模的葬礼。富有戏剧色彩的是,普利策的移民费用来自联邦军队,他又为林肯骑兵效过力,如今却攀上了与联盟国总统有关的亲事。

他们的婚礼在1878年6月19日举行,地点是华盛顿。婚礼的喜讯刊登在《华盛顿邮报》上,这则消息用华丽的辞藻赞美才子佳人如何般配:"戴维斯小姐是杰斐逊·戴维斯的近亲,在最有教养和最文雅的人中间出了名,她在这些人中风度翩翩,被认为是最美丽的点缀。约瑟夫·普利策是圣路易斯市的公民,是一位凭借自己独立的演说家和作家的才能而声名显赫、名利双收的绅士。"

圣路易斯市的上流社会立刻注意到普利策已经今非昔比,他被邀请参加奢华的舞会,也会去公园里骑马。他衣着考究,举止优雅,留着精致的胡子,带着夹鼻眼镜,英语已经十分流利。

在普利策的一生中,他总是对从未经历的生活保持好奇,并努力进入这种生活,而一旦他获得了,就会寻找新的挑战。当普利策成为《圣路易斯邮报》的老板后,他立刻放弃了舞会等交际活动,从早晨到午夜,沉迷在自己可以完全说了算的报纸中,连一个细节也不会放过。很快,他就获得了新的生活体验:运作一张成功的报纸。

成为媒介大亨,让普利策摆脱了圣路易斯市贫民窟里讨生活的流浪汉生活,他依靠个人奋斗和才华,成了像盖茨比那样的新贵。与凯特的婚姻则标志着他被上流社会接纳,获得了一系列新身份标签:美国公民、新教家族的一员、杰斐逊的远方亲戚、优雅迷人生活的代表。

然而普利策向凯特隐瞒了他有犹太血统的事实,凯特知道后,陷入深深的不安中。戴维斯家族是门第森严的新教家庭,如果他们知道普利策的背景,很可能会更加认真地考虑这门亲事。普利策之所以选择隐瞒,有人说普利策害怕得不到凯特的芳心,也有人说普利策害怕反犹主义者伤害凯特,毕竟他曾在圣路易斯市最初的日子被人讥笑为"犹太人乔伊",并长着希伯来人的鼻子。

普利策和凯特的婚礼是在新教教堂举行的，普利策一生中进教堂的次数屈指可数，他的婚礼是其中的一次。普利策不允许人家在他面前谈及宗教和犹太人的事情，尽管他也雇用了不少犹太人，并且为大屠杀受难者捐款。他在犹太身份上的这种态度，后来也成为被竞争对手攻击的地方。

这对新婚夫妇，一起去欧洲度了蜜月，随后在圣路易斯市定居下来。《圣路易斯邮报》为他们带来了财富和名气。他们建设了三层楼的别墅，雇用了仆人，购置了豪华马车。

普利策和凯特一共生了七个子女。其中有两个孩子夭折，包括他最喜欢的女儿露希尔。

抑郁症和静音控：人性的分裂和真实

2016 年 1 月底，华盛顿特区的新闻博物馆展出了一幅约瑟夫·普利策的画像，这是一幅私人收藏画，主人是艾米丽·劳厄·普利策。她允许这幅画展出到 2017 年初，以庆祝普利策奖一百周年。

这幅画的作者叫约翰·辛格·萨金特（John Singer Sargent），他是 19 世纪末 20 世纪初最成功的肖像画家。1905 年，萨金特为普利策的妻子画了肖像，并得到了 5000 美元的酬劳，那时的 5000 美元相当于 2016 年的 13.8 万美元。[1]

普利策显然很满意妻子的肖像画，很快他就安排萨金特给自己也画了一幅，于是就有了本文开头提到的画像。在这幅画中，普利策左手轻搭在左侧脸颊上，右手手执马鞭，放在大腿上，神情忧郁，似乎正在思考，莫名给人一种紧张的感觉。普利策对这幅画的评价是："那就是真实的我，带着我所有的压力和痛苦。"

人们通常只能看到一个成功人士表面的光鲜亮丽，可是如果每个人拥有上帝视角，就会发现成功人士的背后也许还不如自己幸福。普利策

---

[1] Pride, Mike. '*Just as I really am, with all my strain and suffering there*': https://www.pulitzer.org/article/just-i-really-am-all-my-strain-and-suffering-there.

的另一面，是极度悲惨的。

刚到 40 岁的普利策，有一个眼球血管爆裂，这是他废寝忘食工作的结果。不久，另一只眼睛的视力也严重退化。他失明了。对于一个天天看报纸校样的人来说，这是多么大的痛苦和灾难。然而，普利策还患有多种疾病：失眠、抑郁、哮喘、消化不良。他到处寻医问药，跑遍了美国和欧洲，见了很多名医，可是没有人可以医治好他的病，他的情况越来越不好。

在今天看来，普利策身体的疾病可能是心理和认知方面的问题，过度追求完美导致了精神的高度紧张。另一方面，也有家族遗传的可能。普利策的弟弟艾尔伯特，就是那个被母亲期待做传教士的孩子，长大后也干了报纸这一行。他主持的报纸名叫《纽约晨报》。他同样患有失眠症，还患有强迫性多食症，据说他最后肥胖的程度极其可怕。他在普利策去世前两年选择了自杀。

萨金特给普利策画像时，普利策已经 58 岁，他的精神状态已经达到了病态的程度。他连别人吃面包的声音都不能忍受。在前往伦敦的船上，普利策让人在他居住的船舱上方铺了巨大的编织地毯，用来掩盖船员们的脚步声。

他的身边总是有大群人伺候着，包括秘书、看护、看门人、读书人，这些人的个子不能太低，不能让 1.87 米身高的普利策感到屈尊；他们的声音必须悦耳，让害怕噪音的普利策不至于厌烦；还要单身，这样可以没有牵挂，说走就走。高管们也并不轻松，例如《纽约世界报》伦敦分社的詹姆斯·托伊（James Tuohy）的一项工作是，保证普利策的马可以适应伦敦的新环境。

身体的病态加重了他的妄想，为了在休养的地方可以遥控下属，他发明了一种远距离控制报纸的密码。他竟然把两万个密码记住了，而下属们则使用 250 页的密码索引来破解老板的指令。此外，他还在公司员工之间推行互相监督的政策，也在竞争对手那里安排密探。

普利策的肖像画成功地捕捉到了普利策的两面性。据说在萨金特画像的过程中，碰巧看到了普利策发火的样子，这一幕改变了萨金特对他的认识。他开始看到富豪的另一面：凶狠和残忍，而不仅仅是一个仁慈的中年绅士。

在普利策身边工作了 18 年的塞茨，对这幅画的评价是："岁月的痛苦和衰老在他的脸上表现出来，混合着智慧、个性的活力和暴躁的脾气。这是约瑟夫·普利策，是时间和麻烦塑造了他。"

普利策早已不是当年那个在骡马店工作的穷小子了，也无须为了一点征兵的钱背负道德上的压力。他有私人游艇，可是游艇是经过改造的，能够屏蔽噪音；他有别墅，可是别墅的窗户要装上三层玻璃，墙壁中间要夹上隔音材料，地板下面要安装滚珠，防止仆人走动带来噪音。他病情最严重的时候，只能躺在床上，甚至不能从房间的一头走到另一头。糟糕的身体和暴躁的脾气让他无法和他人沟通，包括家人。财富和成功、地位和名气，这些普利策拼命追求的生活到手后，没有想到还带来了失明、抑郁、强迫、妄想。在他创造强大媒介帝国的同时，作为个体却承受着常人难以忍受的痛苦。什么是幸，什么又是不幸？

《世界报》和自由女神像

1878 年，普利策结婚并拥有了《圣路易斯邮报》，到 1882 年，4 年间，邮报为新婚夫妇带来了成功和财富，他们也迎来了拉尔夫、露希尔和凯瑟琳三个孩子。可以说，圣路易斯市是他们的发家之地，也让他们度过了最幸福的一段时光。

普利策在经营《圣路易斯邮报》的时候，展现了他在新闻事业上的才华。在报纸内容上，他发现揭露社会的黑暗面最能增加报纸销路；在人事上，他到全国各地寻找最有才华的人，再用高报酬让其安心工作。这样，邮报发行量从 1878 年出版时的 4020 份，爬升到 1882 年的22000 份。

然而好景不长，普利策最欣赏的编辑约翰·科克里尔（John A. Cockerill）写了一篇社论，这篇文章得罪了一个叫阿朗索·斯莱巴克（Alonzo W. Slayback）的人，结果这个人冲进科克里尔的办公室，对他威胁恐吓，科克里尔把他给打死了。普利策完全站在心爱的下属一边，多方游说，终于让陪审团相信斯莱巴克进来的时候带有武器，因此没有对科克里尔起诉。

这件事情惹恼了圣路易斯市的公众，以至于普利策一家在圣路易斯市再待下去都很尴尬，于是他们安排了一次欧洲旅行。在纽约逗留的时候，偶然得知杰·古尔德（Jay Gould）要出售一家每年亏损 4 万美元的小报《纽约世界报》，普利策抓住机会用 36 万美元买下报纸。

纽约，成了 36 岁的普利策新的新闻战场。

1883 年，普利策把《纽约世界报》改造成了《世界报》。这种改造在发行量上取得了成功。《世界报》创立三个月后，就从之前赔钱小报的 15000 份发行量跃升为 39000 份。

《世界报》在美国新闻史上扮演着极其重要的角色，它主要替民主党发声，是黄色新闻的先驱，最高发行量达到 100 万份。

《世界报》培养了美国首批从事调查报道的记者——内莉·布莱（Nellie Bly），她借凡尔纳的《八十天环游地球》为卖点，在 1889—1990 年间用 72 天环游了地球。布莱也到访了中国，她参观了中国一个麻风病人聚居地。布莱的环球报道迎来了一场新闻界的环游世界时间大比赛，最高的纪录是 36 天环游世界。

我们从布莱的故事可以看出，普利策是多么擅长策划新闻，吸引读者。他在《世界报》的创刊号上表达了他的媒介思想：为大都市服务、价廉、容量大、通俗、揭露黑暗、为市民说话。《世界报》的确实现了这些想法。这份只卖 2 分钱的报纸，成为大众化通俗报纸的翘楚。1890 年，普利策建造了当时世界上最高的办公大楼——纽约世界大厦。

今天的美国地标自由女神像也和这一时期的普利策有关。当时自由女神的底座由美国出资，但是资金一直不到位，普利策想出了一个办法，他承诺无论捐多少钱都会把每位捐款人的姓名印到报纸上，同时他还刊登捐赠者们想要说的话，例如"在这个世界上独自一人的年轻女孩"，"我们省下了去看马戏的钱"。这一下子吸引了 12 万人参加捐款，最后共捐到了 10.2 万美元，其中 80％ 的人所捐数额不到 1 美元。普利策应该是最早玩众筹玩到家的人吧。最终，自由女神像的身体从法国运到贝德罗岛，安装到了底座上。

自由女神像落成的那天，是 1886 年 10 月 28 日。那一天，纽约万人空巷，游行的队伍特意在《世界报》大楼前停留，那一天，纽约开启了纸带游行的新传统，不知道 39 岁的普利策有没有站在《世界报》大楼顶层的半圆形办公室内，欣赏着这精彩的一幕。

来自《太阳报》的攻击

普利策这辈子，受到竞争对手打击最严重的有两次，其中一次是来自《太阳报》的攻击。

《太阳报》被认为是美国第一份成功的便士报。便士报之所以叫这个名字，是因为它只卖一便士。便士报是城市化、工业化、印刷技术提高、识字率上升的产物，也是媒介商品化属性提高、新闻本位提升的产物。

说起《太阳报》，不得不提到 1897 年的一篇社论《世上有圣诞老人吗?》。这篇社论成为美国文化的一部分，后来歌手特里斯·里特（Tex Ritter）用歌曲讲述了其背后的故事。此外，被引用最多的一句话"狗咬人不是新闻，人咬狗才是新闻"是出于《太阳报》的编辑。纪录片这个术语的起源，也来自《太阳报》。1952 年的一部电影《最后期限：美国》大体上是以 1950 年停刊的《太阳报》为原型的。《纽约时报》办公大楼叫"太阳大厦"，有纪念《太阳报》的含义。

攻击普利策的是《太阳报》的查尔斯·安德森·丹纳。他 1868 年成为《太阳报》的编辑和股东之一，直到 1897 年去世都控制着这家报纸。丹纳的办报信条和普利策有相似点，都推崇简单、准确。但是，当普利策在纽约开始他的媒介帝国建设时，触碰到了《太阳报》的发行量。于是丹纳开始在社论中攻击普利策。

丹纳利用纽约犹太人比较多的事实，攻击普利策是"犹太人的叛徒"。由于普利策在自己犹太人身份的问题上始终有一种不愿直接面对和承认的态度，这一次，丹纳可算抓住了他的要害。丹纳还煽动犹太人团结起来，看清普利策的本质，在选举上不要投票给普利策支持的检察长候选人。

丹纳的攻击要是放在一个心胸开阔的人身上，不过是一时之痛。可是普利策，他把选举人的失败看成是自己的失败，他把丹纳的攻击看成是真正砸在心窝子里的伤痛。他被丹纳击碎了。他的身体忠实地反映出这种伤害，很快他的眼睛就看不见了，也陷入抑郁症的折磨中。普利策被迫离开了他的家庭，躲去休养，也再也没有回到《世界报》的编辑室去。

不过普利策内心虽然被困锁，他的意志力没有倒下。他开始在《太阳报》不起眼的楼房对面建造《世界报》的办公大楼，目的就是让丹纳眼睁睁地看着新大楼是如何一层一层地超过他的大楼。丹纳气得要死，却无可奈何。

我们有的时候很难理解这些大佬们的行为，一方面功成名就，不可一世；另一方面，却幼稚得可笑。然而这就是人性，如果身在其中，感受对手那种赤裸裸的叫嚣和挑衅，我们不一定有大佬们做得好。

大楼盖好了，普利策却病得参加不了落成仪式，他的医生认为普利策已经无药可治。但是普利策在这种生不如死的情况下，依然坚持了二十年。这就是选择的问题。普利策这一生在很多事情上都表现出自私、贪婪、狡猾、残忍，唯独在对新闻的执着追求和对困难永不妥协的选择上，表现出鹰一样的气质。

赫斯特和黄色新闻

1895 年，普利策迎来了第二个与他掀起"新闻大战"的人：威廉·兰道夫·赫斯特。

赫斯特比普利策小 16 岁，差不多在普利策坐船来到美国时，赫斯特才出生。赫斯特是含着金汤匙出生的。他父亲曾有一家《旧金山考察家报》的报纸，这让赫斯特从小对办报纸产生兴趣。1885 年，赫斯特进入哈佛学院，他无心学业，状况不断，却乐得研究报纸的煽情手法，还特意去普利策的《世界报》当过见习记者。此后，他担任家族报纸《旧金山考察家报》的主编，只用了不到 5 年的时间，就让这家亏损的报纸每年获利 30 万—50 万美元。《公民凯恩》就是根据赫斯特的生平事迹改编的。

从原生家庭看，赫斯特比普利策幸运，他是家中独子，母亲全力支持他，甚至为了他进军纽约报业市场，卖掉了自家的铜矿。从性格上讲，赫斯特也有一种钻研报纸的痴劲，可是这种痴里有一种玩耍的意味。他给报社员工提了六字方针：发惊、发愕、发呆，而普利策的则是：准确、简练、准确。

如果说普利策第一位敌人丹纳，是个不肯认输的固执老头，那么这一次，他碰到的对手，则是一个比他年轻，比他资源更多，比他更轻松的人。

1895年，赫斯特带着卖铜矿的家产和《考察家报》的利润，来到纽约，买下了普利策的弟弟艾尔伯特的《晨报》，改名《纽约日报》，很快便用极致的煽情主义运作这家报纸。

赫斯特和普利策之间最夸张的是人才大战，双方不惜用高报酬挖人、抢人。以至于那些人刚被赫斯特挖过去，第二天又再被普利策抢回去，一天后再被赫斯特以更高的报酬挖走，堪称奇谈。

《世界报》这边有个漫画家叫奥特考尔特，是著名漫画形象"黄孩子"的创作者。这个人在人才大战中被赫斯特挖去，普利策于是又雇了一个叫乔治·卢克斯的漫画家，让他继续黄孩子专栏的创作。于是两家报纸开始了黄孩子大战，一时间，纽约到处都是黄孩子的形象。"黄色新闻"的叫法由此产生，即用来描述赫斯特和普利策新闻大战中的那种浮夸、煽情的新闻作风。

赫斯特和普利策的这种竞争甚至改变了西班牙的命运。为了争夺纽约的读者，双方发布了对西班牙宣战的社论，派记者从古巴传来假消息，在此煽动下，美西战争开始。赫斯特本人更是塑造了一位古巴起义领袖的外甥女为英雄，然后再派记者将其营救出来，举行盛大仪式欢迎她，并接受美国总统接见。这一切都是为了提高报纸销量，也让人见识到媒介权力失衡后可以操纵社会到什么程度。

普利策在这场新闻竞争中彻底迷失，他背弃了新闻信条，被赫斯特追赶着逐渐变了形。这段历史成为他的污点，也是他矛盾性格在社会责任和商业利润选择中的一次失败。而赫斯特被《美国新闻史》的作者评价为把美国新闻事业的水准拉到最低的人。

普利策后来对"黄色新闻大战"中的表现深感懊悔，而赫斯特不思悔改，继续他的煽情作风。黄色新闻之风也刮到了世界的其他地方。例如西安都市报时期，最风光的《华商报》实际上就是运用的黄色新闻的操作办法。奉行黄色新闻的报纸推行一种下沉到工薪阶层的内容生产方式，用煽情、肤浅的内容迎合快餐口味。黄色新闻之风一旦刮起，报纸在发行量上很快就有很好的回报。例如，当年香港的《苹果日报》就击败很多严肃报纸。而现在的抖音等新媒体，在一定程度上，也是有此味道。

无论怎样，黄色新闻是客观存在的，正如严肃新闻也是客观存在的一样，走什么样的新闻路线依赖于媒介所有者的选择。默多克旗下既有走黄色路线的《太阳报》，也有走严肃路线的《泰晤士报》，而前者的发行量是后者的 9 倍，据说默多克用前者的利润养后者。这个 9 倍的差距，让我们看到，媒介始终要面对大众化市场，那么黄色新闻路线也就总是会有人采纳。但是，有社会责任的媒介人会做出更智慧的选择。

哥伦比亚大学新闻学院

普利策生命中的最后几年，一改他唯利是图的商人形象，干了几件惠及他人的好事，这也帮助他的历史形象多了更多的解读层次。

美西战争的残酷敲醒了普利策，他开始改变《世界报》的风格，更加严肃，更加代表民主党的声音。他继续着他在 1883 年《世界报》创刊号上所倡导的：在这个日益发展的大都市里，这样的报纸才有用——便宜、明白易懂、容量巨大、具有民主精神。忠于人民的事业，不做有钱有势者的奴仆，记录欺诈和黑暗，鞭挞罪恶和弊端，全心全意为人民服务。

他的一些主张，例如对奢侈品、高收入、垄断、有特权的公司征税，改革公务员制度，惩办贪官污吏，惩办贿选等，都已写入法律。由于他的介入，保险业的混乱被遏制，并置于严厉的监管之下。1909 年，《世界报》揭露了美国政府的欺诈行为，遭到政府的起诉，上至总统，下到金融大佬，一起抵制普利策，普利策坚持斗争，终于迎来起诉被驳回，捍卫了新闻自由。

普利策没有上过大学，17 岁就在外打拼，所以他一直渴望年轻人可以获得大学的教育。他计划在大学里建立一所新闻学院。他在遗嘱中写道:我对新闻业的进步和提高深感兴趣,因为我毕生从事这一职业,我认为这是一种崇高的职业,其对人们的思想和道德的影响是无与伦比的。而其他职业都有严格的训练和教育,新闻记者也应该如此。

普利策向哥伦比亚大学捐赠了 200 万美元,起初大学拒绝了这笔捐赠,但在普利策的努力下,1912 年,哥伦比亚大学新闻学院建立。今天,哥大新闻学院是全世界最顶尖的新闻学院之一,他的教学以提供务实的、扎实的、严格的新闻训练出名,秉承了普利策那种"实践出真知"的风格。在哥伦比亚大学,普利策的新闻信条被镌刻在墙上:

> 国家与媒介上下沉浮,同生共死。一个公正有为的新闻媒体,它培养常识和智慧,知道如何做是正确的,并有勇气去做。它保存了公众的德行,没有这些,政府就会沦为骗局和笑柄。一个玩世不恭、唯利是图、煽风点火的媒体迟早会制造出一个和它一样卑鄙的民族。塑造国家的权力掌握在未来几代记者的手里。

每年,普利策奖颁奖的那一天,都是在哥伦比亚大学进行,每一个获奖人都要从哥伦比亚大学校长那里接过奖状。

普利策还拿出了 25 万美元,建立普利策奖学金,这就是百年普利策奖的启动资金。

逝世和百年普利策奖

1911 年 10 月 29 日,在南卡罗来纳州查尔斯顿港,停泊着一艘长 82 米的游艇,这艘游艇名叫"自由号"。

游艇的主人 17 岁来到北美大陆,怀揣着梦想,他崇尚自我奋斗,热爱自由,他从一个不会说英语的打工仔到成为这个国家的顶级富豪,开创两家大报,为新闻自由与总统作对,为发行量与对手死磕,为国家法律的完善不断在报纸上出谋划策,为自由女神像发起 12 万人的捐款,为步入工业化的美国和崛起的工薪阶层提供廉价的报纸和发声的渠道。他为这些付出了身体的代价,40 岁就失去视力,为噪音所控,不得安息。

这个人就是约瑟夫·普利策，一个成就美国梦的匈牙利移民，一个载入美国史册的新闻人。

死亡带走了运气、财富、名气和一切，也带来了解脱和安息。据说，普利策临死前的最后一句话是："轻柔，相当轻柔。"当时他的秘书正在为他朗读法国国王路易十一的故事，当故事接近尾声的时候，普利策留下这句话就去世了。普利策狂飙突进的一生以这句话作为句号。"原谅我一生放纵不羁爱自由"，这句话中的"原谅"是想获得人们对普利策那些不道德行为的宽恕，但这终究是后来者的一种意愿，不知道倔强的普利策愿不愿意与自己和解，与世界和解？

1917 年，在普利策离开这个世界 6 年后，他所倡导并设立的普利策奖终于颁发了第一次奖励。

作为普利策奖的总设计师，普利策在 1904 年就提出了设想，他的设想奠定了普利策奖的基础。

第一，非卓越不奖励。普利策是一个很苛刻的人，他对新闻报道一向严苛，对文学艺术有很高的品位，只对上一年表现最优异的人和作品奖励。此外，普利策奖坚持保密评审原则，排斥有关奖励的辩论，捍卫自己的决定，保持评奖的独立性。因此就出现过有些获奖的小说，并不会进入畅销书之列，这显示了与大众品味的距离。

第二，确立奖励的大类。一是奖励新闻界；二是奖励文学、戏剧界（普利策本人很喜欢和别人讨论文艺问题）；三是奖励教育界，谁写了优秀的新闻论文或者谁的学业优秀就受到奖励。除了第三项，前两项都保留了下来。

第三，赋予管理委员会自由裁定权。普利策这个人心思细腻，他在设计的时候也考虑到时代在发展、社会在变化，于是就授权管理委员会可以终止或暂停某些奖励，如果上一年入选的作品水平不够，委员会也有权不颁奖。这样一来，普利策奖具备了与时俱进的能力，在线上新闻和数据新闻到来时，做出了积极的呼应。

2016 年 4 月 18 日，普利策奖迎来了第 100 届颁奖礼。这届大奖最引人注目的就是美联社四位女记者一起获得了公共服务奖。报道使得两千名奴隶渔民获得了自由，并引发了行业改革。普利策奖走过百年，见证了美国新闻业的变化，但不变的是依然在改写着底层人民的命运，尽管一次只是解救一个小群体，但是有星火，就有希望。①

第二节　普利策新闻奖

普利策奖评奖制度及奖项

美国东部时间 2019 年 4 月 15 日下午 3 点，在哥伦比亚大学新闻学院著名的普利策厅，普利策奖历史上第一位女性主席、也是第一位黑人主席达娜·坎迪（Dana Canedy）宣布了 2019 年的获奖者名单。

达娜·坎迪作为评委会主席，是资深的新闻从业者，也是传奇的时代女性。2001 年她凭借着《美国的种族如何生活》获得了普利策国家报道奖。达娜在《纽约时报》工作了二十年，做过财经记者和国内突发新闻编辑。同时，她也是深情的母亲和妻子，达娜的畅销书《乔丹日志》，记录了她和她死于伊拉克战争的丈夫一起写给儿子的话。

在普利策官网公布的 2019 颁奖视频里，普利策奖的精神被片头的名人话语再次点亮。达娜在颁奖视频中说："普利策奖之所以重要，是因为新闻是美国民主的基石。普利策奖所有奖项告诉我们这个国家是谁，从哪里来，到哪里去。""普利策奖之所以富有名望，是因为我们从不降低标准。"

普利策奖，根据美国报业巨头约瑟夫·普利策（Joseph Pulitzer）的遗愿设立，1917 年第一次颁奖的普利策奖，在新闻单元只设立了两个奖项，报道奖和社论奖。二十世纪七八十年代普利策奖已发展成为美国新闻界的一项最高荣誉。普利策新闻奖获奖名录几乎囊括了 20 世纪以来美国最杰出的记者和最优秀的新闻作品。2020 年，普利策新闻奖的奖项已经扩展到 15 项，其中音频报道奖是新设立的奖项，获奖者是《美国生活》的工作人员、《洛杉矶时报》的莫莉·奥图尔（Molly O'Toole）、自由职业者艾米丽·格林（Emily Green）。他们的作品名叫《人群》，这则

---

① 道格拉斯·贝茨.美国普利策奖金内幕[M].贾宗谊,译.北京:新华出版社,1993.

新闻富有启发性，也很贴心，阐明了特朗普政府的"留在墨西哥"政策对个人的影响。

普利策奖从设立之初就是一个旨在鼓励美国的奖，从1917年开始就大致分为两个部分，一个是新闻界奖，一个是书籍、音乐和戏剧奖。截至2020年，新闻奖单元已经发展出15个奖项，艺术单元则有7个奖项。新闻界的获奖者可以是任何国籍，但是获奖文本必须在美国媒体发表。创作界获得者必须是美国公民，唯一例外是历史奖，只要是关于美国历史的书都可获奖，作者不必是美国人。

每年1月份，大约有1100个新闻参赛作品被提交到普利策官网。参赛的作品必须是上一年发表在美国报纸、杂志和新闻网站上的作品，遵循最高的新闻准则。提交的作品篇数是有限制的，比如公共服务和摄影类别可以提交20篇文章，其他类目限制为10篇。2月下旬，70多名编辑、出版家、作家和教育工作者在一起评判15个新闻奖项中的所有作品，他们会在各个奖项中提名三个作品。这些作品最终被提交给普利策奖董事会，董事会成员再决定获奖者名单。自从普利策奖设立以来，就保持了和美国新闻业的发展同步，比如在1942年设立了摄影奖，2020年设立了音频报道奖。新闻单元的奖项，都设定了清晰的评奖标准。我们以2019年的获奖作品为例，对每个奖项进行解释。

1. 公共服务奖（PUBLIC SERVICE）

获奖者可以是报纸或新闻网站，可以利用故事、社论、卡通、照片、图形、视频、数据库、多媒体、互动演示或其他视觉材料，向公众提供优异的公共服务。公共服务奖的奖品除了奖金外还有一个奖牌。2019年的获奖者是《南佛罗里达太阳哨兵报》，该报揭露了学校和执法官员在校园致命枪击案前后的失职行为。

2. 突发新闻报道（BREAKING NEWS REPORTING）

获奖作品要以尽可能快的速度捕获事件发生时的准确信息，并在后续报道中提供更多的背景信息。2019年的获奖媒体是《匹兹堡报》，他们对匹兹堡生命之树犹太教堂大屠杀后续的报道赢得了该奖。突发新闻是最能反映新闻业准则的报道类型，本书特别以2010年《西雅图时报》的获奖作品《克莱蒙斯枪杀四警察》为话语分析的案例，对突发新闻的文本特征进行分析研究。

3. 调查报道奖（INVESTIGATIVE REPORTING）

奖励在调查报道中杰出的作品，报道可以使用任何可用的新闻工具。2019 年的获奖者是《洛杉矶时报》，该报是得奖专业户，他们对南加州大学的妇科医生在过去 25 年侵犯百名年轻女性的报道，使其再次赢得了 2019 年的普利策奖。

4. 解释性报道奖（EXPLANATORY REPORTING）

获奖报道阐明了一个重要而复杂的主题，并使用任何可用的新闻工具展示了对该主题的精通，作品拥有清晰的文字和清晰的呈现。得奖专业户《纽约时报》拿到了 2019 年的解释性报道奖，该报对特朗普的财务状况进行了 18 个月的调查，揭穿了他自称白手起家的说法，对其商业帝国的逃税问题也有涉及。由于该报道，特朗普和《纽约时报》结怨，特朗普甚至在推特三连骂《纽约时报》。

5. 地方报道奖（LOCAL REPORTING）

这个奖是鼓励那些使用任何可用的新闻工具来报道当地重大新闻的报道，这些报道需要展示创意和社区专业知识。当地报道奖是 2006 年由原来的专题报道奖（BEAT REPORTING）改来的。2019 年的获奖媒体是《倡导者》，报道了歧视性定罪制度。

6. 国家报道奖（NATIONAL REPORTING）

该奖奖励那些对国家新闻报道做出贡献的记者。2019 年的获奖媒体是《华尔街日报》，它调查了特朗普竞选期间向两名声称与他有染的妇女提供报酬，引发刑事调查和要求弹劾的事件。

7. 国际报道奖（INTERNATIONAL REPORTING）

该奖项奖励国际事务报道方面的杰出事例。美联社在 2019 年夺得此奖，它揭露了也门战争的残酷行为，包括盗窃食品援助、部署儿童兵和对囚犯的酷刑。少见的是，2019 年的国际报道奖是"双黄蛋"，路透社也获此殊荣。路透社揭露了军队和佛教村民从缅甸驱逐和谋杀穆斯林的事件，记者因为勇敢的报道被关进了监狱。

8. 特稿写作奖（FEATURE WRITING）

该奖项奖励写作质量高，具有原创性和简洁性的报道。2019 年的获奖媒体是 ProPublica，他们报道了萨尔瓦多移民在纽约长岛的生活，被联邦政府对国际犯罪团伙 MS-13 的拙劣镇压所摧毁。

9. 评论奖（COMMENTARY）

评论奖奖励在媒体上开设专栏发表的评论。2019 年的获奖媒体是《圣路易斯邮报》，获奖作者是托尼·曼森哲（Tony Messenger）。托尼的专栏充满了勇气，揭露了密苏里州的不公正行为，被指控犯有轻罪的穷人，支付不起罚款或被送进监狱。本书特别选取托尼的十篇获奖文本，进行了叙事和消息来源的话语分析。

10. 批评奖（CRITICISM）

批评奖是一个偏文艺范的时评奖。2019 年的获奖者是《华盛顿邮报》的卡洛斯·洛萨达（Carlos Lozada）。卡洛斯的书评对涉及政府和美国经验的大量书籍进行了敏锐的评论和细致的分析。

11. 社论奖（EDITORIAL WRITING）

社论奖看重作品是否具有清晰的风格，是否具有道德目的，是否具有合理的推理能力，以及在作家认为正确的方向上是否有能力影响公众舆论。《纽约时报》2019 年再次砸中大奖，获奖者是布伦特·斯台普斯（Brent Staples）。他的作品描述了美国历史上一个两极分化的时刻，以非凡的道德清晰度描绘了美国的种族断层线。

12. 社论性漫画奖（EDITORIAL CARTOONING）

社论性漫画奖开设于 1922 年，奖励独创性又具有时事批评性质的漫画作品，平面或者动画作品都可以参评。达林·贝尔（Darrin Bell）作为自由职业者获奖，其作品运用美丽而大胆的社论漫画批评了政府。

13. 突发新闻摄影奖（BREAKING NEWS PHOTOGRAPHY）

这个奖 1942 年设立，1968 年分为两个奖项，一个是现场新闻摄影奖，一个是特写摄影奖。参赛作品可以是黑白，也可以是彩色照片。路透社摄影人员获得 2019 年的大奖，作品运用生动而令人震撼的画面，讲述了移民从中美洲和南美洲前往美国时的紧迫性、绝望和悲伤。

14. 特写摄影奖（FEATURE PHOTOGRAPHY）

《华盛顿邮报》的洛伦佐·图格诺利（Lorenzo Tugnoli）获得 2019 年的特写摄影奖。照片讲述了也门的悲惨饥荒。

第二章　话语分析要略

第一节　批判取向、主体意识与话语理性

现代人类社会物欲的驰骋带来了人欲边界的扩张，也使我们常常置身于理性失控的恶果之中。在伦理、政治、经济、文化等各领域发作的长效危机与突发性危机冲淡了物质进步带给我们的幸福感与超越感，显露出人性的愚蠢与软弱，也使我们如同置身于艾略特笔下的"荒原"，在精神的迷茫与困惑中迫切寻找着"意义"的意义。大众媒介是现代人日常化的信息供给选择，也是危机发作时积极的信息传播解释载体。然而正是大众媒介再一次使人们经历了意义的剥蚀，"拟态环境"仿佛是加之于大众媒介的一个魔咒，其效力似乎在危机传播中表现得更甚。地沟油、毒奶粉、汶川地震、动车出轨、富士康跳楼、小悦悦惨死……危机魔怪般地变化着形态一次次侵袭我们，而大众媒介的话语则变得冗长而不得要领，夹杂着成见和噱头。看起来"最有生命力的假设是新闻和真相并非同一回事"① 并不是过分悲观的判断。但即便是做出该假设的李普曼也没有彻底放弃大众媒介。本节也尝试从《合法化危机》入手，探索危机传播话语实践的救治之道。

20 世纪 70 年代初，哈贝马斯针对晚期资本主义出现的各类危机进行了哲学阐释，《合法化危机》由此诞生。《合法化危机》力图从整体上对当代资本主义社会由于制度结构的内在矛盾所引发的经济危机、合理性

---

① 沃尔特·李普曼.公众舆论[M].阎克文,江红,译.上海:上海世纪出版集团,2006:256.

危机、合法化危机、动机危机进行批判性分析，揭示了危机与认同性的关系，为我们从理性层面认识危机提供了理论大纲。然而在危机传播领域却少见对该理论资源的借鉴。很可能是《合法化危机》采取了宏观、系统、批判的理论导向，对危机的讨论也往往在制度和社会层面进行，而结论又在价值层面产生，因此限制了通常只在事实和个案层面进行研究的危机传播的借鉴和运用。这种限制情况的形成正反映了危机传播的狭隘性，危机传播绝不仅仅等同于危机信息公关或危机信息管理，我们所缺乏的正是从价值层面理解危机的发生，看到危机爆发所牵涉的系统整合与社会整合的混乱，洞见社会成员达成共识的困难。总之，我们迫切需要用一种批判的视角重新理解危机传播。

"他者的审视"：批判取向

"危机是什么"，对这一问题的回答制约着危机传播话语实践。我们习惯于将危机理解为非正常状态或者处境异常的事件，只从事实层面理解危机，因此危机传播也就相应地只注重危机事实信息地传播了。这样一来，危机作为事实存在的客观性就被过分强调，由此引发了我们对信息控制问题的关注。认识到这一点，就不难解释为什么危机传播受到了公关思维和管理思维的深刻影响，因为公关学和管理学都比较重视控制问题。在相当长的时间里，危机传播实际上简化为危机应对、处置、善后环节中的信息控制实践，而危机传播效果也局限在减少或规避危机事件的破坏性上。有些学者已经注意到了这种现象，胡百精提出的"危机—事件"模式[①]就包含着对这种现象的批判。

事实与价值的二分法早在休谟时期就已经谈到，"是"与"不是"绝不能推导出"应该"或"不应该"。仅仅从事实层面理解危机，只突出危机的实然面，也就忽视了危机的应然面。在《合法化危机》中，哈贝马斯一开始就抛弃了这种简单的思维，他强调危机从个体层面理解首先是一个挑战旧有规范的问题，而从社会层面理解则是系统整合的持续失调

---

①胡百精.中国危机管理报告[M].北京：中国人民大学出版社,2007:3.

所导致的，哈贝马斯的这两种回答都落脚于对危机的价值内涵的判断上。

史安斌曾经对西方危机传播研究的三种路径，即管理取向、修辞取向和批判取向进行介绍。[①] 这使我们认识到，危机传播也应该有更加多元的视角。以危机管理、危机公关为目的的可称之为管理型的危机传播；以反映和疏导舆论为目的的可称之为话语型的危机传播；以价值反思和建构为目的的可称为批判型的危机传播。与管理型和话语型不同，批判型的危机传播不单单从事实层面理解危机，不简单将危机理解为事件的爆发、发展、解决的线性过程，而是认识到危机的发生有着复杂的原因，应该从历史和社会层面对危机做出更全面深刻的思考，然后将这种思考通过话语实践的方式在危机传播中表现出来。简单而言，我们不仅要让公众看到危机的全貌，更重要的是让他们看到人与社会。正如史安斌所言："'管理取向'和'修辞取向'关注的是危机传播如何做到'入眼、入耳'，而'批判取向'则关注的是危机传播如何做到'入脑、入心'。"[②] 总之，批判取向的危机传播更重视挖掘并呈现危机包含的价值异化问题，这正是胡百精所倡导的"危机—价值"模式。

无论危机有着怎样残酷和多样的外表，本质上无非是人与社会欲望、恐惧、善恶选择的呈现过程，倡导一种批判性的危机传播，即并非不假思索地在话语实践中接受那些占有统治地位的观念，而是通过危机信息的分享对人的行动与社会关系进行反思，整合生产领域与公共领域内的关系，促使人们去认识危机现象背后的本质因素，了解危机产生的真正社会基础，建立社会发展和人的发展的新动力。总之批判的危机传播其根本目的是帮助人们认识危机本身及危机对人类社会的真正影响。

"只有主体才会被卷入危机"：人的危机

作为西方马克思主义的继承者，哈贝马斯坚持了马克思哲学中将人

---

①史安斌.危机传播研究的"西方范式"及其在中国语境下的"本土化"问题[J].国际新闻界,2008(6):24.

②史安斌.危机传播研究的"西方范式"及其在中国语境下的"本土化"问题[J].国际新闻界,2008(6):26.

的主体性和解放性联系在一起的实践哲学特征。"只有主体才会被卷入危机"①，哈贝马斯通过挖掘危机作为医学用语和戏剧用语的前科学概念得出了这一结论。这为危机传播的主体意识建构找到了坚实的理论依据。

"危机"最初是一个医学用语，表示主体因疾病暂时失去了维持身体健康的能力，并对自己的处境深刻体认。主体既有肉体的客观反映，也有精神的卷入，这两方面的共存显示出主体的危机处境。哈贝马斯恢复了危机与人的关系，使我们意识到危机不仅仅是对主体自然生命的威胁，更重要的是对主体精神生命和社会生命的考验。理解危机根本上还要落到人的问题上进行思考，既要看到客观力量对人的身体功能的破坏，也要看到危机中人的价值冲突问题。危机还展示了人与一种客观力量的狭路相逢。这一点当危机概念被运用到戏剧中时表现得十分突出。陷入危机的戏剧主角被命运的神秘力量所控制，一步步走进命运布置好的陷阱。如果戏剧主角不能建立一种新的自我认同来破除命运之魔咒，那么等待他的就是被命运吞噬。危机在这个意义上的使用，展示了它本身携带着的规范性价值，危机使人遭遇困境，也提供了摆脱困境实现蜕变的机遇。

受到专业主义的影响，危机传播注重在危机信息供给时采取及时性和客观性的判断标准，这本无可厚非，但人们却发现由此产生的传播效果并不总是理想。例如在"富士康跳楼事件"中，媒体的"第N跳"报道造成了新闻"围观"现象，助长了社会"看客"心态，可以说十分客观但又异常冷血，究其原因就是丧失了对人的关怀。"危机不能脱离陷于危机中的人的内心体会"②，危机传播不应该简单关注生命和财产损失数字，或者处置善后是否符合程序，残酷的数字与理性的分析替代不了对人的价值危机的思考。2010年《西雅图时报》获得了普利策奖，获奖报道的内容是关于一名杀人犯的逃亡与追捕故事。《西雅图时报》没有采取肤浅的话语逻辑，而是将精神心理分析与社会环境相互作用机制结合起来，将罪犯的成长背景、人际关系、行为心理、犯罪记录以及造成他屡

---

①尤尔根·哈贝马斯.合法化危机[M].刘北成，曹卫东，译.上海：上海世纪出版集团，2009：5.

②尤尔根·哈贝马斯.合法化危机[M].刘北成，曹卫东，译.上海：上海世纪出版集团，2009：3.

次减刑保释的司法制度漏洞进行了全面深刻的分析。《西雅图时报》的做法值得危机传播借鉴。

危机概念所包含的规范性意义，则使我们认识到危机传播在对客观力量警醒的同时，应积极寻找并建构促成主体摆脱困境获得解放的精神力量，实现对人的救赎。每个社会的力量归根结底是一种精神的力量，我们只有认识到这一点，才能真正实现进步。危机传播主要是通过话语实践的方式实现观念的解放，观念的解放将促成其他方面的解放。首先是促成个体命运的解放。危机中的个体在遭遇客观力量巨大威胁时，也获得了通过自由选择来重新塑造自我的机会，危机传播应提供这种促使主体做出正确选择的价值根据和情感鼓励。近年来，社会发生的伦理性危机往往暴露出个体人性的堕落，或者是精神性疾病酿成灾难，或者是功利教育结出苦果，都反映了传统社会的某些不合理性，这是社会病痛的根源。如果我们可以从"南坪杀童案"中窥见精神疾病的危险，就应当在危机传播中增强对个体精神健康的关怀；如果我们在"药家鑫案"中发现功利教育的毒害，就应当在危机传播中陈述功利主义对人性的剥蚀。其次是促成群体命运的革新。危机传播应关心人类的前景和共同命运，将对人性沉沦与人之出路的思考放置进去。危机传播不能只是通过危机的解决来加强对这个世界的维护和美化，而是要彻底暴露危机中隐含着的对人的肉体和精神的双重压抑，使人们意识到现实世界异化的严重程度，帮助人们超越异化的现实和日常生活经验，使人的感官和精神重新得到解放，寻找理想的生存处境。

"人对意义有一种渴求"：话语理性

哈贝马斯对危机概念的第三重阐释是在社会科学层面进行的，在这个意义上，危机表现为"系统整合的持续失调"，即"当社会系统结构所能容许解决问题的可能性低于该系统继续生存所必需的限度时，就会产生危机"[1]。导致此类危机的根本原因是社会成员的认同性出了问题，正如哈

---

[1] 尤尔根·哈贝马斯.合法化危机[M].刘北成,曹卫东,译.上海:上海世纪出版集团,2009:4.

贝马斯所说，"社会成员感受到他们的社会认同受到威胁时才会说产生了危机"①。我国社会已进入社会危机多发、频发阶段，这些危机从表面上看是经济生产的活跃引发的一系列系统因素失衡所导致的结果，但根本上却反映了经济理性主导下的社会成员利益分配不平衡与意义失落导致的共识达成的困难。以食品安全危机为例，"毒奶粉"、"瘦肉精"猪肉、"地沟油"、"苏丹红"等的出现显示了食品行业生产的无序与混乱，而无序和混乱的根本原因还在于伦理意义的缺失与规范认同危机。而近年来发生的一些由交通事故引发的舆论危机中，则更容易看到社会成员的意见分歧，"杭州飙车事件""我爸是李刚""药家鑫案""动车出轨""小悦悦案"之所以掀起如此剧烈的公众舆论风暴，其力量来自社会利益群体与非利益群体的认同撕裂与对立。

哈贝马斯始终相信"实践问题是可以用话语来处理的"②。面对社会认同性危机，哈贝马斯主张应通过建立"理想的话语环境"③ 加以解决，而建立的方法则是普遍遵守话语交往的有效性，即真实性、规范性与真诚性。哈贝马斯相信在社会实践中追求话语交往的有效性，将保证民主、公正、合理程序的建立。由此，在危机传播话语实践中也存在着对话语交往有效性的实践问题，即话语理性的建立。诉诸话语理性，体现了主体对正义和善的道德选择，也体现了主体对意义的追求。"人对意义有一种渴求"，危机传播从其根本上来说应该成为积极价值的输出实践。

真实性强调通过真实的陈述使主体与客观世界发生关系。在危机传播中，话语实践以真实性为标准，不仅符合新闻伦理，同时将使受众分享到有效的信息。追求话语的真实性将抵制话语空洞的出现。危机的异常性、突发性、灾害性常常导致媒介信息供给不能有效满足公众的信息需求，于是变相的信息补充如成见、流言、谣言等畸变信息得以更快速地传播。畸变信息呈现出信息源的含混性、陈述的重复性、判断的虚假性，其根源在

---

① 尤尔根·哈贝马斯.合法化危机[M].刘北成,曹卫东,译.上海:上海世纪出版集团,2009:5.

② 尤尔根·哈贝马斯.合法化危机[M].刘北成,曹卫东,译.上海:上海世纪出版集团,2009:129.

③ 章国峰.关于一个公正世界的"乌托邦"构想——解读哈贝马斯《交往行为理论》[M].济南:山东人民出版社,2001:151.

于意义的亏缺。真实性法则的捍卫将使危机传播成为"精确的检验"①，将不断地提供可供话语交往产生意义的有效资源，也将扭转大众的怀疑取向，使他们对政府处理危机与媒介报道危机的过程投入更多的大众忠诚。

规范性注重通过合乎规范的言说使主体与社会世界建立关系。这里的规范包括积淀在语言中的文化传统，以及话语交往双方都能够认可的背景信息、道德原则。危机传播的目的是实现与受众的话语交往，而话语交往的目的是能够促进话语共识的产生。规范性的话语实践本身体现了理论探讨和论证的结果，同时也是为了保证危机传播与社会一致的规范符合，从而能够产生积极的传播效果。

真诚性强调通过真诚性的言说使主体与主观世界发生关系。在危机传播中，传者应诉诸能够使受众产生信任的意向选择，在公开性与公益性的标准下通过话语构建传受双方的良好互动关系。危机导致社会进入应急状态，公众生命存在的坐标发生了动摇，公开性的危机传播将使公众获得更多的安全确认。公益性则要求危机传播与日常的话语实践分别出来，更加注重话语实践的伦理取向，尤其避免媒介收视率等经济理性思维对危机传播的影响。

危机传播诉诸话语理性的根本目的是达成共识。此共识不是绝对真理，不具有完美和普适性，而是通过主体参与在对话过程中不断被论证并最终被参与者确认的意见，因此它是平等对话、自由发言、民主协商的结果。只有在危机传播中诉诸真实性、规范性与真诚性的话语理性，才能瓦解话语权力，才能使那些因话语权力关系所产生的交往阻隔消除，实现危机传播的本真性，化解社会压抑，促成人格养成，完善个体生命，呈现出美好而有生命力的媒介形象。

第二节　新闻格局、主题与言语反应

"生活在文明的火山上。"②《风险社会》的作者德国学者乌尔里希·

------

①沃尔特·李普曼.公众舆论[M].阎克文,江红,译.上海:上海世纪出版集团,2006:257.

②乌尔里希·贝克.风险社会[M].何博闻,译.南京:译林出版社,2004:13.

贝克这样描述我们的时代。一次危机发作就如同一次火山爆发，将使社会系统遭遇危机状态。然而现代社会所遭遇的最大危机则是危机的屡见不鲜。掌握着一部分界定、报道、化解危机权力的大众媒介，何以能够真正有效地减弱危机频发带给人类身心的恐惧和苦痛？况且由于媒介传播，发生在地理上特定区域的危机，往往产生了超越地理界限的影响力，这种影响既可能警示公众化解矛盾，也可能扩大焦虑强化积弊。心理学家告诉我们，减少恐惧和苦痛最有效的方法是直面事实，探究真相。如此，奉真实、客观为圭臬的大众媒介则应在再现危机的媒介话语生成中建构出作为社会真实有效补充的媒介真实，以此抚慰人心、安顿民生。如何建构这种真实，如何使这种真实的建构更加有效，路径的选择并不是单一的，我们习惯了从传播政策、媒介组织、意识形态等宏观角度的探索，本文将从媒介话语生成的微观角度，从新闻文本的结构和组织的策略出发，探索格局、主题、言语反应如何弥补理性裂痕，培植一种解读当下，放眼未来的风险意识。

第一时间之外：完构新闻格局

新闻格局，英语对应为 News Schemata，也被翻译成新闻图式。新闻格局由心理学及认知科学领域一个重要概念"格局"发展而来，荷兰语言学家冯·戴伊克将其引入了新闻领域，他指出："我确信，不论从实证角度，还是从理论角度，我们都有理由假设新闻格局是存在的。这种新闻格局可以描写为话语的抽象结构特征，或者再现，或者社会共知的、使用新闻的规则、规范和意识形态系统。"[①]

新闻格局是新闻话语的常规范式。所谓常规范式，是指新闻格局应当是新闻话语生成的基础性和共识性策略。但与这个常规范式相比，"第一时间"报道显然更加受到媒介追捧。这与人们对于危机特征的认识层次有关。詹姆斯·鲁宾逊和查尔斯·赫尔曼对危机有一个经典界定，给出了构成危机的三个要素，即目标受到威胁、做出反应的时间有限、意

---

①冯·戴伊克.话语 心理 社会[M].施旭,冯冰,编译.北京:中华书局,1993:69.

外性。① 这种偏重危机特征的认识显示出人们对于危机客观力量的关注，营造了要求媒介迅速介入报道的压力环境，也产生了通过信息的及时补充来减少危机破坏性的媒介认同，因此"第一时间"报道被确立为危机话语的黄金法则。刘建明肯定"第一时间"报道既是信息发布提速的代名词，也是遏止不良信息扩散的监控力。②

"第一时间"报道作为话语生成规则在危机话语中获得普遍认同自有显著的价值和意义，但是面对成因复杂、性质敏感的危机事件，媒介的话语生成规则不能只局限于此。哈贝马斯指出从客观角度看危机表现出"系统整合的持续失调"③，而从主观方面看危机与主体的卷入密切相连，也就是说只有社会成员感受到社会认同的威胁才能够说危机产生，由此他特别强调通过话语行为及其体现出来的逻辑性来重建社会认同从而真正地解决危机，即"能够用来讨论'社会矛盾'的逻辑应该是一种在言语行为和其他行为中所使用的命题内容的逻辑"④。单纯地强调"第一时间"报道只是增加了传递危机客观力量的时效性，在有些情况下一味求快却适得其反，从"富士康跳楼事件"就可看出媒介在缺乏完整新闻格局意识下迅速地捕捉跳楼信息，极易造成社会恐慌并被指责诱发"维特效应"，不仅不利于媒介形象建构，甚至扩散了危机的破坏力量。因此，在"第一时间"报道之外，面对危机，媒介应确立的首要话语规则应是：通过完整的新闻格局的建构，培植一种整合性的话语认知系统，从而恢复受到损伤的社会心理机制，建构产生新的社会认同的话语系统。

新闻格局具体通过标题、导语、故事、背景、情节、结果、反应、评价等范畴的演绎构建话语系统。对新闻话语长期关注的学者曾庆香认为一则新闻里包括所有的范畴才能够体现新闻格局的完构性。⑤ 完整的新闻格局所构建的话语系统提供了完整的认知结构，有助于全面认识危机

---

① 王忠武,吴焕文.试析社会危机的类型与成因[J].河南社会科学,2003(9):34.

② 邹建华.突发事件舆论引导策略[M].北京:中共中央党校出版社,2009:13.

③ 尤尔根·哈贝马斯.合法化危机[M].刘北成,曹卫东,译.上海:上海世纪出版集团,2009:4.

④ 尤尔根·哈贝马斯.合法化危机[M].刘北成,曹卫东,译.上海:上海世纪出版集团,2009:30.

⑤ 曾庆香.新闻叙事学[M].北京:中国广播电视出版社,2005:47.

事件。获得 2010 年普利策突发新闻奖的《西雅图时报》在这一方面给了我们重要启示。克莱蒙斯袭警事件发生在早上 8 点 15 分，《西雅图时报》在 10 点 14 分就发出了第一份电子邮件警报，并于当天在线发布了 36 则信息。《西雅图时报》的报道很好地诠释了"第一时间"报道，然而普利策评委会则更看重"全面的报道"。新闻格局的完构性比新闻格局本身更加重要。因为在实际中，比较容易实践的范畴是标题、导语、故事，而其他范畴则需要记者投入更多的精力。危机情境的特殊性增加了调查采访的难度，也容易造成对一些范畴的忽视。偏颇的新闻格局实践导致了媒介对危机的成因等复杂命题很难进行深入的探讨，而对一些肤浅的表象问题却花费了太多的笔墨，由此造成一种"媒介狂欢"现象，而受到破坏的认知结构重建的程度是极其有限的。完构的新闻格局重视各范畴的实践，主张在新闻话语中充分实现各范畴的平衡。

在危机话语生成中强调新闻格局的完构性，其目的不在于维持一种表象的平衡，而根本目的在于达成共识。哈贝马斯强调危机本身蕴含着规范的意义，因为攻克危机需要提供新的价值认同来化解危机造成的认同性困难。罗森塔尔也提出危机严重威胁了社会结构和社会基本价值规范。对共识的强烈诉求也符合新闻格局定义的后半段，新闻格局一方面是话语的抽象结构特征，另一方面也是约定俗成的新闻规范系统的再现。因此新闻格局及其完构性在媒介危机话语生成中的重要价值在于：面对复杂多变的危机，积极主动地将一种整合型的认知结构和客观公正的共识认同在话语生成中最终体现出来。台湾学者翁秀琪谈到新闻报道是一种媒介真实，新闻事件是一种社会真实，媒介总是通过符号或者话语来反映社会真实。但是社会真实的"正身"无法验明，人们感知到的社会真实，是某种建构的结果。媒介真实正是一种重要的建构方式。[①] 媒介的建构要产生真实性、客观性的效果，在主、客观的辩证关系中尽其可能地反映社会真实的多个面向是一条有效的话语规则，这正是新闻格局的意义。

---

① 翁秀琪等.新闻与社会真实建构——大众媒体、官方消息来源与社会运动的三角关系[M].台北：三民书局，2004:2.

天灾抑或人祸？主题的设置与实现

主题是话语表达中最重要、最中心的内容，是话语的纲要和主旨。费尔克拉夫认为"所谓话语，是对主题或者目标的谈论方式"[①]，从这个得到普遍认可的定义也可以看出，主题对于话语的重要性恰恰在于那种统摄和引领的作用。主题的确立实际上对事实的选择做出了区分，媒介迅速地将危机重组为话语。这样做的好处正如麦库姆斯所言，媒介对主题的精确实际上向受众传达了一种强烈的信息，告诉他们当前最重要的是什么。[②]

面对危机事件，媒介话语的主题设置首先要考虑的是危机的性质。危机按照成因可以分为天灾与人祸两大类，天灾由自然力导致，人祸为社会性灾难。2012年普利策突发新闻获奖作品报道的正是"飓风袭城"这一自然灾害事件。而2010年的作品则反映了克莱蒙斯袭警这一社会性危机事件。在媒介话语生成中应充分考虑到危机性质的不同，根据不同的危机类型对主题的选择做出不同的安排。《塔斯卡卢萨新闻》对待飓风袭城事件，设置了两个报道主题，其一为"飓风来袭"，其二为"我们不能掩埋我们自己"。"飓风来袭"的主题突出了自然灾害类危机所通常强调的报道重点，即客观全面地报道灾难事实。"我们不能掩埋我们自己"则充分显示了主题立意之特点，表达了灾难新闻常见的价值诉求——人文关怀。而《西雅图时报》则围绕一个主题，即屡屡犯罪的危险分子克莱蒙斯何以能够获得保释进而造成袭警恐怖事件？由此可见，对待自然性危机，媒介话语重在呈现；而社会性危机，媒介话语重在反思。

主题并不是铁板一块，而是一种层级结构组织，具有等级特征，有中心主题和次级主题的区分。中心主题往往通过标题表达或者暗示，如《塔斯卡卢萨新闻》连续两天以黑色粗体通栏标题"飓风来袭"和"我们不能掩埋我们自己"表达主题。但也存在中心主题未在标题中明确出现

①诺曼·费尔克拉夫.话语与社会变迁[M].殷晓蓉,译.北京:华夏出版社,2003:1.
②马克斯韦尔·麦库姆斯.议程设置:大众媒介与舆论[M].郭镇之,徐培喜,译.北京:北京大学出版社,2008:19.

的情况，如《西雅图时报》就克莱蒙斯事件共发表了 10 组报道，分别是《4 警员被杀，追捕开始》《嫌犯一星期前从皮尔斯郡监狱释放》《霍克比长期执行减刑》《资深警员也都是父母》《追捕加剧》《克莱蒙斯被巡警击毙》《有说服力的恳求帮助克莱蒙斯赢得宽容》《五月四天里上演的悲剧》《叔叔：他一切为了钱，突然，一切又为了上帝》《电子邮件："希望他未获保释"》，从这些偏重叙述的标题中看不出中心主题。根据冯·戴伊克的研究，对待这种情况可以通过删略原则即删略掉不影响内容理解的信息得到中心主题。

次级主题的结构有两种，纵向结构与平行结构。纵向结构体现主题结构的归属性，低级主题可以归属到高级主题中去。平行结构体现主题结构的组装性，通过平行关系的主题组装丰富更高级别的主题。对于人祸，主题实现偏向纵向结构，探知危机成因。在"克莱蒙斯袭警案"中，次级主题沿着两个方向纵向发展，第一方向追问是谁放走了克莱蒙斯？前任州长霍克比先生过度仁慈的减刑计划，阿肯色州与华盛顿州关于克莱蒙斯保释令的签署纠纷，显然这些次级主题讨论的是系统失控问题；第二个方向则从人道关怀的角度深刻反思了惨剧发生的人性危机以及危害，如克莱蒙斯的性格成因、精神危机，被杀警察的家庭关系等等。而天灾往往由不可知力导致，因此主题的实现偏向横向结构。危机的发生发展反映了时间的连续性，归属性和组装性的结构发展打破了这种连续性，前者从话语深度上，后者从话语广度上使媒介话语不按照时间顺序编码，打破了事件的固有框架，组合了能够直接揭示最高主题的事件。

主题的实现最终要落实到具体的句子和情节，这体现了新闻话语的详述原则。详述原则的具体运用表现在：按照从重要到次重要，从高层次到低层次的顺序详细表达信息；对事件的发生时间、地点、性质、情势、影响以及参与者的相关信息详细表达；循环陈述主旨性信息；通过言语反应对记者不便言及的主观感受、评价性信息进行反映。

谁在生成话语？言语反应及其功能

谁在生成话语？新闻话语与其他话语类型的区别在于，它的生成者是多元的。媒介是新闻话语的授权单位，记者是新闻话语的组装者，此外各种新闻来源作为新闻事件的实际介入或者参与者也成为新闻话语的生成者。新闻来源所拥有的新闻信息经过记者的引用，转化成了新闻话语。言语反应便是这类被记者转化的引语信息中的一部分。言语反应英语对应为 verbal reaction，也可翻译为口头反应，指的是新闻事件直接参与者的引语信息，它是后果范畴一个重要的下属范畴。危机所引起的灾难性后果，其影响范围与程度往往超过了危机本身。因此在媒介危机话语生成中后果范畴的建构就显得非常重要。后果范畴属于新闻格局的一个组成部分，表示由主要新闻事件引起的主客观结果。危机必然带来如环境破坏、财产损失、系统毁损等客观问题，同时也会带来心理失衡、情绪恐慌、共识困惑等主观问题。后果范畴除了记者通过观察、调查行为进行自建构外，还会通过言语反应的方式进行他者视角的呈现。

言语反应一般会顺应新闻价值规律，重视权威人物和权威机构的话语信息。曾庆香指出"新闻中真正的说话者是各种各样的处于当权者位置的新闻来源"[①]，权威人物和权威机构掌握着话语权力，引用他们的信息将增加新闻话语的权威性和说服力。特别是在危机报道中，由于权威人物和权威机构往往比普通公众对危机的情况掌握得更加全面，重视他们的言语反应将帮助记者呈现危机成因，揭示敏感问题，并对事件做出客观、可靠的评价。报道"克莱蒙斯案"的记者深知挖掘袭警案背后隐藏的美国司法制度漏洞绝不能依靠记者主观的论断，通过权威人物和机构的言语反应来说明危机成因将更能说服公众。在《电子邮件："希望他未获保释"》一文中，针对造成克莱蒙斯获得保释继而犯下重罪的责任究竟应该由阿肯色州还是由华盛顿州承担这一问题，记者分别采集了皮尔斯郡发言人，华盛顿惩教部的管理人员，阿肯色的保释官员，阿肯色社区矫正部的主管官员，皮尔斯郡的检察官和探员，华盛顿惩教部的秘书等 12 位人物的言语反应。透过这些言语反应，读者知道阿肯色州与华盛顿州在罪犯保释问题上矛盾激烈，用皮尔斯郡长发言人的话说，"如果这两个州相邻一场边境战争将会爆发"，读者也感受到双方公务往来中的硝

①曾庆香.新闻叙事学[M].北京:中国广播电视出版社,2005:18.

烟弥漫，从中理清了事件的来龙去脉。例如华盛顿惩教部的管理人员"希望嫌犯未获得保释"，但阿肯色的保释官员却回复说授权华盛顿不对克莱蒙斯施行保释的授权令取消了，"将重新考虑案件"。又如阿肯色发布文件说授权令被召回是由主管官员与罪犯的妻子和母亲交谈决定的。但记者通过调查发现克莱蒙斯的妈妈去世很多年了，这意味着所谓的谈话是不可能进行的。总之，通过言语反应的互相比对参照，读者终于知道正是美国州际之间公务行为中存在的矛盾导致了克莱蒙斯能够在身负多项罪名的情况下大步迈出监狱，使一个危险分子终于酿成更大的惨剧。

　　危机的爆发、处置、善后都受到公众的高度关注，其后果和影响也具有扩散性，如果能在媒介危机话语生成中重视亲历事件的普通公众的言语反应，将增加媒介话语的沟通效果。媒介、记者或者权威人物都只承担着一部分话语建构的责任。媒介是社会公器，新闻话语也应当呈现公众意见，反映公众的话语建构能力。《生还者爬出碎石堆》是 2012 年普利策突发新闻奖作品"飓风袭城"报道中的一篇文章，该文经翻译后约有 4000 字，而言语反应的字数约在 1400 字。经统计，有 16 位亲历飓风的生还者接受了采访，他们职业、性别、年龄以及在危机中的遭遇大有不同，但身份都是普通的市民，例如有牛排馆的经理，刚刚经历卡特里娜飓风的司机，努力保护顾客的饭店女雇员，躲进浴缸的母亲，照顾卧病在床父亲的女儿，坚信爱邻如己到处寻找伤者的基督徒，共同经历灾难的同居室友，飓风来袭时依然熟睡的 73 岁老人。这些普通公众描述了他们在飓风中的经历，他们的描述在危机报道中变成了鲜活的、清晰的危机场面，带给读者直观真实的危机感受。例如："树根被拔起、每个物体都在移动、房子被破坏了、我们不得不从窗户爬出去"；"我转过来看见一团黑云落下并贴近地面、其余两个烟柱在旁边出现"；"我看见它正朝我们而来并且将碎片吐到各处"；"我姐夫喊着并说它直接冲着我们而来，我往窗外看去发现它在湖上盘旋"；"它特别巨大，你所能看见的只是黑色的，而它将树木和物品吐到各处"。这些言语反应从不同的角度对飓风来临时的可怕景象进行了描述，呈现危机的客观现象和细节，使读者获得直观真实的体验。

　　从宏观角度看，言语反应对主题的实现也有重要的价值。言语反应会配合主题，呈现相应的言语信息，在克莱蒙斯案报道中针对罪犯犯罪历史和背景、被害警员为人父母的事实、美国司法制度漏洞等主题，言语反应也相应地呈现了罪犯家人、被害警员亲友、司法人员和政府公务人员的言语信息。其次言语反应还会反复出现，以此来强化主题，如针对霍克比对克莱蒙斯的减刑，其中一组言语反应，"那将是阿肯色和华盛顿两州刑事司法体系一连串失误的结果"被三次引用，暗示主题。

第三章　普利策突发新闻奖案例库及话语分析

第一节　消息来源的选择和设置

　　新闻是建构媒介信任和社会信任的重要文本。但是，消息来源数量的缺乏和设置的不合理是导致我国新闻文本无法满足公众对新闻真实性要求的重要原因。所谓消息来源，就是新闻话语中出现的提供消息的源头。新闻以事实影响舆论，消息来源则是新闻建构事实的最基本和最重要的要素，缺乏消息来源的新闻将会产生扭曲的舆论。这就是为什么在类似彭宇案的新闻被多次报道后，社会的舆论并没有进步，反而陷入"扶还是不扶"这样无意义的讨论循环中。

　　为了规范我国新闻话语文本的生产，本文将选取新闻领域公认的普利策新闻奖典范文本作品进行研究，特别针对消息来源进行内容分析并探讨新闻话语的规范化如何产生，而重视消息来源的新闻文本又如何在议题的开掘上更加自由和多元，从而避免社会舆论僵化的存在。

　　我们的样本来自《西雅图时报》，样本报道了轰动美国的案件即一名男子枪杀四名警察的新闻，文本总字数为 7867 个英文字符，文本量 7 个，各样本标题如下：文本 1《嫌犯一星期前离开皮尔斯县监狱》（*Person of interest let out of Pierce County jail one week ago*）；文本 2《霍克比长期执行减刑》（*Huckabee commuted long term*）；文本 3《资深警官也是为人父母》（*Veteran officers were parents , too*）；文本 4《有说服力的上诉帮助克莱蒙斯获得宽大处理》（*Persuasive appeal helped Clemmons* win clemency）；文本 5《悲剧在五月的四天中酿成》（*Four days in May set stage for tragedy*）；文本 6《叔叔：他满嘴都是钱，但突然又全是上帝》（*Uncle*：'*He was all about money—suddenly, he was all about God*'）；文本 7《电子邮件：希望他未获保释》（*E-mail*：'*Hopefully he will not get out on bail*'）①

消息来源的数量显露新闻的良心

电影《头版内幕》的主演老卡尔在片中呈现最多的镜头就是不厌其烦地给消息来源打电话，必要时还需要亲自去接触消息来源。他是《纽约时报》的资深记者，他对待消息来源的态度也是这个获得过普利策奖最多的媒体对待严肃新闻的基本态度。事实上，只要在文本中数一数消息来源的数量，就可以判断出新闻是如何生产出来的。当然也有消息来源造假的情况，老卡尔的同事朱迪斯在报道伊拉克是否拥有大规模杀伤性武器新闻中就亲自承认自己有 6 到 7 个消息来源是错误的。但即便如此，她其实还是变相承认了消息来源数量的重要意义。②

遗憾的是，重视消息来源的数量在我国的新闻报道中并没有成为新闻生产的普遍话语范例。"药家鑫事件"是轰动我国的一个新闻，我们将药案中的一篇关键新闻《大学生撞人后捅死伤者续：据称其父母欲登门道歉》③ 与克莱蒙斯案同样字数的文章作对比，一千字左右的消息源"药案"文本有 11 个，而"克莱蒙斯案"文本有 26 个。并且"药案"文本的消息来源还存在具名不清晰、不完整、重复性高的特点。"药案"和"克莱蒙斯案"同为骇人听闻的新闻事件，新闻媒体本该通过对事件周密的调查来重塑一种社会认知状态，但因缺乏消息来源"药案"报道最终流入平庸，而《西雅图时报》的"克莱蒙斯案"却塑造了一个新闻改变认知的经典。

---

①文本来源 https://www. pulitzer. org/winners/staff-71。
②信息来源 *Page One*：*Inside The New York Times*。
③文本见《华商报》，载于 2010 年 12 月 1 日。

【文本示例】

Person of interest let out of Pierce County jail one week ago①

（全文 1104 个英文单词）

1. Maurice Clemmons，the 37-year-old man wanted for questioning in the killing of four Lakewood police officers Sunday morning，has a long criminal record punctuated by violence，erratic behavior and concerns about his mental health.

2. His criminal history includes at least five felony convictions in Arkansas and at least eight felony charges in Washington. That record also stands out for the number of times Clemmons has been released from custody despite questions about the danger he posed.

3. Mike Huckabee，while governor of Arkansas，granted clemency to Clemmons nine years ago，commuting his lengthy prison sentence over the protests of prosecutors. "This is the day I've been dreading for a long time," ①Larry Jegley，prosecuting attorney for Arkansas' Pulaski County，（拉里·杰格里，阿肯色州普拉斯基县的检察官）said Sunday night when informed that Clemmons was being sought in connection with the killings.

4. In Pierce County，Clemmons had been in jail for the past several months on a child-rape charge that carries a possible life sentence. He was released from custody one week ago，even though he was staring at eight felony charges in all.

5. Clemmons posted $15,000 with a Chehalis company called Jail Sucks Bail Bonds. The bondsman，in turn，put up $150,000，securing Clemmons' release on the child rape charge.

6. Clemmons moved to Washington from Arkansas in 2004. He was placed under the supervision of the Washington State Department of Corrections (DOC) for an Arkansas conviction，according to ②a department spokesman（部门发言人）. The DOC classified him as "high

———————————

①本示例截取自"克莱蒙斯枪杀四警察案"中的文本 2，请参考案例库部分。

risk to reoffend. " His supervision was to continue until October 2015，③the spokesman said（发言人，和 2 消息来源是同一个）.

7. He lives in Tacoma, where he has run a landscaping and power-washing business out of his house. He is married，but the relationship has been tumultuous，with accounts of his unpredictable behavior leading to at least two run-ins with police this year.

8. Clemmons punched a Pierce County sheriff's deputy in the face during one confrontation，according to④ court records（法庭记录，这是一个证明材料消息来源）. Two days later，at his home，Clemmons allegedly gathered his wife and two younger relatives at around 3 or 4 a. m. and had them all undress. He told them that families need to "be naked for at least five minutes on Sunday," ⑤a Pierce County sheriff's report says（皮尔斯县警长的报告）.

9. The family complied because they were afraid of Clemmons and thought he was growing increasingly erratic. "The whole time Clemmons kept saying things like trust him，the world is going to end soon，and that he was Jesus," ⑥ the report（报告，和 5 为同一个） says.

10. The Sheriff's Office interviewed Clemmons' sister in May. She said her brother "is not in his right mind and did not know how he could react when contacted by law enforcement," ⑦a sheriff's report says.（这里容易把消息源误判成克莱蒙斯的妹妹，但实际上是报告） "She stated that he was saying that the Secret Service was coming to get him because he had written a letter to the president. …She suspects he is having a mental breakdown," ⑧the report says（报告，这个消息来源如果不读上下文，会被误判为一个匿名消息来源。消息来源判断的难度在于必须建立在熟悉文本的基础上，如果不熟悉文本，那么很多都会误判。这在研究方法上的启示是，定量分析中对消息来源的统计必须考虑熟读文本的重要性。而克莱蒙斯文本的话语分析是建立在多年熟读经验上的）.

11. ⑨Family members（家庭成员，这个消息来源根据上下文也应该是从报告中体现的。） also told deputies that Clemmons claimed he could

fly and expected President Obama to visit to "confirm that he is Messiah in the flesh."

12. While investigating this incident, deputies uncovered evidence that led to a charge that he had raped and molested a 12-year-old relative.

13. Prosecutors in Pierce County recently had requested a mental evaluation for Clemmons at Western State Hospital. On Nov. 6, a judge concluded that Clemmons was competent to stand trial on the child-rape and other felony charges, according to ⑩ court records（法庭记录）.

Long record in Arkansas

14. News accounts out of Arkansas offer a confusing—and, at times, conflicting description of Clemmons' criminal history and prison time.

15. In 1990, Clemmons, then 18, was sentenced in Arkansas to 60 years in prison for burglary and theft, according to a ⑪news account（新闻报道）. Responding to a circuit judge's comment that Clemmons had broken his mother's heart, ⑫Clemmons（克莱蒙斯）said, "I have broken my own heart."

16. Newspaper stories describe a series of disturbing incidents involving Clemmons while he was being tried in Arkansas on various charges. During one trial, he was shackled in leg irons and seated next to a uniformed officer. The presiding judge ordered the extra security because he felt Clemmons had threatened him, ⑬court records（法庭记录）show. At other times, Clemmons was accused of hiding a piece of metal in his sock to use as a weapon; throwing a lock at a bailiff, and instead hitting his mother; and reaching for a guard's pistol while being transported to court.

17. Clemmons was arrested when he was a junior in high school for having a. 25-caliber pistol on school property. Clemmons told police that he brought the gun to school because he had been "beaten by dopers" and that if they got after him again, he had "something for them," ⑭a newspaper account（新闻报道）says. When Clemmons received

the 60-year sentence, he already was serving 48 years on five felony convictions and facing up to 95 more years on charges of robbery, theft and possessing a handgun on school property, according to ⑮a story in the Arkansas Democrat-Gazette （阿肯色州民主党公报上的一个故事）.

18. Clemmons served 11 years before being released. Then-Governor Huckabee, who was a Republican presidential candidate in 2008, commuted Clemmons' sentence. He cited Clemmons' young age, at the time the crimes were committed, according to ⑯news reports （新闻报道）.

Huckabee's statement

19. Huckabee, in ⑰ a statement （声明） released Sunday night, said Clemmons' release from prison had been reviewed and approved by the Arkansas parole board. If Clemmons is found responsible for the police killings, "it will be the result of a series of failures in the criminal-justice system in both Arkansas and Washington State," ⑱Huckabee （霍克比） said.

20. After his release, Clemmons remained on parole. Soon after, he found trouble again. In March 2001, he was accused of violating his parole by committing aggravated robbery and theft, according to ⑲ the Democrat-Gazette （民主党公报）.

21. He was returned to prison on a parole violation. But in what appears to have been a mistake, he wasn't served with the arrest warrants until leaving prison three years later.

22. Clemmons' attorney argued that the charges should be dismissed because too much time had passed. Prosecutors thereafter dropped the charges. On Sunday night, ⑳Clemmons' sister Latanya （克莱蒙斯的妹妹拉塔尼亚） said her brother is the second-oldest of six children.

23. "Maurice is a fairly good person, good heart," ㉑she （克莱蒙斯的妹妹拉塔尼亚） said. He came over to her place on Thanksgiving for about an hour and seemed fine, ㉒she （克莱蒙斯的妹妹拉塔尼亚） said.

24. ㉓Clemmons' maternal grandmother，Lela Clemmons，82，of Marianna，Ark.（克莱蒙斯的外祖母，住在玛丽安娜方舟地区的 82 岁的里拉·克莱蒙斯。具名清晰度高）said her grandson lived in Marianna when he was young. Later，as a teen，he lived in Little Rock，㉔another relative（另一个亲戚，匿名消息来源）said.

25. "All I know is he is a pretty good guy," ㉕Maurice Clemmons' grandmother（莫里斯·克莱蒙斯的祖母）said. ㉖She（莫里斯·克莱蒙斯的祖母）said both of his parents died years ago. His mother worked in a nursing home，and his father was a factory worker.

序号	消息来源	翻译
①	Larry Jegley，prosecuting attorney for Arkansas' Pulaski County	拉里·杰格里，阿肯色州普拉斯基县的检察官
②	a department spokesman	部门发言人
③	the spokesman	发言人，和 2 消息来源是同一个
④	court records	法庭记录
⑤	a Pierce County sheriff's report	皮尔斯县警长的报告
⑥	the report	报告，和 5 为同一个
⑦	a sheriff's report says	报告
⑧	the report	报告
⑨	Family members	家庭成员
⑩	court records	法庭记录
⑪	news account	新闻报道
⑫	Clemmons	克莱蒙斯
⑬	court records	法庭记录
⑭	a newspaper account	新闻报道
⑮	a story in the Arkansas Democrat-Gazette	阿肯色州民主党公报上的一个故事
⑯	news reports	新闻报道
⑰	a statement	声明
⑱	Huckabee	霍克比
⑲	the Democrat-Gazette	民主党公报
⑳	Clemmons' sister Latanya	克莱蒙斯的妹妹拉塔尼亚

续　表

序号	消息来源	翻　译
㉑	she	克莱蒙斯的妹妹拉塔尼亚
㉒	she	克莱蒙斯的妹妹拉塔尼亚
㉓	Clemmons' maternal grandmother, Lela Clemmons，82，of Marianna，Ark.	克莱蒙斯的外祖母，住在玛丽安娜方舟地区的 82 岁的里拉·克莱蒙斯。
㉔	another relative	另一个亲戚，匿名消息来源
㉕	Maurice Clemmons' grandmother	莫里斯·克莱蒙斯的祖母
㉖	She	莫里斯·克莱蒙斯的祖母

【文本示例】

大学生撞人后捅死伤者续：据称其父母欲登门道歉

大三学生药家鑫驾私家车撞伤女行人，不是及时抢救反而持刀连刺受害者张萌（化名）8 刀，夺走其生命。

（全文字数 1081 个字）

①据死者张萌的丈夫王辉称，昨日他接了一个陌生电话，一女子在电话里称，药家鑫的父母欲登门致歉。但截至昨晚 11 时，嫌疑人父母仍未出现。

昨晚，记者来到王辉的住处，西安市长安区兴隆乡宫子村的一座平房。客厅及卧室都凌乱不堪，唯一整洁的，是张萌的灵堂，和墙壁上张贴着的、依然嫣红的双喜字。王辉坐在沙发上，翻看着夫妻俩的结婚照，一边是墙上的双喜字，一边是灵堂上的烛火。

②据王辉说，昨日上午，他接到一个陌生女子的电话，对方称，嫌疑人药家鑫的父母欲登门致歉，"由于当时在车上，再加上我的代理律师不在，我就告诉对方，要谈和我的律师谈"之后，王辉打电话让父母在家里等候，但等了一天，仍未等到嫌疑人家属。"我的妻子躺在太平间里，我想尽早让她入土为安，但是，如果对方家属不提出道歉，我要是将妻子安葬，那就等于玷污了她生命的尊严了。"③王辉说。

昨日下午，④读者罗师傅打来电话称，药家鑫曾给他 10 岁的儿子带过两年钢琴家教。罗师傅说，"他能做出这样的事，让人匪夷所思……"

药家鑫父母曾委托警方送来 1 万元安葬费

目前，药家鑫已被逮捕，羁押在看守所内。⑤警方介绍，每天清晨 6 时 30 分，药家鑫和被关押在同一监舍的人员一起起床，然后，出早操，整理内务，每晚 10 时熄灯号后准时休息。

⑥药家鑫自称"当时慌乱，未考虑后果"。

事发 40 多天来，张萌的父亲张平选、丈夫王辉等人陷入巨大悲痛中。⑦张平选称，女儿被杀害十多天后，凶手药家鑫的父母委托公安长安分局郭杜派出所民警转交了一万元钱，说这是给女儿的安葬费。对此，张平选分文未动，"我不是为了钱。我娃都没命了……我只是要替我娃讨一个说法，看双方父母能不能坐在一起，协商解决后事……""身为在校大学生，驾车撞伤人不是救助，而是持刀杀人，手段还极其残忍！"就药家鑫的杀人动机和犯罪时的心理活动，昨日下午，⑧公安长安分局一名警察说，药家鑫供述称，怕自己车号被受害者记住而遇到麻烦，还说"当时慌乱，没有考虑到后果……"法医鉴定显示胸腹背手多处刺伤，手段残忍。"如果你当时及时救人，而不是持刀杀人，你会怎样？"药家鑫被警方抓获后，曾有人这样问他。⑨他说，"如果没有这件事（即连刺 8 刀杀人），我现在应该还在学校里"。

但是，⑩一位警察认为，无论疑犯药家鑫事后如何陈述，仍无法掩盖其在杀人时的残忍手段。法医鉴定时发现，受害人张萌除腿部骨折和后脑部磕伤外，其腹部、胸部、背部及双手共有大小 8 处刀伤。张萌惨遭杀害后，⑪其丈夫王辉从法医处得知，张萌的腹部中了一刀，背上有 3 刀，右侧颈部还有一处明显致命的刀伤，此外双手也有明显的刀伤。（华商网—华商报 2010-12-01）

序号	消息来源
①	据死者张萌的丈夫王辉
②	据王辉
③	王辉说
④	读者罗师傅
⑤	警方介绍

序号	消息来源
⑥	药家鑫自称
⑦	张平选称
⑧	公安长安分局一名警察说
⑨	他说
⑩	一位警察认为
⑪	其丈夫王辉从法医处得知

　　根据沈丽羽对"扶老人"事件350篇新闻报道消息来源的统计分析，有22％的新闻报道没有明确的消息来源，而运用消息来源的报道又存在消息来源单一化、近用性的特点。[①] 消息来源的使用缺乏认知和规范，这造成了"扶老人"新闻难以向公众提供促使其讨论纵深化发展的事实要素。而普利策奖作为美国新闻作品规范标准的引导和确立者，它的评价标准无疑是新闻文本生产的重要参照。根据马云飞对35篇普利策奖新闻作品的分析，共出现832个消息来源，平均每篇文章的消息来源达到23.7个。[②] 如果我们可以把一篇文章的消息来源数量设定为一个基本的新闻文本写作规范，那么新闻的采访和写作实际上就有了门槛。当我们谈论专业化的时候，就不会停留在概念和道德层面，而是可以量化的。

　　消息来源的数量是一个非常直观的衡量新闻话语可信性的指标。消息来源的数量几乎可以直接换算成记者的采访投入，因此是建构新闻可信性的刻度。在克莱蒙斯一文中，消息来源共出现了183个。其中文本1出现消息来源38个，文本2出现消息来源9个，文本3出现消息来源35个，文本4出现消息来源33个，文本5出现消息来源27个，文本6出现消息来源17个，文本7出现消息来源24个[③]。笔者在新闻专业外语本科课堂连续多年以这组文章进行读者感受性测试，均发现学生对消息来源的数量与新

---

①沈丽羽. 网络热点事件新闻报道话语分析——以"扶老人"事件为例[D]. 2017年长安大学硕士论文。

②马云飞. 美国财经新闻的媒介呈现研究——以2013—2017年普利策奖财经主题新闻为例[D]. 2018年长安大学硕士论文。

③本处数据采用的第二次统计的结果。

闻话语可信性之间关系的密切性有强烈的感受。虽然还不能得出消息来源的数量与新闻话语可信性成正比的关系，但实际上那些消息来源越多的文章会立即让读者产生文本可信性强、记者下了功夫的直观感受。通过消息来源我们可以轻易地看出新闻话语生产的惯例和规训如何，也可以感知到新闻话语的可信性和客观性，消息来源是新闻话语的一个标志性的策略。消息来源数量本身就是检测新闻话语可信性的标准。

消息来源的类型、具名程度和非近用媒体性

消息来源大致可以分为三类：分别是以人为源头的消息源（human source）；以物为源头的消息源（material source），例如法庭记录、公权力机构的文件证明、参考文献等；以及在线消息源，例如以网络数据库或在线文本为源头的消息来源。在克莱蒙斯案报道中，统计发现人的消息源出现 129 次，物的消息源出现 54 次。其中物的消息来源中又可以细分为文献来源 42 次，媒体来源 12 次。①

一篇新闻文本的消息来源如果表现出类型多元化的特征，其主题就越容易获得信赖感。因为类型丰富的消息来源昭示着信息获得渠道的多样化，有助于对主题的建构形成相互佐证的效果，使得主题获得由不同类型证词证言所搭建的信任体系的支持。不同的消息来源对主题可信度的建构效果也不同，一般来讲，物的消息源的可信度建构效果要高于人的消息源。在线消息源的情况则比较复杂，某些权威的在线消息源，如专业数据库其可信度要高于人的消息源。但是以 QQ 空间、博客评论、微博微信文字为源头的消息来源其对主题可信度的建构效果值得怀疑。本研究采用复旦大学黄洋中毒案的一篇文章《与自己的战争：复旦研究生为何毒杀室友》② 来验证这一结论，这篇发表在公信力颇高的《南方周末》上的文章大量采用了 QQ 空间和 BBS 论坛里的信息源，结果主题的

---

①此文最初发表时的数据统计如下：统计发现人的消息源出现 139 次，物的消息源出现 44 次。其中物的消息来源中又可以细分为机构来源 1 次，文献来源 34 次，媒体来源 9 次。这是一个很好的例证，证明统计消息来源的时候是存在偏差的，这种偏差形成的主要原因在于对文本的理解和判断。

②文本见《南方周末》，2013 年 4 月 25 日。

可信度也打了折扣。原因在于这种用虚拟世界里的自白式的信息代替真实世界中的人证和物证的做法降低了采访的难度和工作量,降低了对人物社会性一面的了解程度,对新闻主题的可信度是一个损害。

尽管出于对消息来源安全性的考虑,新闻文本有对消息来源进行匿名处理的传统。但从新闻主题可信度出发,消息来源应尽可能具名化。具名清晰有助于建构新闻主题的现实感。具名清晰的消息来源会对消息来源的背景、特征直接指明或者在上下文中有所交代。具名清晰不仅昭示了采访工作的细致,而且带给文本有据可查的可信任性。为了对文本进行消息来源具名性的分析,我们将消息来源分为三种:A 具名清晰;B 上下文交代清晰;C 匿名。在克莱蒙斯案文本 1《嫌犯一星期前离开皮尔斯县监狱》中,共统计出 38 个消息源,其中有 10 个消息源具名清晰,指示了人物的身份及关系特征,另外有 21 个消息来源从上下文来判断也是清晰的,只有 7 个消息源涉及隐私性具名不清晰。我们在对比文本《大学生撞人后捅死伤者续:据称其父母欲登门道歉》中发现,使用的消息来源分别是死者张萌的丈夫王辉、读者罗师傅、警方、药家鑫本人、死者的父亲张平选、公安长安分局一名警察。我们看到,作为拥有公权力背景具有发言权威性的消息来源——警方的具名不清晰,消息来源多为事件的涉事者,来自第三方的消息源缺乏,这充分暴露了文本采访的不足,因而文本的可信度也较低。

近用媒体消息来源的概念是与新闻价值联系在一起的。由于受到重要性、显著性、权威性等新闻价值观念的影响,媒介在采用消息来源的时候实际上有一些使用偏好,对代表官方、研究机构、专家消息来源的使用更为频繁。这种特点被 Hall 描述为结构性偏好,是由于媒介在截稿压力下偏好使用可信赖度高的消息来源导致的。然而这也造成有权力和有特权的消息来源获得更多接近媒体机会的现象,从而影响了新闻的平衡与客观。[1] 臧国仁也认为媒介在使用消息来源的时候比较依赖常规渠道,不同背景的消息来源在新闻话语中使用的比例并不平等。[2] 权力机

---

①翁秀琪等.新闻与社会真实建构——大众媒体、官方消息来源与社会运动的三角关系[M].台北:三民书局印行,2004:136.

②臧国仁编.新闻工作者与消息来源[M].台北:政大新闻研究所,1995.

构、政府发言人、名人、经济强人更容易被媒介作为消息来源。换句话说政治权力和经济权力可以赢得更大的话语权力。因此，新闻话语的可信性指标就产生了一个非近用媒体的消息来源。也就是观察文本中是否更多地采用了一些缺少话语权力的消息来源。例如普通的公众、具有私人性的机构和人物、受害者及其亲属等等。在"克莱蒙斯案"报道中，我们将人的消息来源分为以下三种，A 拥有公权力背景的；B 一般公众；C 私人领域关系中的。文本 1《嫌犯一星期前离开皮尔斯县监狱》中，这个比例是 A：B：C＝4：6：9。在文本 3《资深警官也是为人父母》中，这个比例是 A：B：C＝15：9：6。在这里，非近用媒体的消息来源即一般公众和私人领域内的消息源所占比例超出了拥有公权力背景的消息来源。这样做实现了新闻话语的真实、平衡，使得公领域和私领域都得到了话语呈现，新闻的可信性自然得到提高。

消息来源的设置：建构丰富的层级关系

消息来源的数量、类型、具名性及非近用媒体的消息来源使用比例是影响新闻主题可信度的硬指标。我们通过对新闻话语的初步分析和直接感知就可以对这些要素进行判断。但是对新闻话语可信度建构更为复杂和关键的要素则表现为消息来源的层级关系。层级关系丰富、平衡的新闻话语其主题可信性要高于层级关系单一、偏向的新闻话语。

消息来源层级关系的设置是围绕着新闻主题进行的，通过深入的话语分析，就可以感知消息来源是如何与主题互动的。克莱蒙斯案的主题延续了普利策奖揭丑和问责的传统，记者提问：为什么一个有着长期的犯罪记录、暴力倾向、古怪行为和心理问题的高危分子却可以获得保释，继而犯下更大的罪行？问题出在哪一个环节？谁应该为这个悲剧负责？

消息来源层级关系中能够界定主题，并使主题获得稳定性的往往是初级界定者。"这一天是我害怕了很久的日子"——这句话来自克莱蒙斯案文本中第一个消息来源。这个消息来源的具名高度清晰，他是阿肯色州普瓦斯基县的公诉律师拉里·杰格里。杰格里的悲叹是来自他明知道克莱蒙斯是极危险的罪犯，但是却无力阻止其多次获得减刑及保释，以至于终于等来了克莱蒙斯犯下杀死四名警官这一悲剧。此话奠定了主题，即为什么屡次犯下重罪的克莱蒙斯却可以获得保释继而犯下更大的罪行？在克莱蒙斯案中，拉里·杰格里是一个关键的初级界定者，作为克莱蒙斯一案的公诉律师，他在整组报道中出现了 5 次，是媒介问责议题的主要建构者，他认为克莱蒙斯是一个时刻需要留意的危险分子，却在州长霍克比饱受争议的减刑计划中提前取得了保释资格，为日后惨案发生埋下了祸根。

初级界定者是对新闻主题建构起到决定性作用的消息来源。在众多的消息来源中如何选择对主题承担主要建构功能的初级界定者，考验的其实是各个消息来源之间关系的合理性问题。如果初级界定者没有设置或者设置不恰当，新闻主题的稳定性就会减弱，因而可信性也会受损。

有趣的是，初级界定者往往存在相对的同级界定者。前阿肯色州州长霍克比在整组报道中出现了 35 次，其中作为对立面的初级界定者消息来源出现了 12 次。这个消息来源提供了对以杰格里为代表的舆论的反驳，他认为克莱蒙斯的保释是阿肯色州和华盛顿州刑事司法体系一系列失败的结果，而不应将舆论的矛头导向他。杰格里与霍克比的针锋相对，在文本中形成了初级界定者之间的舆论辩论场域，不仅使得主题更加稳固，而且使得新闻报道的客观性、辩证性更好地彰显出来。

消息来源的次级界定者对主题进行佐证和补充，使主题更饱满。在文本 1 中，拉里·杰格里是初级界定者，当其出现后，华盛顿惩教署及其发言人作为次级界定者分别出现 3 次，提供了罪犯被监管的事实，紧接着法庭记录和治安官报告作为文献消息来源又出现了 5 次，提供了克莱蒙斯殴打治安官、虐童以及反常言行的事实。在接下来的叙述中，文本又以新闻报道作为消息来源提供了克莱蒙斯的犯罪经历，以邻居的证词反映了克莱蒙斯糟糕的邻里和家庭关系。可以看出，后续的次级界定者都在对杰格里的话表示回应，即克莱蒙斯迟早要酿成惨剧，而这正是建构问责州长霍克比减刑计划的铺垫。

谁才是新闻的主人：消息来源是新闻文本的重要特征

长期以来，我国的新闻文本习惯在"主题＋叙事"的模式下生产内容，主题先行和叙事升华是两大特征，这使新闻文本表现出文艺性、伦理化的特征。因此，思辨代替了实证，道德论取代了真实论。新闻话语的认知框架往往以伦理问题为逻辑起点展开，而不是一个事实追问。比如"扶老人"事件，新闻文本设置的主题往往是"该不该扶老人"，而不是"老人是如何跌倒的"，结果舆论完全陷入道德逼问的循环中。其实改变这一现象的关键环节就是在文本中增加消息来源的数量，丰富消息来源的层级关系。

《圣彼得斯堡时报》的一位记者汤姆·佛伦奇，曾写过一篇受到公众热烈关注的作品。这篇名为《暗夜尖叫》的作品建立在 50 多个消息来源和 6000 多页法庭文件的基础上。人们评价说读这篇作品好像正在目击事件的发生。汤姆后来回忆说他非常依赖消息来源提供的信息，甚至死去的消息来源也绝不放过，想方设法让其在文字中发声，他还用三个星期的时间核对了所有消息来源，把每个字都读出来，确保无误。[1]

Cohen 和 Young 将消息来源建构媒介内容的模式划分为市场模式和操纵模式两种。[2] 在操纵模式中，消息来源的作用往往被忽视。而在市场模式中，消息来源则成为真正的主人。卡罗尔指出："把消息源看作书中的主人公，让读者看到、听到并关心他们。"[3] 新闻文本只有确立消息源为主，记者才愿意花大量的时间和精力去接触消息来源，根据消息来源所提供的信息挖掘值得被公众关注的主题，再通过消息来源之口将这个主题在文本中还原出来。如此，新闻话语的叙事性才能够成立，新闻话语的真实性才能够彰显，新闻话语对公共舆论的生成才完成了使命。

话语是我们思想的存在方式，福柯提醒我们回到话语本身去发现问题。因此我们应回到新闻话语本身的生产制作中来。新闻话语是如何生产出来的，什么样的要素在新闻话语生产中起关键作用，是真实性为主导的要素，还是意识形态为主导的要素，这些问题都在追问我们：谁才是新闻的主人？

---

[1]卡罗尔·里奇.新闻写作与报道训练教程[M].钟新,主译.北京:中国人民大学出版社,2004:231.

[2]Stanley Cohen and Jock Young. *The Manufacture of News*：*Deviance*，*Social Problems and the Mass Media*. Constable. 1981.

[3]卡罗尔·里奇.新闻写作与报道训练教程[M].钟新,主译.北京:中国人民大学出版社,2004:232.

第二节 普利策突发新闻的框架基模

从"武昌火车站恶性砍人事件"到陕西"米脂中学惨案",从"重庆公交车坠江事件"到"乐清滴滴杀人事件",公众总是通过新闻报道来了解和评估恶性突发事件,也建构对于事件的认知和想象。作为媒介,如果新闻报道框架是扭曲和偏颇的,那么公众对于社会安全感的认知和社会美好走向的思索也将产生偏差,如果这个媒介的报道框架是浅薄和粗糙的,那么从一开始公众的认知和思索就注定会陷入困惑之中。

恶性突发事件有两个特点,第一是突发性,第二是暴力性。这就不难解释为什么恶性突发事件的发生总是伴随着舆论中恐慌情绪的蔓延和谣言的传播。唯有真实是刺透黑暗的光。因此,恶性突发事件报道最重要的框架选择就是对真相的曝光。臧国仁指出:"框架的选择不但受到历史情境与文化的限制,也创造了新的历史情境与文化,两者互为因果。"[1]一次恶性突发事件是悲剧,也是契机,帮助我们再次堵塞导致悲剧发生的制度漏洞,填补意识盲区,也就为我们的人民和社会创造了美好生活生发的新的情境和文化。因此本节将通过对美国普利策恶性突发新闻获奖作品的框架分析,得出此类新闻谋篇布局的经验。

"克莱蒙斯案"之所以值得研究,是因为它曾是震惊美国的恶性突发事件,施暴者克莱蒙斯在 2009 年 11 月的一个早上持枪杀害了四名警察。事件发生后,西雅图时报在一个小时内就发出了现场连线报道,并在第一时间确认了犯罪嫌疑人的身份和犯罪历史。接下来的几天里,西雅图时报组织记者采访了 9 篇稿件,这些稿件被普利策奖冠以"精准、详细"[2],创造了一个恶性突发新闻事件的经典报道框架。这个经典的报道框架将恶性突发新闻的框架基模完美地呈现出来:对事件发生的真相探索构成了真相框架,对受害者和施暴者的报道构成了受害者框架和施暴者框架,我们把这个称为"一体两翼"模式。

---

①臧国仁.新闻媒体与消息来源——媒介框架与真实建构之论述[M].台北:三民书局,1999:49.

②https://www.pulitzer.org/winners/staff-71.

本文对真相、受害者和施暴者框架采取的分析方法，运用了臧国仁对框架结构层次进行高、中、低分析的方法：即对真相框架进行高层次结构的分析，简而言之就是主题分析；对受害者框架进行中层次结构分析，看文章如何通过选择和重组主要事件、先前事件、结果、影响、评估等要素塑造主题；对施暴者框架进行低层次结构分析，主要通过消息来源和引语以及语句、修辞来勾勒主题。

真相框架：倾向有推理基础的批判

一起恶性突发事件发生，人们最大的关注点总是：为什么会发生这件事？新闻媒体最简单但是也可能最被挑战的做法就是回应受众的疑问，去探索事件发生的原因，本文把新闻报道对突发事件发生原因的呈现称之为真相框架。真相框架应该是恶性突发新闻报道首要的框架选择，也就是本文所称呼的"一体"。

臧国仁指出：框架总是有着高层次（macrostructure）的意义，往往是对某一事件主题的界定。①冯·戴伊克也强调新闻的整体格局（这里的"整体格局"完全是"新闻框架"的另一种概念创造）塞满了话语内容，而谁来界定话语内容呢，就是主题。② 主题会决定框架中层方向中事件的选择，也会决定框架下层方向中语言的选择。对于克莱蒙斯案的真相框架来讲，设置了怎样的主题？

van Dijk 认为：主题（theme）乃由命题（proposition）组成。③因此我们可以借由对命题的寻找拼凑出主题。我们在文章 *Person of interest let out of Pierce County jail one week ago*（《嫌犯一星期前从皮尔斯监狱出来》）中找到四个命题。

---

① 臧国仁.新闻媒体与消息来源——媒介框架与真实建构之论述[M].台北:三民书局,1999:34.

② 冯·戴伊克.话语 心理 社会[M].施旭,冯冰,编译.北京:中华书局,1993:71.

③ 臧国仁.新闻媒体与消息来源——媒介框架与真实建构之论述[M].台北:三民书局,1999:35.

Proposition1	拥有多项重罪记录的克莱蒙斯被数次释放
Proposition2	霍克比作为前州长顶着检察官的反对减免克莱蒙斯的刑期
Proposition3	即使身披重罪，克莱蒙斯还是在袭警案前一周被保释
Proposition4	霍可比声明释放克莱蒙斯获得了州假释裁决委员会的批准

这些命题塑造出一个主题：罪行累累的嫌犯何以被保释。按照 Goffman 的说法，就是提出："这是什么事（what is it that's going on here)?"[1] 周末发生在咖啡馆里四名警察被杀的案件真相是什么？是关于一个危险的身披重罪的人被多次保释的事情。警察被杀只是罪犯被保释的结果，而媒体真正要调查的问题是：我们的州长、监狱、司法、保释公司都做了什么？

臧国仁强调：主题经常会以一些特定的形式出现，如在标题、导语和直接引语中被提到。[2]《嫌犯一星期前从皮尔斯监狱出来》这篇文章的标题突出了嫌犯被保释的事实，而在标题下面的提示语 'Facing 8 felony charges, he had been held months'（面对 8 项重罪指控，他已经囚禁了几个月），'Prison time, at least 5 convictions in Arkansas'（服刑期间，在阿肯色州至少有五项罪名），再次突出了他犯罪的严重性。导语对主题的反映就更加明显。'Maurice Clemmons, the 37-year-old man wanted for questioning in the killing of four Lakewood police officers Sunday morning, has a long criminal record punctuated by violence, erratic behavior and concerns about his mental health.'（莫里斯·克莱蒙斯，37 岁，被怀疑在星期天早上枪杀了四名莱克伍德市的警察，他有着长期的犯罪记录，这个记录充满了暴力、古怪行为和对他心理问题的关注。）

命题的下一个层次还可以是微观命题（Microposition），试举一例：

---

①臧国仁.新闻媒体与消息来源——媒介框架与真实建构之论述[M].台北：三民书局,1999:34.

②臧国仁.新闻媒体与消息来源——媒介框架与真实建构之论述[M].台北：三民书局,1999:35.

Proposition 1	拥有多项重罪记录的克莱蒙斯被数次释放
Microposition 1	前州长霍克比顶着检察官的反对减免了他漫长的刑期
Microposition 2	他在袭警案发前一星期被释放即使他身负重罪指控
Microposition 3	保释公司用重金把克莱蒙斯从强暴儿童的指控中保释
Microposition 4	霍可比认为克莱蒙斯的释放获准于州假释裁决委员会

由此我们可以看到，报道的主题正是通过宏观命题和微观命题不断被塑造出来。克莱蒙斯案主题的塑造有三个特点：

第一，根据倒金子塔原则，直接提出核心命题。新闻话语的倒金字塔原则要求直接在标题和导语中把事件的关键问题抛出，这体现了记者直面真相、刺破黑暗的勇气和信心。劣质的新闻往往不提或故意模糊核心问题，或者产生偏向。比如对施暴者妖魔化，然而一个被妖魔化的人就可以成为事件发生的理由吗？把问题归因为偶发因素是思想懒惰的表现，而深究出刺激个体施暴的必然因素才是核心命题追问的所在。

第二，高度重视消息来源和引语对真相的推理。报道开头克莱蒙斯案的检察官拉里·杰格里惊呼："这是我长期以来一直担心的那一天！"由此引出了不顾检察官的反对执意对克莱蒙斯进行减刑的前任州长霍克比的线索。然后又巧妙地借助霍克比踢皮球的话语，"克莱蒙斯案是阿肯色州和华盛顿州刑事司法体系一系列失败的结果"，将真相的探索引向美国司法制度的漏洞。最后在《电子邮件："希望他未获保释"》一文中，又引用皮尔斯县治安官发言人艾得·托伊尔的说辞，把阿肯色州和华盛顿州在克莱蒙斯案中的互相推诿描述成一场随时会爆发的边境战争。

第三，对制度漏洞和文化刻板观念保持批判。虽然霍克比的减刑并不是导致克莱蒙斯犯下杀人案的直接原因，但是这条线索让读者看到过于宽松以及州长拥有过多决定权的赦免制度成为一些罪犯寻求法外开恩的途径。文章也对美国宗教文化所倡导的宽恕观念以及宗教领袖的影响力，还有对青少年犯罪同情姑息的文化观念提出了反思，因为这些间接成为克莱蒙斯寻求保释机会的借口。由于两个州之间在授权令责任方面不予深究的处置，最终导致克莱蒙斯在交纳天价保释金后走出了监狱。记者不放过任何细节的记录，让美国司法体系中州与州之间合作的间隙与拖延完全暴露出来。正是这种纠结于公文和责任大小的思路导致了本可以阻止克莱蒙斯出狱的授权令被拖延,这才是克莱蒙斯杀人案的直接原因。问题分析到这里,读者们从对案件的神秘揣测和恐惧焦虑中跌落到事实的真相面前,原来这样血腥恐怖的枪杀案最初都是从一纸授权令导致的,如果当初……这样残酷的真相通过侦探式的推理一步步呈现出来,漏洞因为太过普通导致人们对残酷结果感到更加遗憾,也促成了所有人沉默着的思考。

受害者框架:通过选择和重组修复核心价值观

对真相的挖掘承担起了报道的筋骨,也刺透了社会的黑暗和腐败。但是新闻报道的使命并不仅仅在于揭露,也在于修复和重建。克莱蒙斯杀害四名警察的事情对美国主流文化价值产生了冲击,人们的怀疑和困惑必须通过对信仰的再次确认来获得希望的延续。受害者框架和施暴者框架就好比飞机的两翼,起到了平衡作用。

受害者框架是突发恶性事件中人们第二关心的框架,因此也是突发恶性报道的常态框架之一。我们对受害者框架的分析将采用框架的中层结构分析方法。框架的中层是由主要事件、过去的事件、结果、影响等环节构成的一种结构层次。

在"克莱蒙斯案"中,记者用《久经沙场的警察也是为人父母》这样的标题组织了一篇独立的报道。整篇文章用"集装箱"式的写法对四名受害者进行了呈现。

受害者	主要事件	以前事件	结　果	他人的评价	影　响
Tina	被克莱蒙斯枪杀,终年 40 岁。	获得过救生奖,是反恐特警队员,战术小组唯一的女性。	留下 21 岁的女儿和 8 岁的儿子。	可爱的,享受生活的;自信,勇敢,擅长处理高危情况,体能超常,可以做 30—40 个引体向上;勤奋,和她工作有乐趣,乐于陪伴家人。	令同事和家人感到震惊不已。

受害者	主要事件	以前事件	结　果	他人的评价	影　响
Gregory	被克莱蒙斯枪杀,终年 42 岁。	有 8 年的执法经验,警员摇滚乐队的鼓手。	留下妻子,一个女儿和两个儿子。	亲切,乐于与之共事;受人尊敬和爱戴;聪明、天使般的人。	他的死让人难过;家人们聚在一起悼念他。
Mark	被克莱蒙斯枪杀,终年 39 岁。	获得授勋的资深警员;警察协会的主席;反恐特警组课程的教官。	留下妻子和三个孩子。	专业、敬业;慈爱的父亲、丈夫和家庭成员;受欢迎的同事、爱帮助他人。	被家人深深怀念;网上的悼念页面上很快有大量悼念信息。
Ronald	被克莱蒙斯枪杀,终年 37 岁。	国家巡逻骑兵;他在曾经作为侦探的父亲去世后成为警察。	单身父亲。留下一个女儿	专业的警察和慈爱的父亲;"理想的房客";好邻居、善良。	听到消息让人说不出话来。

我们看到,关涉四位受害者被枪杀的主要事件只是强调了受害者的年龄,并未对具体的被杀细节和动作进行描述,这种处理无疑会淡化事件的恐怖气息。而先前的事件,则是突出并着重使用"选择"机制呈现了四位警官从业经历的资深性,这样至少可以证明四名警官的被害完全是遭到偷袭的结果,而并不是警察的无能导致的,这有利于维护公众对公共安全保障的信心。

"结果"和"影响"是由主要事件引起的后果。其中"结果"强调的是直接性,"影响"强调的是间接性。警察被枪杀的直接结果是亲人生死相隔,间接影响到亲戚、同事、邻居等周围人的生活,在这里把悲伤和缅怀的情绪释放出来。"归因"环节是缺省的,因为在"真相原因"框架中已经处理过了。值得注意的是体现对事件好恶的"评估"环节是没有的,记者并没有在文章中反映人们对警察被杀案的价值判断,通常在恶性突发新闻中这个环节是最容易发泄人们怒气和抱怨的环节,但是普利策奖的这组作品并没有这个环节。也就是说在框架偏向上它避免了进入对事件进行负面反馈的"诅咒"和"妖魔化"的环节。相反,这组作品选择了一个"他人对受害者的评价",而使文章包含了浓浓的温情和深深的缅怀,这些评价突出了美国文化所倡导的伦理价值观,诸如家庭第一,和睦友爱,乐于助人,使大家看到,逝者远去,但留下的价值信念依然是你我熟悉和愿意继续的美好。

"哀而不怨"是受害者框架带给人的整体感觉，这种感觉是通过框架中层次方向的选择和重组完成的。通过对框架中层次结构所包含环节的取舍，记者没有使文章陷入苦毒和抱怨的负能量之中，也没有陷入恐怖和无力的绝望气息中，而是带给人平安、盼望和带着微笑的悼念。

这种文化塑造能力正是新闻报道体现价值，建构人们共享信仰系统中的同一性和美好性的基础。臧国仁说："选择意指从芸芸众生中撷取少数特殊项目，转换为有意义的结构，重组则系将撷取的项目按重要性排列，借以显示重视程度。选择与重组俱为真实转换之必备手法，也是彰显社会意义的重要过程。"① 恶性突发新闻报道通过这样的过程呈现了更重要的真实：盼望和救赎。

施暴者框架：不对施暴者妖魔化

施暴者框架也是恶性突发新闻报道常态的框架之一。我们对施暴者框架的分析方法采用了框架的低层次结构分析法。这既是臧国仁所强调的对语句和修辞的分析，也是冯·戴伊克所说的对文章句子、话语、语义的分析。② 福勒（Fowler）曾把这种作用看得很高，认为可以写出作者不同的世界观。③ 施暴者框架的确可以反映出人们对待人性的不同态度。人们惯于对罪大恶极的人报以仇恨和抛弃的态度，然而新闻报道要随从大众情绪，附之以"妖魔化框架"或者"诅咒框架"吗？如何看待一个罪犯，体现了社会意识的宽容和理性程度。我们当然可以把一个罪大恶极的人钉死在耻辱柱上，这是轻松和容易的，难的是透过这一个人看到人性堕落的层次，看到人性堕落背后可能有的温良的挽留，看到人性堕落的伤痛和教训，这是我们写尽一个人的恶与狠所做不到的。

掩卷"克莱蒙斯案"，激发不了人的仇恨和恐惧，相反是深深的沉默和反思。记者通过数十个消息来源的话语勾勒出了一个真实、全面的克

---

①臧国仁.新闻媒体与消息来源——媒介框架与真实建构之论述［M］.台北：三民书局,1999:57.

②冯·戴伊克.话语 心理 社会［M］.施旭,冯冰,编译.北京:中华书局出版,1993:44.

③臧国仁.新闻媒体与消息来源——媒介框架与真实建构之论述［M］.台北：三民书局,1999:41.

莱蒙斯。

克莱蒙斯的亲人	克莱蒙斯的妹妹拉塔尼亚	"相当不错的人，他心地善良。"
	克莱蒙斯的祖母	"在我看来他是一个非常好的小伙子。"
	克莱蒙斯的叔叔雷·克莱蒙斯	"他远离真实的自己。" "他心中苦涩。" "他觉得他被虐待。他不喜欢警察，而且他不希望再回到监狱里去。" "我们穷，但是回到那时，没有犯罪。" "我们把时间花在林间穿梭，在藤蔓间荡漾。做孩子们所做的事情。"
	他的家人	克莱蒙斯声称他可以飞，他要拯救地球。
克莱蒙斯本人	克莱蒙斯写给霍克比的申请信	"我屈服于同龄人以及在新处境中我必须被其他年轻人需要的压力，由此和不法之徒混在一起，导致了一个将我送进监狱的历时七个月的犯罪活动。"
	克莱蒙斯的上诉辩护书	"这里站着一个曾经那么年轻的……但误入歧途的傻瓜，他无法掌握自己的人生。如今这里站着的是一个27岁不再年轻的男子，已在逆境中认识到欣赏并尊重他人的权利。在监狱生活的严酷现实中他已学会了必要的能力来站稳脚跟，而不是如同曾经那个只有16岁的孩子一样跟随众人行恶。"
其他受害者	邻居	克莱蒙斯曾经向窗户和汽车扔石头。
	邻居	在此之前，克莱蒙斯一直很亲切友好，没有给任何人找麻烦。
	被抢劫女子	"他的眼神我永远也忘不了。"
反对克莱蒙斯假释的人	迈克·考密克：克莱蒙斯公诉律师的代理人	"他是一个时刻需留意的人。""在法庭上你只想和他保持距离。"
	华盛顿惩教署的发言人	"高危性重犯"
对克莱蒙斯假释负有责任的人	霍克比	"我能在九年前就知道这一切并且能预知未来吗？我能在没有假释委员会的建议下顺利行动吗？当然不能。"

从这些引用可以看出，亲人们对克莱蒙斯主要是同情和肯定，也反映了他混乱的内心世界；克莱蒙斯的自述使一个罪犯的心声被听见。其他受害者客观陈述了事实，没有抱怨诅咒。反对克莱蒙斯假释的人看到

了克莱蒙斯的危险性。而对克莱蒙斯假释负有责任的人则忽视了他的危险性，看到了他的年轻，对他施以宽容。透过消息来源和引语内容，我们看到了一个家境贫困、成长受到社会邪恶势力引诱，缺乏自控，一再犯罪，然而又有着狡黠、良善、值得同情一面的克莱蒙斯。对施暴者的呈现是全面、理性、深刻的。这就形成了错而不斥：施暴者框架弱化施暴细节，不对施暴者妖魔化的表达。

错误的框架偏向：诅咒、妖魔化、自救锦囊

行文至此，反思一下近年来我国恶性突发新闻报道存在的一些问题：诅咒、妖魔化、自救锦囊是三个错误的框架偏向。这三个框架偏向的产生都和事故发生的真正原因没有被报道清楚有关。像普利策获奖作品克莱蒙斯案这样，呈现出事故发生的必然性原因、制度性原因、公共性原因，报道就会避免通过对罪犯进行妖魔化、诅咒化来释放公众焦虑情绪，也无须画蛇添足般地编写自救锦囊的文章，滥竽充数。再回到本文的主旨，面对恶性突发新闻，媒体报道需要设定新闻文本的"巨命题"[1]，这个巨命题就是真相框架。真相框架就是用剥洋葱的方法去建构，而意识形态的重建则可以通过受害者和施暴者框架去完成。

第三节 案例库：克莱蒙斯枪杀四警察案[2]

1. 奖励标准

普利策突发新闻奖颁给卓越的当地新闻报道，特别看重初始报道的速度和准确性，可以是印刷版本，也可以是在线版本，奖励1万美金。

---

[1] 臧国仁.新闻媒体与消息来源——媒介框架与真实建构之论述[M].台北：三民书局，1999：133.

[2] 该案例库英文文本版权属于原作者和首发媒体,本书作者通过电子邮件等形式联系《西雅图时报》和相关记者,但均未收到关于版权的回复。本书作者最终决定在书中收录英文文本,一是方便读者感受英文突发新闻的特色,二是在文本中标注了大量话语分析符号和记录文字,供读者学习使用。本书作者会继续保持和原作者的沟通联系,并承诺保护原作者的版权权益。

2. 获奖致辞

授予《西雅图时报》的工作人员,他们的作品采用报纸和网络两方面呈现新闻,报道了在一家咖啡屋里四名警官被枪杀,以及对嫌犯 40 小时追捕的过程,这份报道体现了综合性。

3. 入围者

2010 年入围普利策突发新闻奖的记者还有:新泽西州纽瓦克市《星报》的人员,他们对一次牵涉面广的腐败丑闻关涉的 44 个被捕者进行了周全的报道,这个丑闻使得当地官员、一些宗教领袖和其他人深陷其中。另一个入围者是《华盛顿邮报》。他们对一名陆军精神科医生进行了引人入胜的报道,此人与华盛顿方面有长期联系,他在得克萨斯军事基地胡德堡的枪击案中杀了 13 人。

4. 获奖作品

日 期	英文题目	中文题目
November 28, 2009	4 officers shot; manhunt begins (online exhibit)	4 警官被枪杀,追捕开始(在线展示)
November 29, 2009	Person of interest let out of Pierce County jail one week ago	嫌犯一星期前从皮尔斯监狱出来
November 29, 2009	Huckabee commuted long term	霍可比长期执行减刑
November 29, 2009	Veteran officers were parents, too	资深警官也是为人父母
November 29, 2009	Manhunt intensifies (online exhibit)	搜捕变得更加严峻(在线展示)
November 30, 2009	Persuasive appeal helped Clemmons win clemency	有说服力的上诉帮助克莱蒙斯获得宽大处理
November 30, 2009	Four days in May set stage for tragedy	五月的四天为悲剧做准备
November 29, 2009	Clemmons killed by patrolman (online exhibit)	克莱蒙斯被巡警击毙(在线展示)
December 1, 2009	Uncle: 'He was all about money—suddenly, he was all about God'	叔叔:"他满嘴都是钱,突然,又全是上帝。"
December 1, 2009	E-Mail: 'Hopefully (he) will not get out on bail'	电子邮件:"希望他未获保释。"

【2010 年普利策突发新闻奖 1 号文本】①

4 officers shot; manhunt begins（online exhibit）

4 警官被枪杀，追捕开始（在线展示）

online coverage of breaking news

在线突发新闻报道

November 29，2009

2009 年 11 月 29 日

Following the 8：15 a. m. shooting，seattletimes. com first posted an AP item and linked to reports from the scene—about an hour south of Seattle. But the staff mobilized quickly and began posting its own reports. The first e-mail alert was sent shortly after 10 a. m. Throughout the day，more than three dozen stories were posted or updated online. Seattletimes. com was the first to identify the suspect and detail his criminal history.

早上 8：15 枪杀案发生后，西雅图时报网站第一时间发布了美联社的新闻并从现场连线报道——一小时后在西雅图南边。但是全体员工立刻行动开始发出他们自己的报道。10 点后发出了第一封电子邮件报警信。一天内，发出三打以上报道或者在网络更新。西雅图时报网站第一时间确认了嫌疑人和他的犯罪历史细节。

【2010 年普利策突发新闻奖 2 号文本】

Person of interest let out of Pierce County jail one week ago

嫌犯一星期前从皮尔斯监狱出来

Facing 8 felony charges，he had been held months（副标题）

面对 8 项重罪指控，他已经被关押了几个月

By：Seattle Times Staff

西雅图时报员工

Susan Kelleher，Jonathan Martin，Ken Armstrong，Steve Miletich，Jennifer Sullivan，Mike Carter and Jim Brunner，and news researchers Gene

---

①文本 1 是一则消息，用来展示突发新闻的报道时效性。

Balk and Miyoko Wolf

November 30，2009

苏珊·凯勒赫，乔纳森·马丁，肯·阿姆斯壮，斯蒂文·米欧可，詹妮弗·苏文，麦克·卡特和吉姆·布伦纳，以及新闻研究者詹·巴克和米优克·沃夫。

2009 年 11 月 30 日

Prison time，at least 5 convictions in Arkansas

服刑期间，在阿肯色州至少有五次定罪

1　Maurice Clemmons，the 37-year-old man wanted for questioning in the killing of four Lakewood police officers Sunday morning，has a long criminal record punctuated by violence，erratic behavior and concerns about his mental health.

　　莫里斯·克莱蒙斯 37 岁，被怀疑在星期天早上枪杀了四名莱克伍德市的警官，他的犯罪记录很长，这个记录充满了暴力、古怪行为，并使人注意到他的心理问题。

2　His criminal history includes at least five felony convictions in Arkansas and at least eight felony charges in Washington. That record also stands out for the number of times Clemmons has been released from custody despite questions about the danger he posed.

　　他的犯罪史包括：在阿肯色州至少有五起重罪定罪，在华盛顿州至少有八起重罪指控。这一犯罪记录令一些人注意的地方在于：尽管他被怀疑是一个危险人物，但仍然多次被刑拘释放。

3　Mike Huckabee，while governor of Arkansas，granted clemency to Clemmons nine years ago，commuting his lengthy prison sentence over the protests of prosecutors. "This is the day I've been dreading for a long time," ①Larry Jegley，prosecuting attorney for Arkansas' Pulaski County（拉里·杰格里，阿肯色州普拉斯基县的检察官），said Sunday night when informed that Clemmons was being sought in connection with the killings.

　　麦克·霍克比，在他当阿肯色州州长时，九年前他赦免了克莱蒙斯，顶着检察官的反对减免了他漫长的刑期。"这一天是我害怕了很久的日子"，①拉里·杰格里，阿肯色州普瓦斯基县的公诉律师，周天晚上，当他了解到正在被追捕的克莱蒙斯与这起谋杀案有关的时候说了这句话。

4 In Pierce County, Clemmons had been in jail for the past several months on a child-rape charge that carries a possible life sentence. He was released from custody one week ago, even though he was staring at eight felony charges in all.

　　在皮尔斯县，克莱蒙斯因为一个强暴儿童的指控，过去的几个月里被监禁，他将可能面临终身监禁。他一星期前被释放，即使他身负8个重罪指控。

5 Clemmons posted $15,000 with a Chehalis company called Jail Sucks Bail Bonds. The bondsman, in turn, put up $150,000, securing Clemmons' release on the child rape charge.

　　克莱蒙斯花了15000美元与奇哈利斯公司旗下的监狱吸纳保释金公司签订了合约。担保人反过来用150000美元把克莱蒙斯从强暴儿童的指控中保释出来。

6 Clemmons moved to Washington from Arkansas in 2004. He was placed under the supervision of the Washington State Department of Corrections (DOC) for an Arkansas conviction, according to ②a department spokesman（部门发言人）. The DOC classified him as "high risk to reoffend." His supervision was to continue until October 2015, ③the spokesman said（发言人，和消息来源是同一个）.

　　克莱蒙斯2004年从阿肯色州搬到了华盛顿州。由于在阿肯色州的一项罪名，克莱蒙斯处于华盛顿惩教署的监管之下，②依照一位部门发言人的说法。华盛顿惩教署将他列为"高危性重犯"。③这位发言人说，对他的监管将持续到2015年的10月。

7 He lives in Tacoma, where he has run a landscaping and power-washing business out of his house. He is married, but the relationship has been tumultuous, with accounts of his unpredictable behavior leading to at least two run-ins with police this year.

克莱蒙斯居住在塔科马，他在家门外经营景观美化和动力清洗生意。他已婚，但夫妻关系动荡不安。今年，他至少被备案两次，原因是出乎意料的行为举动导致和警察争吵。

8 Clemmons punched a Pierce County sheriff's deputy in the face during one confrontation，according to ④court records（法庭记录，这是一个证明材料消息来源）. Two days later，at his home，Clemmons allegedly gathered his wife and two younger relatives at around 3 or 4 a. m. and had them all undress. He told them that families need to "be naked for at least five minutes on Sunday，"⑤a Pierce County sheriff's report says（皮尔斯县警长的报告）.

④根据法庭记录，克莱蒙斯在面对一项对峙时打了皮尔斯县州长副官的脸。两天后，在他家，据称克莱蒙斯大约在早上 3 点到 4 点让他的妻子和两个年纪轻轻的亲戚一丝不挂。他告诉他们家庭需要"在周末的时候至少裸体五分钟"，⑤一份皮尔斯县的州长报告这样说道。

9 The family complied because they were afraid of Clemmons and thought he was growing increasingly erratic. "The whole time Clemmons kept saying things like trust him，the world is going to end soon，and that he was Jesus，"⑥the report（报告，和⑤为同一个）says.

家里人照着做是因为他们害怕克莱蒙斯，而且觉得他变得越来越不稳定。"克莱蒙斯无时无刻不在说着一些话，比如要相信他，这个世界就快要灭亡了，而且还说他就是耶稣。"⑥报告说道。

10 The Sheriff's Office interviewed Clemmons' sister in May. She said her brother "is not in his right mind and did not know how he could react when contacted by law enforcement，"⑦a sheriff's report says.（这里容易把消息源误判成克莱蒙斯的妹妹，但实际上是报告。）"She stated that he was saying that the Secret Service was coming to get him because he had written a letter to the president…She suspects he is having a mental breakdown，"⑧the report says（报告）.

五月份州长办公室访问了克莱蒙斯的妹妹。她说她的兄弟"头脑不清楚而且当他面对执法机关联系时不知如何反应"，⑦一个警长的报告如是说。"她说他不断说秘密服务组织将要来抓他，因为他给总统写了一封信。……她怀疑他正遭受精神崩溃。"⑧报告陈述。

11　⑨Family members（家庭成员，这个消息来源根据上下文也应该是从报告中体现的。）also told deputies that Clemmons claimed he could fly and expected President Obama to visit to "confirm that he is Messiah in the flesh."

　　⑨他的家人也告诉副官，克莱蒙斯声称他可以飞，还期待奥巴马总统可以来访，"证实他是尘世中的救世主"。

12　While investigating this incident, deputies uncovered evidence that led to a charge that he had raped and molested a 12-year-old relative.

　　调查这个事件，副官发现了证据，导致了对他的一项指控，他强奸猥亵一个 12 岁亲戚。

13　Prosecutors in Pierce County recently had requested a mental evaluation for Clemmons at Western State Hospital. On Nov. 6, a judge concluded that Clemmons was competent to stand trial on the child-rape and other felony charges, according to ⑩court records（法庭记录）.

　　皮尔斯县的检察官最近要求对克莱蒙斯在西部州立医院进行精神评估。⑩据法庭记录，11 月 6 日，法官做出了克莱蒙斯可以就强奸儿童罪和其他重罪指控受审的结论。

Long record in Arkansas
阿肯色的长记录

14　News accounts out of Arkansas offer a confusing—and, at times, conflicting description of Clemmons' criminal history and prison time.

　　来自阿肯色州的新闻报道对克莱蒙斯的犯罪历史和服刑时间的描述令人困惑，有时甚至相互矛盾。

15　In 1990, Clemmons, then 18, was sentenced in Arkansas to 60 years in prison for burglary and theft, according to a ⑪news account（新闻报道）. Responding to a circuit judge's comment that Clemmons had broken his mother's heart, ⑫Clemmons（克莱蒙斯）said, "I have broken my own heart. "

　　⑪根据一份新闻报道：1990 年，克莱蒙斯那时 18 岁，因入室行窃和偷盗行为在阿肯色州被判 60 年监禁。在回应一位巡回法官的评价时，克莱蒙斯伤透了他母亲的心，⑫克莱蒙斯说："我自己的心也被伤透了。"

16　Newspaper stories describe a series of disturbing incidents involving Clemmons while he was being tried in Arkansas on various charges. During one trial，he was shackled in leg irons and seated next to a u-niformed officer. The presiding judge ordered the extra security be-cause he felt Clemmons had threatened him，⑬court records（法庭记录）show. At other times，Clemmons was accused of hiding a piece of metal in his sock to use as a weapon；throwing a lock at a bailiff，and instead hitting his mother；and reaching for a guard's pistol while being transported to court.

　　报纸上的故事描述了一系列令人不安的事件，这些事件涉及克莱蒙斯曾经在阿肯色州因各种指控受审。在一次审讯中，他戴着脚镣坐在一个警察旁边。⑬法庭记录显示：主审法官命令增加额外的安全警戒，因为他感觉到克莱蒙斯威胁到他。在其他时间，克莱蒙斯被控在他的袜子里藏了一块金属用来当作武器；向一个法警扔锁但却砸到了他的母亲；在被押解到法庭过程中欲接触一个警卫的手枪。

17　Clemmons was arrested when he was a junior in high school for having a. 25-caliber pistol on school property. Clemmons told police that he brought the gun to school because he had been "beaten by dopers" and that if they got after him again，he had "something for them，" ⑭a newspaper account（新闻报道）says. When Clemmons received the 60-year sentence，he already was serving 48 years on five felony con-victions and facing up to 95 more years on charges of robbery，theft and possessing a handgun on school property，according to ⑮a story in the Arkansas Democrat-Gazette（阿肯色州民主党公报上的一个故事）.

克莱蒙斯在高中一年级时被捕，因为在学校里持一个 0.25 口径的手枪。⑭一家报纸这样报道：克莱蒙斯告诉警察，他带着手枪去学校，是因为他曾被"兴奋剂使用者殴打"，如果他们再次招惹他，他就会"为他们准备些东西"。⑮根据《阿肯色州民主党公报》的报道，克莱蒙斯获得 60 年刑期时，他已经因五项重罪定罪要服刑 48 年，并面临着因抢劫、盗窃以及在学校持枪而被判 95 年以上刑期。

18　Clemmons served 11 years before being released. Then-Governor Huckabee，who was a Republican presidential candidate in 2008，commuted Clemmons' sentence. He cited Clemmons' young age，at the time the crimes were committed，according to ⑯ news reports（新闻报道）.

克莱蒙斯在被释放前已经服刑 11 年。当时的州长霍可比是 2008 年共和党总统候选人，他缩减了克莱蒙斯的刑期。⑯依据新闻报道，他列举了克莱蒙斯是在 17 岁年纪轻轻的时候，犯下的罪行。

Huckabee's statement 霍可比的声明

19　Huckabee，in ⑰ a statement（声明）released Sunday night，said Clemmons' release from prison had been reviewed and approved by the Arkansas parole board. If Clemmons is found responsible for the police killings，"it will be the result of a series of failures in the criminal-justice system in both Arkansas and Washington State，" ⑱ Huckabee（霍克比）said.

霍可比在周日晚上发了⑰一个声明，他说克莱蒙斯从监狱里释放，已经获得了阿肯色州假释委员会的审核和批准。如果克莱蒙斯为袭警事件负责，⑱霍可比说，"那么这是阿肯色州和华盛顿州刑事司法系统一系列纰漏的结果"。

20　After his release，Clemmons remained on parole. Soon after，he found trouble again. In March 2001，he was accused of violating his parole by committing aggravated robbery and theft，according to ⑲ the Democrat-Gazette（民主党公报）.

克莱蒙斯被释放后仍然处于假释状态。不久他再次遇上了麻烦。

⑲根据《民主党公报》报道，2001 年 3 月，他被控告违反了假释条件，因为犯下严重的抢劫和盗窃案。

21　He was returned to prison on a parole violation. But in what appears to have been a mistake, he wasn't served with the arrest warrants until leaving prison three years later.

他因为违反保释条例而被送回了监狱。但这看起来是个错误，他的逮捕令直到三年后他离开监狱才送达。

22　Clemmons' attorney argued that the charges should be dismissed because too much time had passed. Prosecutors thereafter dropped the charges. On Sunday night, ⑳Clemmons' sister Latanya（克莱蒙斯的妹妹拉塔尼亚）said her brother is the second-oldest of six children.

克莱蒙斯的律师辩称，由于过去了太长时间应当撤销指控。检察官此后撤销了指控。星期天晚上，⑳克莱蒙斯的妹妹拉塔尼亚说她的兄弟在六个孩子中排行第二。

23　"Maurice is a fairly good person, good heart," ㉑she（克莱蒙斯的妹妹拉塔尼亚）said. He came over to her place on Thanksgiving for about an hour and seemed fine, ㉒she（克莱蒙斯的妹妹拉塔尼亚）said.

㉑她说："莫里斯是一个相当不错的人，他心地善良。"㉒她说，他在感恩节那天前来拜访过她，待了大约一个小时，看起来很好。

24　㉓Clemmons' maternal grandmother, Lela Clemmons, 82, of Marianna, Ark.（克莱蒙斯的外祖母，住在玛丽安娜方舟地区的 82 岁的里拉·克莱蒙斯。具名清晰度高）, said her grandson lived in Marianna when he was young. Later, as a teen, he lived in Little Rock, ㉔another relative（另一个亲戚，匿名消息来源）said.

克莱蒙斯的外祖母莱拉·克莱蒙斯已经 82 岁了，住在阿肯色州玛丽安娜这个地方，㉓她说她的孙子小时候住在玛丽安娜。㉔另一亲戚说，后来，青少年时期，他住在小石城。

25　"All I know is he is a pretty good guy," ㉕Maurice Clemmons' grandmother（莫里斯·克莱蒙斯的祖母）said. ㉖She（莫里斯·克莱蒙

斯的祖母）said both of his parents died years ago. His mother worked in a nursing home, and his father was a factory worker.

㉕莫里斯·克莱蒙斯的外祖母说："在我看来他是一个非常好的小伙子。"㉖她说他的父母多年前就已经去世。他妈妈曾在疗养院工作,他爸爸是工厂工人。

26 In addition to the child-rape charge, Clemmons faces seven felony charges and a misdemeanor count stemming from a May 9 disturbance outside his home, according to ㉗a probable-cause declaration（可能原因的声明）.

㉗根据一项可能原因的声明,除了强奸儿童指控,克莱蒙斯将面临七项重罪指控,以及一项 5 月 9 日在他家门口的骚乱导致的轻罪指控。

Trouble at home
家中的麻烦

27 When a Pierce County sheriff's deputy went to Clemmons' home at 12: 45 p. m. ,two men, Eddie Lee Davis and Joseph Denton Pitts, were standing outside, ㉘the declaration（声明）says. They told the deputy that Clemmons was inside the house. But when the deputy tried to go in, Davis grabbed him by the wrist.

㉘该声明说,当皮尔斯县州长副官在下午 12:45 去克莱蒙斯家时,有两名男子站在外面,即艾迪·里·戴维斯和约瑟夫·丹顿·皮兹。他们告诉副官克莱蒙斯在屋子里。但是当副官想进去时,戴维斯抓住他的手腕。

28 Pitts joined in, and, while the three men struggled, Clemmons ran out of the house and punched the deputy in the face, ㉙the declaration（声明）says.

㉙声明说,皮兹也加入进来,当三名男子挣扎时,克莱蒙斯跑出了家门,一拳打在副官的脸上。

29 Another deputy arrived, and the two officers were able to gain control over Clemmons, Davis and Pitts. Both deputies suffered injuries

during the fight，③court records（法庭记录）say. Afterward，③neighbors（邻居）told deputies that Clemmons had been throwing rocks through windows and at cars.

　　另一副官抵达后，两名警官能够控制住克莱蒙斯、戴维斯和皮兹。③法庭记录上说，两名警官都在争斗中受了伤。后来，③邻居告诉警官说克莱蒙斯曾经向窗户和汽车扔石头。

30　One resident was struck by a rock that crashed through the window. At least five cars and three houses were damaged，including a car that belonged to Clemmons and his wife，③the declaration（声明）says.

　　③声明说，一位居民被一块从窗口坠落的石头击中。至少有五辆汽车、三间房屋遭到损坏，其中包括克莱蒙斯夫妇的汽车。

31　His wife "declined to complete domestic-violence paperwork，" ③ the declaration（声明）says，"but did tell deputies that she and Clemmons argued over a newly discovered child and theorized that this argument precipitated the rampage."

　　③声明说，他的妻子"拒绝完成家庭暴力的笔录工作"，"但她告诉警官们，她和克莱蒙斯为了一个新发现的孩子争论，并推断是这个争论加剧了克莱蒙斯的暴行"。

32　On Sunday，④one neighbor（邻居）said the fight ended only when an officer pulled a gun and threatened to shoot Clemmons. ⑤This same neighbor（邻居）said one officer came to his door afterward with a black eye.

　　周日，④一个邻居说，直到一名警察拔出一支枪并威胁要枪杀克莱蒙斯时，争斗才结束。⑤这位邻居还说，后来一名被打青眼睛的警察来到他家门口。

33　Clemmons moved into the home a couple of years ago and had a number of loud parties，⑥this neighbor（邻居）said. ⑦Another neighbor，a 70-year-old man（另一位邻居，70 岁），said that Clemmons threw rocks through two of his plate-glass windows.

　　⑥这个邻居说，几年前克莱蒙斯搬到这里，办了许多嘈杂的聚会。另一位邻居，⑦一名 70 岁的男子说，克莱蒙斯朝他的两个玻璃

窗扔过石头。

34 After he tried talking to Clemmons，the neighbor walked way，only to have Clemmons throw a rock that hit him in the hand，splitting it open.

　　在他试图跟克莱蒙斯交谈后，这位邻居走开了，克莱蒙斯向他扔石头，砸中了他的手，石头裂开了。

35 Until that day, Clemmons had been cordial and friendly and never had given anyone trouble，㊳this neighbor（邻居）said.

　　㊳这个邻居说，在此之前，克莱蒙斯一直很亲切友好，没有给任何人添麻烦。

【2010 年普利策突发新闻奖 3 号文本】

Huckabee commuted long term

霍可比长期执行减刑

Clemmons freed in 2000

克莱蒙斯 2000 年获得自由

By：Jim Brunner，Seattle Times staff reporter

吉姆·布伦纳，西雅图时报记者

Times reporter Susan Kelleher and researcher Miyoko Wolf contributed to this report，which also includes material from The Associated Press.

时报的记者苏珊·凯勒赫和研究员米优克·沃夫也对此文有贡献，还包括来自美联社的资料。

November 30，2009

2009 年 11 月 30 日

Former Arkansas governor issued 1，033 commutations and pardons over 10 years

前阿肯色州州长在十多年间颁布了 1033 桩减刑和赦免案。

1 Former Arkansas Gov. Mike Huckabee's record of freeing criminals from prison was controversial even before news that the man sought for questioning in the killing of four Lakewood police officers had a

lengthy prison sentence commuted by Huckabee.

前阿肯色州州长迈克·霍克比把罪犯从监狱释放的记录是饱受争议的，甚至在获知那个涉嫌枪杀四名莱克伍德警官的男子被霍可比减免掉长的刑期之前就受到争议。

2　The one-time Republican presidential contender granted twice as many pardons and commutations as the previous three governors of Arkansas combined，①The Associated Press reported in 2007（美联社 2007 年的报道）.

①据美联社 2007 年的报道，这位昔日的共和党总统竞选人施行的诸多减刑和赦免是他三位前任的纪录总和的两倍。

3　In all，he issued 1，033 pardons and commutations during more than 10 years as governor—an average of about one every four days.

在他担任州长的十多年间，总共签署了 1033 份赦免令和减刑令——平均大约每四天一份。

4　Maurice Clemmons，the man police were searching for Sunday night，faced decades in prison for robberies and other charges when his sentence was commuted by Huckabee in 2000. Clemmons later was sent back to prison after violating parole，but was released again five years ago.

莫里斯·克莱蒙斯，是周日晚上被警方搜捕的那名男子，当 2000 年他的刑期被霍克比减免时，因抢劫和其他指控仍面临着数十年的牢狱之灾。随后因违反假释条例，克莱蒙斯又被送进监狱，但在五年前再次被释放。

5　Clemmons was released from jail in Pierce County six days ago after posting bond. He'd spent the past several months in jail on a charge of child rape. His release came even though he faced seven additional felony charges in Washington state.

六天前，在提交保释金后，克莱蒙斯从皮尔斯县监狱被释放。因强奸儿童的指控，他过去几个月在监狱里度过。在华盛顿州，尽管他面临着七项其他的重罪指控，还是被释放了。

6　Huckabee issued a written ②statement（声明）Sunday night through his daughter and spokeswoman, Sarah Huckabee, saying the "sense-less and savage execution" of the police officers "has saddened the nation."

霍克比通过他的女儿兼发言人萨拉·霍克比在周日晚间发布了一个书面声明，②声明说对警员"愚蠢和野蛮的杀戮令举国悲痛"。

7 If Clemmons is found to be responsible, ③Huckabee's statement（霍克比的声明）said, "it will be the result of a series of failures in the criminal justice system in both Arkansas and Washington state."

③霍克比的声明表示如果克莱蒙斯被发现是有责任的，"那这将是阿肯色州和华盛顿州刑事司法体系一系列失败的结果"。

8 ④The statement（声明）said Clemmons had been recommended for commutation and that his release was approved by the state parole board.

④这份声明称克莱蒙斯曾被建议减刑，并且他的释放是得到州假释委员会核准的。

9 ⑤Huckabee（霍克比）noted that Clemmons later was arrested for parole violations but was released after prosecutors failed to press new charges that could have kept him in prison.

⑤霍克比提到克莱蒙斯后来，因假释违规行为被捕，但是却因公诉人无法提供能使他待在监狱里的新指控而被释放。

10 "It appears that he has continued to have a string of criminal and psychotic behavior but was not kept incarcerated by either state. This is a horrible and tragic event and if found and convicted the offender should be held accountable to the fullest extent of the law," ⑥he（霍克比）said.

⑥他（霍克比）说："看来他仍在继续一连串的犯罪行为和精神异常行为，但两个州似乎都不能将他关进监狱里。这是一个可怕又悲哀的事件，如果发现并被判罪名成立，那罪犯应在最大程度上担负法律责任。"

11 Huckabee's clemencies became a campaign issue when he ran for the Republican presidential nomination last year. He was criticized by

prosecutors and political rivals for releasing prisoners who went on to commit more crimes.

去年当霍克比竞选共和党总统提名时，他的仁慈变成一项竞选议题。他由于释放有可能接着犯罪的囚犯被检察官和政治对手批评。

12　"It's a crying shame that a sitting governor would be so insensitive to victims' rights," Pulaski County Prosecuting Attorney Larry Jegley told an Arkansas newspaper，⑦ The Leader（阿肯色州的报纸《领袖》。这里的消息来源看起来是拉里·杰格里，但实际上拉里的话是从报纸上得来的，消息来源应该是报纸。还有一个判断来由是拉里说这个话是在 2004 年，显然拉里的采访发生在过去，是记者从报纸报道中获取的消息）in 2004.

"这是一位对受害者权利漠不关心的现任州长的奇耻大辱"，2004 年普瓦斯基县检察官拉里·杰格里对⑦阿肯色州的报纸《领袖》这样说。

13　In one high-profile case，castrated rapist Wayne DuMond was set free by the Arkansas parole board at Huckabee's urging，according to ⑧ news accounts（新闻报道）. DuMond later suffocated a mother of three in Missouri and was sentenced to life in prison，where he died in 2005.

⑧根据新闻报道，在一个备受瞩目的案件中，在霍可比的敦促下强奸犯韦恩·杜蒙德被阿肯色州假释委员会释放。后来杜蒙德在密苏里使得一位有三个孩子的母亲窒息而死并被判处终身监禁，2005 年死在那里。

14　A Southern Baptist preacher，Huckabee sometimes was motivated to release prisoners at the urging of pastors or other acquaintances，according to ⑨news accounts（新闻报道）.

⑨根据新闻报道，一位南方浸礼会传教士说，霍克比有时在牧师或其他熟人的敦促下去释放囚徒。

15　His clemencies also benefitted the stepson of a staff member，and e-ven Rolling Stones guitarist Keith Richards，who received a pardon for a 1975 traffic offense. Huckabee，who sometimes jammed on the bass guitar with his band at campaign events, pardoned Richards after meeting him at a concert.

他的大赦也使得一位员工的继子受益，甚至滚石吉他手基斯·理查兹也在 1975 年的一起交通违规中接受了赦免。这位时常在竞选中和理查兹乐队猛弹低音吉他的霍克比，在一场音乐会中遇见理查兹后赦免了他。

16 In an appearance on "Fox News Sunday" — before the news about Clemmons was out—Huckabee said he was leaning slightly against running for president in 2012.

在《周日福克斯新闻》中——在克莱蒙斯消息传出之前——霍克比说他略微倾向于参与竞选 2012 年总统。

【2010 年普利策突发新闻奖 4 号文本】
Veteran officers were parents, too
资深警官也是为人父母
By：Jack Broom, Lynda V. Mapes, Bob Young and Susan Kelleher, Seattle Times staff reporters
杰克·布鲁姆，琳达 V. 曼普，鲍勃·扬和苏珊·凯勒赫，西雅图时报记者。
November 30，2009
2009 年 11 月 30 日

1 The four victims of Sunday morning's shooting were veteran officers who brought a range of talents to the fledgling Lakewood Police Department when it was created in 2004，according to ①Lakewood Police Chief Bret Farrar（莱克伍德警察局长布雷特·法勒）.

①据莱克伍德警察局长布雷特·法勒说，周日上午枪击案的四个受害者是经验丰富的警官，2004 年创建莱克伍德警察局时，正是他们将一系列的人才带到这个羽翼未丰的地方。

2 "This is a very difficult time for our families and our officers," ②he（莱克伍德警察局长布雷特·法勒。这个消息来源的判断必须从上下

文中来判断，否则会被误判为匿名消息来源）said. "Please keep our families and Lakewood Police in your prayers."

　　"对于我们大家庭和我们警员来说这是一个非常艰难的时刻，" ②他说，"请在你们的祷告中纪念我们的家庭和莱克伍德警方。"

3　The slain officers "all have been outstanding professionals," ③he（莱克伍德警察局长布雷特·法勒）added.

　　③他补充说，被杀害的警员"都是出类拔萃的专业人才"。

Officer Tina Griswold
警员蒂娜·格里斯沃尔德

4　Tina Griswold, 40, joined the Lakewood Police Department in 2004 and earlier this year won its Lifesaving Award.

　　蒂娜·格里斯沃尔德40岁，2004年加入莱克伍德警察局，并在2004年年初获得了救生奖。

5　"She was likable and enjoyed life," said ④her former father-in-law, Carroll Kelley of Shelton, Mason County（前岳父梅森县谢尔顿市的卡洛尔·凯利，具名清晰度高）.

　　④她前岳父梅森县谢尔顿市的卡洛尔·凯利说："她讨人喜欢，过着快乐的生活。"

6　She and Kelley's son met when both were students at Shelton High School, ⑤Kelley（凯利）said. Griswold became a police officer after they divorced, ⑥he（凯利）said.

　　⑤凯利说，她和凯利的儿子相识于谢尔顿高中做学生时。⑥他说，他们离婚后格里斯沃尔德成了一名警察。

7　She is survived by her husband, a daughter, 21, and a son, 8, ⑦police and relatives（警察和亲戚们。这是一个复合的匿名消息来源，不过这里的匿名不影响信息的真实性判断）said.

　　⑦警察和亲戚说，她的遗属包括丈夫、一个21岁的女儿和一个8岁的儿子。

8　She previously worked as a police officer in Shelton for three years, ⑧ public records（公共档案）show. She was an officer and SWAT team member for the Lacey Police Department from 1998 to 2004，according to ⑨Sgt. Scott Eastman，her former supervisor（前任主管斯科特·伊士曼军士）. The group was responsible for serving high-risk warrants and conducting high-risk entries，⑩he（伊士曼军士）said.

⑧公共档案显示，她先前在谢尔顿做了 3 年警察。⑨她的前任主管斯科特·伊士曼军士说，从 1998 年到 2004 年她曾是莱西警察局的警员和反恐特警组的队员。⑩他说，那个组织负责服务高风险的授权以及执行高风险的项目。

9　"Tina was an outstanding officer，" ⑪Eastman（伊士曼）said. "She was very assertive，and had no fear in dealing with high-risk situations and suspects that were larger than her. She had this presence about her that was in charge and you were going to do what she said. She had the verbal skills and the confidence to pull it off."

　　"蒂娜是个杰出的警员，" ⑪伊士曼说，"她非常有主见，对处理高危情况和个头比她大的犯罪嫌疑人毫不畏惧。她自身有一股掌控全局的气势，而你只需要按她说的做。她有着很好的谈话技巧和信心来解决这些难题。"

10　Griswold was avid about physical fitness，and lifted weights and ran regularly，⑫Eastman（伊士曼）said. She stood about 5 feet and weighed less than 100 pounds.

　　⑫伊士曼说，格里斯沃尔德对于体能、举重、定跑非常痴迷。她身高是 5 英尺，体重不到 100 镑。

11　"She could do 30 to 40 pull-ups，" ⑬Eastman（伊士曼）said. "A lot of the guys were talking about that this morning. We'd always joke that she didn't have much to lift."

　　"她可以做 30 到 40 个引体向上，" ⑬伊士曼说，"今天早上很多人都在谈论这一点。我们总是开玩笑说，她没有更多的提升了。"

12　Griswold was one of the first members of Lacey's tactical team，and the first woman to hold the job，⑭Eastman（伊士曼）said.

　　⑭伊士曼说，格里斯沃尔德是莱西战术小组第一批成员之一，也是第一位担任这个工作的女性。

13　"She was a very hard worker and just a fun person to work with," ⑮ he（伊士曼）said.　"She spent most of her free time with family… That was her priority."

　　"她是个工作努力的人，和她工作很有乐趣，"⑮他说，"她花了大量的业余时间陪家人。……那是她优先考虑的。"

14　"Although she left Shelton to join the Lacey department，she still lived in town and would run into her former colleagues."

　　"尽管她离开谢尔顿加入了莱西部门，她仍住在镇上并能经常碰见她以前的同事。"

15　"The young officers looked up to her," ⑯ Eastman（伊士曼）said. "And she was a great partner for the experienced officers.　She knew what she was doing."

　　"年轻的警察尊敬她，"⑯伊士曼说，"而对经验丰富的警察而言她是一个伟大的合作伙伴。她知道她在做什么。"

16　Lacey officers are still in shock over the news，⑰ he（伊士曼）said，adding，"We're looking for an opportunity to honor her and her family."

　　莱西的警察听到这消息后仍感到震惊不已，⑰他补充说："我们正在寻找机会向她和她的家人表示敬意。"

Officer Gregory Richards
警察格雷戈里·理查兹

17　He was known as one of the sweet guys, the one everyone liked to work with.

　　他被誉为一个亲切的家伙，每个人都喜欢与之共事。

18　Gregory Richards，42，of Graham had eight years of law-enforcement experience，starting with work as a patrol officer in Kent.

　　格雷戈里·理查兹，42 岁，格雷汉姆人，有 8 年的执法经验，起初是肯特郡的一名巡警。

19　He worked there from September 2001 until October 2004，before hiring on with the Lakewood Police Department.

在受雇莱克伍德警察局之前，从 2001 年 9 月到 2004 年 10 月，他在那儿上班。

20　The Kent department was going through layoffs because of budget cuts, and Richards sought a more secure situation for his family, said ⑱Lt. Lisa Price, public-information officer for the Kent department（肯特部门公共信息官中尉丽莎·普瑞斯）.

⑱肯特部门公共信息官中尉丽莎·普瑞斯说，由于预算削减，肯特部门正在经历裁员，理查兹为他的家人找到了更安全的处境。

21　"He was a very well-respected and well-liked co-worker, and when he left we were sad to see him go," ⑲Price（普瑞斯）said. "People loved working alongside him. I firmly believe Greg would still be with Kent if we hadn't been going through layoffs."

"他是一个非常受人尊敬且受人欢迎的同事，当他离开时大家都很难过，"⑲普瑞斯说，"大家都很喜欢与他一起工作，如果我们没有经历裁员，我坚信格雷戈仍在肯特郡。"

22　"He was just a nice, cute, angelic guy."

"他实在是一个很不错的、聪明的、天使般的家伙。"

23　He had a lighter side too. Richards was the drummer in an all-police officer rock band called Locked Down. The band played at social gatherings, including a recent police officers' motorcycle rally in Ocean Shores.

他也有轻松的一面。理查兹是名鼓手，在一个名为锁定的警员组成的摇滚乐队。乐队会在社交聚会上演奏，包括最近一次海岸边的警察摩托车聚会。

24　The killing was devastating news. "It was a complete shock to my system, it's a horrific crime and it hits close to home," ⑳Price（普瑞斯）said.

杀害事件是毁灭性的消息。⑳普瑞斯说："这对我的认知是彻底的震撼，这是一个可怕的犯罪并且它就发生在我家附近。"

25　Richards is survived by his wife, Kelly, a daughter and two sons.

理查兹的遗属包括妻子凯莉、一个女儿和两个儿子。

26 "Everyone is just here," said ㉑Melanie Burwell，a sister-in-law（嫂子梅勒妮·布鲁威尔）answering the door at Richards' home. "We are staying together."

"每个人都在这里，"㉑理查兹家中开门的嫂子梅勒妮·布鲁威尔说，"我们都待在一起。"

27 ㉒Burwell（布鲁威尔）said she last saw Richards at Thanksgiving. "It was wonderful，"㉓she（布鲁威尔）said，fighting tears. "All he ever wanted was his family. He didn't want to do anything but be with them.

㉒布鲁威尔说她上一次见到理查兹还是在感恩节。"太棒了，"㉓她边说边强忍泪水，"他曾经所想的都是他的家人。除了与他们在一起他别无所求。"

28 "If there were more people in this world like Greg，nothing like this would ever happen."

"如果这个世界上有更多像格雷戈里这样的人，那么就不会有这样的事情发生。"

Sgt. Mark Renninger
中士马克·雷宁格

29 A decorated veteran officer and popular law-enforcement instructor，Sgt. Mark Renninger，39，is survived by his wife and three children.

马克·雷宁格中士，授勋的资深警员，受人欢迎的执法教练，39岁，死后留下妻子和三个孩子。

30 "Mark was a professional，dedicated police officer who made the ultimate sacrifice. More importantly，he was a loving and devoted father，husband and family member who will be missed by many，" said Renninger's brother，Matt，on ㉔a statement published on the Web site of WFMZ-TV（WFMZ-TV 的网站发表的声明）in Pennsylvania's Lehigh Valley，where Renninger grew up.

"马克是一名专业的、敬业的警察，他做出了最后的牺牲。更重要的是，他是充满爱心的慈爱父亲、丈夫和家庭成员，他将被很多人怀念。"雷宁格的兄弟马特在雷宁格成长的地方宾夕法尼亚州利哈伊谷的㉔一个 WFMZ-TV 网站上发表的声明中提到。

31 He joined the Tukwila Police Department shortly after leaving military service in 1996. He was a patrol officer, a SWAT team member and was, for a time, president of the Tukwila police officers' guild.

　　1996 年退伍后，他加入了塔克维拉警察局。他是一名巡警，反恐特警组的队员，有一段时间，他是塔克维拉警察协会的主席。

32 "Mark was an outstanding police officer and a well-liked member of the department during his time with us," said a ㉕statement issued by the Tukwila Police Department（塔克维拉警察局发布的声明）.

　　"马克是一位杰出的警察，与我们相处时他也是受欢迎的同事。"㉕塔克维拉警察局发布的一份声明这样说道。

33 He moved to the Lakewood department in 2004. ㉖According to the program for a state 2008 law-enforcement conference（2008 年州执法会议的计划）, Renninger was an instructor in SWAT courses and served as an instructor for courses in firearms, chemical munitions and patrol responsibilities.

　　他 2004 年来到莱克伍德警察局。㉖根据一项 2008 年州执法会议的计划，雷宁格是反恐特警组课程的教官，教授有关枪支、化学武器和巡逻职责的课程。

34 On a Facebook tribute page set up by his relatives Sunday, more than 1,000 message of tribute were posted by early evening.

　　周日在脸书上，一个由他亲戚创建的致敬页面上，傍晚前已经有超过 1000 条的致敬信息。

35 Among the postings was one from Rick Fisher, who said he coached Renninger's daughter in fastpitch softball two seasons ago. "Mark was a fun and compassionate man," ㉗Fisher（费舍尔）wrote. "He was always willing to help me and the girls out when he could. He was a tremendous help."

　　在这些帖子中有一条来自里克·费舍尔，他两个赛季前指导雷宁格女儿训练快掷垒球。"马克是一个有趣的富有同情心的人，"㉗费舍尔写道，"他总愿意尽可能地帮助我和女孩们外出。他的确帮助很大。"

Officer Ronald Owens
警官罗纳德·欧文斯

36　Friends describe Ronald Owens，37，as a dedicated officer and devoted father．He was also an "ideal tenant," said ㉘Toni Strehlow（托尼·史特瑞劳），who managed a property Owens rented，a house with a white-picket fence near downtown Puyallup.

　　朋友形容罗纳德·欧文斯，37岁，是一个专业的警察和慈爱的父亲。他也是一个"理想的房客"，负责管理出租给欧文斯物业的㉘托尼·史特瑞劳说，这所有白色栅栏的房子靠近普亚洛普市中心。

37　"When he rented from us，the first thing he did was replace walls and a patio door and he never charged us，never wanted a rent deduction．He just wanted to do for people," said ㉙Strehlow（史特瑞劳）.

　　"当他从我们这里租到房子，他所做的第一件事就是更换壁纸和露台的门。他从来不会让我们付钱，也没有要求我们减租。他只是为人们着想。"㉙史特瑞劳说。

38　He was a good neighbor，too，said ㉚Charley Stokes（查利·斯托克斯）who lived next door to him in Puyallup．"We'd talk over the back fence，have a beer once in a while."

　　住在普亚洛普欧文斯隔壁的㉚查利·斯托克斯说，他也是一个好邻居，"我们会在栏杆后面交谈，有时还喝杯啤酒"。

39　Owens，who was divorced，was very proud of his daughter，㉛he（查利·斯托克斯）said.

　　㉛他说，离了婚的欧文斯为他的女儿感到骄傲。

40　㉜Strehlow and Stokes（史特瑞劳和斯托克斯）said Owens was excited about going from his job as a State Patrol trooper to the Lakewood Police Department in 2004，saying Owens looked forward to more regular hours and better advancement opportunities.

㉜史特瑞劳和斯托克斯说，2004 年作为莱克伍德警察局一名州巡逻官，欧文斯感到兴奋，他们说欧文斯期待着更多的固定工作时间和更好的发展机会。

41 ㉝Strehlow（史特瑞劳）said she was speechless when she heard the news. "It's just wrong. He was truly an unforgettable man and a kind, kind person."

㉝史特瑞劳说，当她听到这个消息她说不出话来，"这是绝对错误的。他是一个真正令人难忘的人，一个善良的人"。

42 Owens went into police work because his father, who died in 2006, was a detective, according to ㉞a neighbor, Edie Wintermute（邻居艾迪·温特默特）.

㉞据邻居艾迪·温特默特说，欧文斯进入警方工作是因为他的父亲，他的父亲在 2006 年去世，是一名探员。

43 Owens checked in on her husband after surgery, ㉟she（邻居艾迪·温特默特）said. "He was a good father and very caring guy."

欧文斯在她丈夫手术后探访了她，㉟她说："他是一个好父亲，有爱心的人。"

【2010 年普利策突发新闻奖 5 号文本】

Manhunt intensifies
搜捕变得更加严峻
online coverage of breaking news（突发新闻在线报道）
November 30，2009
2009 年 11 月 30 日

Sunday night, the manhunt for Maurice Clemmons took focus on Seattle, specifically his aunt' home in the Leschi neighborhood. Photographer Cliff DesPeaux, perched on a neighbor's balcony, chronicled the hours long standoff on Twitter, which was posted at the top of seattletimes. com. (We created ♯washooting, which became the region's primary hashtag to track the story.) The home page—and DesPeaux—attracted followers throughout the night as he described police using megaphones, tear gas and robots as they surrounded the house. But Clemmons eluded them. Monday and into Tuesday, police chased tips, identified hoaxes, searched homes and stopped potential suspects throughout the city.

周日晚上，对克莱蒙斯的搜捕范围已经集中到西雅图，特别是位于莱斯基附近他姑妈家。摄影师克利夫·戴斯皮克斯待在邻居的阳台上，在推特上记述了长达几小时的对峙情况，并把它顶帖于西雅图时报网站上。（我们创建了＃washooting标签，成为该地区追踪这个故事的主要标签。）在戴斯皮克斯的主页上，他描述了警方在包围整个房子时使用扩音器、催泪弹和机器人的情况，吸引了用户整晚跟帖。但是克莱蒙斯逃离了他们的包围。从周一到周二，警方根据追捕信息才发现并确定了这是一个骗局，开始在全市范围内搜查住房和搜查可能的嫌疑人。

【2010 年普利策突发新闻奖 6 号文本】
Persuasive appeal helped Clemmons win clemency
有说服力的上诉帮助克莱蒙斯获得宽大处理
A changed man
脱胎换骨的人
By: Jim Brunner and Susan Kelleher, Seattle Times staff reporters
西雅图时报的记者 吉姆·布伦纳和苏珊·凯勒赫
December 1, 2009
2009 年 12 月 1 日

The repeat felon convinced Gov. Mike Huckabee and the Arkansas Parole Board he had learned from his mistakes.
重复犯下重罪的犯人使州长霍克比和阿肯色州假释委员会确信他已从其错误中吸取了教训。

1　Maurice Clemmons likely would still be sitting in an Arkansas prison cell if he hadn't convinced former Gov. Mike Huckabee and the state's parole board that he'd reformed while behind bars for a teenage crime spree.

如果莫里斯·克莱蒙斯没有说服前任州长麦克·霍克比和州假释委员会,他已经在青少年犯罪狂潮之后待在监狱里接受了改造,他仍可能被关在阿肯色州的监狱里。

2　Clemmons,a suspect in Sunday's slaying of four Lakewood police officers,had been sentenced to about 100 years in prison for several felonies,including bringing a gun to school and a robbery in which he punched a woman in the face.

克莱蒙斯,这名在星期日杀害四名莱克伍德警察的犯罪嫌疑人,因数项重罪已被判处 100 年的监禁,这些罪名包括持枪入学和抢劫一名被他用拳打中脸部的妇女。

3　He would not have been eligible for parole until 2015 or later,according to ①Arkansas court documents and prosecutors(阿肯色州法庭文件和检察官们).

①根据阿肯色州法庭文件和检察官的说辞,他要到 2015 年或更晚才有假释的资格。

4　But Clemmons was set free in 2000-over the objections of prosecutors-after Huckabee commuted the long prison sentence,making him immediately eligible for parole.

在霍克比减免漫长刑期后,克莱蒙斯立刻获得了假释的资格。顶着检察官的反对,他在 2000 年被释放。

5　In ②his appeal(上诉)to Huckabee,Clemmons apologized for his actions but complained he'd received overly harsh sentences.

在他向霍克比的②上诉中,克莱蒙斯为他的行为道歉,但是也抱怨他受到过于严厉的刑罚。

6　③Clemmons(克莱蒙斯)said he started his crime spree at 16,after he had moved from Seattle to a high-crime neighborhood in Arkansas.

③克莱蒙斯说他十六岁时开始无节制的犯罪活动,这发生在他从西雅图搬到阿肯色州一个高犯罪率的社区之后。

7　"I succumbed to the peer pressure and the need I had to be accepted by other youth in my new environment and fell in with the wrong crowd and thus began a seven month crime spree which led me to prison,"

Clemmons wrote in his clemency ④application（申请）to Huckabee.

克莱蒙斯写④信给霍克比，寻求宽大处理，他写道："我屈服于同龄人的压力，以及在新处境中我必须被其他年轻人接受的压力，由此和不法之徒混在一起，导致了一个将我送进监狱的历时七个月的犯罪活动。"

"Good Christian family"

"好基督徒家庭"

8 ⑤Clemmons（克莱蒙斯）wrote he came from "a very good Christian family" and "was raised much better than my actions speak……"

⑤克莱蒙斯写道，他来自"一个非常好的基督徒家庭"，并且"被牧养的情况要比我的行为更有说服力……"

9 In a 1989 aggravated robbery, Clemmons, 17 at the time, and two accomplices accosted a woman at midnight in the parking lot of a Little Rock hotel bar and robbed her of $16 and a credit card.

1989年一起恶劣的抢劫中，17岁的克莱蒙斯和两个同伙在午夜的小石城旅馆酒吧的停车场与一名女子搭讪，抢劫了那名女子16美元和一张信用卡。

10 The woman, ⑥Karen Hodge（凯伦·霍奇）, testified at trial that Clemmons threatened her by pretending to have a gun in his pocket. "Give me your purse or I'm going to shoot you," he told her.

这个女人名叫⑥凯伦·霍奇，在听审时作证说，克莱蒙斯威胁她假装他的口袋里有一把枪。"把你的手袋给我否则我就开枪"，他告诉她。

11 Hodge, who'd had a glass of scotch, responded, "Well…why don't you just shoot?" Clemmons punched her in the head and tore the purse off her shoulder, according to⑦court records（法庭记录）.

霍奇喝了杯苏格兰威士忌，回答道："那么……你为什么不直接开枪？"⑦根据法庭记录，克莱蒙斯用拳猛击她的头部并且将手袋从她的肩膀扯下。

12 He was sentenced to 35 years in prison for that incident.

他因为这件事被判入狱35年。

13   In ⑧ his appeal（上诉）for clemency，Clemmons said he had
changed.

⑧在克莱蒙斯寻求宽恕的上诉中，他说他已洗心革面。

14   "Where once stood a young ... misguided fool，who's（sic）own life
he was unable to rule. Now stands a 27 year old man，who has learned through 'the school of hard knocks' to appreciate and respect the
rights of others. And who has in the midst of the harsh reality of
prison life developed the necessary skills to stand along（sic）and not
follow a multitude to do evil，as I did as a 16 year old child."

"这里站着一个曾经年轻的……但误入歧途的傻瓜，他无法掌
握自己的人生。如今这里站着的是一个 27 岁不再年轻的男子，已在
逆境中认识到欣赏并尊重他人的权利。在监狱生活的严酷现实中他
已学会了必要的能力来站稳脚跟，而不是跟随众人行恶，如同曾经
那个只有 16 岁的孩子。"

15   ⑨ Clemmons（克莱蒙斯）added that his mother had recently died
without seeing him turn his life around and that he prayed Huckabee
would show compassion by releasing him.

⑨克莱蒙斯补充说，他的母亲刚刚死去，并没有看到他作出改
变，他祈祷霍可比在释放他这件事上给予他同情。

16   His clemency application was supported by Pulaski County Circuit
Court Judge Marion Humphrey，who cited Clemmons ' youth at the
time of his crimes and called his cumulative sentence excessive.
Clemmons' release was unanimously approved by the parole board.

克莱蒙斯请求宽恕的申请得到了普拉斯基县巡回法院法官马里
恩·汉弗莱的支持，他列举了克莱蒙斯犯罪时的少不更事，并称他
叠加的刑期过重。假释委员会一致通过克莱蒙斯的释放。

17   The Pulaski County prosecutor's office twice objected to parole recom-
mendations for Clemmons.

普拉斯基县检察官办公室两次驳回了对克莱蒙斯的假释推荐。

18   "For us to prosecute a 17-year-old，and for him to get a 95-year sentence without a homicide，you've got to be a bad little dude to draw

that kind of a sentence," said ⑩Mark Fraiser（马克·弗雷泽），who prosecuted the early cases against Clemmons in Pulaski County.

　　"让我们起诉一个 17 岁大的，对他来说没有杀人却得到一个 95 年的刑期，你必须是个坏家伙才能作出那种判决。"在普拉斯基县起诉了针对克莱蒙斯的早期案子的⑩马克·弗雷泽说。

19　Clemmons had insisted on separate trials for each charge，⑪Fraiser（弗雷泽）said，and the judge who presided over the cases had a strong tendency to issue consecutive sentences that reflected the judgment of jurors in each case.

　　克莱蒙斯坚持对每起案件进行独立审判，⑪弗雷泽说，主审案件的法官有很强的意愿进行连续的判决，以反映每起案件中陪审员的判断。

20　Clemmons "had an obvious propensity for future violence," ⑫Fraiser（弗雷泽）said Monday. "To wake up this morning and turn on the news and hear his name，I can't even imagine the suffering of those families and the suffering of people in those communities."

　　克莱蒙斯"显然有可能发生未来的暴力行为"，⑫弗雷泽周一说，"今早醒来，打开新闻听到他的名字，我无法想象那些家庭和那些社区的人们所遭受的痛苦。"

21　⑬Humphrey（汉弗莱）said Monday he remembers Clemmons and believed he was genuinely remorseful and wanted to change.

　　⑬汉弗莱周一说，他记得克莱蒙斯，而且相信他是真心悔改并希望改过自新。

22　"I figure young people make some mistakes," ⑭he（汉弗莱）said. Also a Presbyterian minister，⑮Humphrey（汉弗莱）said he believes in giving people a second chance.

　　"我认为年轻人会犯一些错误。"⑭他说。同样作为一个长老会牧师，⑮汉弗莱说他相信应给予人们第二次机会。

23　Humphrey in 2004 also officiated Clemmons' wedding，according to⑯ a copy of the marriage certificate（结婚证的副本。这个消息来源的获得可以看出作者的采访功力。）.

⑯根据一份结婚证的副本，汉弗莱在 2004 年主持了克莱蒙斯的婚礼。

24　"It would be the furthest thing from my mind that he would go out and kill four police officers，if in fact he did，" ⑰Humphrey（汉弗莱）said.

　　"我根本不会想到他会出来，还杀了四个警官，如果那确实是克莱蒙斯做的。"⑰汉弗莱说。

25　Huckabee also cited Clemmons' young age at the time of his crimes in an official proclamation commuting his sentence. ⑱The proclamation（公告）said Clemmons faced a 95-year sentence but ⑲corrections officials（惩教官员）in that state said he likely would have served far less than that.

　　霍克比在一份官方减刑公告中，列举了克莱蒙斯犯罪时年纪轻轻。⑱公告说克莱蒙斯面临 95 年的刑期，但那个州的⑲惩教官员说他可能不会监禁那么久。

26　The proclamation was one of 1,033 commutations and pardons Huckabee issued during his more than 10 years as governor. That's about twice the number issued by his three predecessors combined.

　　该公告是霍可比十多年的州长生涯中所发布的 1033 份减刑和特赦令中的一份。这个数字是他三个前任州长总和的两倍。

Back in prison

回到监狱

27　Clemmons was released from prison in August 2000 but was sent back on a parole violation—a robbery charge—in July 2001，according to⑳ Dina Tyler（迪娜·泰勒），spokeswoman for the Arkansas Department of Corrections.

　　⑳据阿肯色州惩教局的发言人迪娜·泰勒所说，2000 年 8 月克莱蒙斯从监狱释放，但在 2001 年 7 月因抢劫控告违反了假释条件而被送回监狱。

28　He received a 10-year sentence，㉑Tyler（泰勒）said，but ㉒records（记录）show he was paroled again in March 2004.

㉑泰勒说，克莱蒙斯获得了十年刑期，但是㉒记录显示他在 2004 年 3 月再次被假释。

29　㉓Pulaski County Prosecutor Larry Jegley（普拉斯基县的检察官拉里·杰格里）said that by his count，Clemmons should have been in jail until 2021.

　　㉓普拉斯基县的检察官拉里·杰格里说，根据他的计算克莱蒙斯应该在监狱待到 2021 年。

30　"Mr. Huckabee made him parole-eligible 21 years before he would have been，"㉔Jegley（杰格里）said.

　　"霍克比先生使他早了 21 年获得假释资格。"㉔杰格里说。

31　Clemmons' volatile behavior in court gave officials little reason to show leniency.

　　克莱蒙斯在法庭上不稳定的行为使公职人员几乎不愿对他宽大处理。

32　"He was one you always kept an eye on，" said ㉕W. A. McCormick（W. A.迈克考密克），chief deputy for Jegley in the years Clemmons was prosecuted. "You just wanted to keep your distance with him in the courtroom."

　　"他是一个时刻需留意的人，"克莱蒙斯被起诉的几年间杰格里的主要代理㉕W. A.迈克考密克说，"在法庭上你只想和他保持距离。"

33　㉖Fraiser（弗雷泽）recalled how Clemmons dismantled a pneumatic metal door stop and hid it in his sock，possibly to use as a weapon. A bailiff discovered it and took it away.

　　㉖弗雷泽回忆起克莱蒙斯如何拆卸一个气动金属门挡，并把它藏在他的袜子里，可能是用作武器。一位法警发现并拿走了它。

34　㉗A judge also accused Clemmons of threatening him，and，in yet another case，Clemmons took a lock from his holding cell and threw it at a bailiff，missing him and hitting Clemmons' mother instead.

　　㉗法官还指责克莱蒙斯威胁他。在另一个案例，克莱蒙斯从他的拘留室里拿了一把锁并把它扔向法警，锁没有打中法警却打中了克莱蒙斯的妈妈。

35 Clemmons moved to Washington state in 2004 while still on parole, a move approved by Arkansas authorities. He spent the past several months in jail on a child-rape charge but was released last week after arranging for a bail-bond company to post his $150,000 bond. His release here came despite seven other pending felony charges, according to㉘ court records (法庭记录).

2004 年，克莱蒙斯在假释期搬到了华盛顿州，此举得到阿肯色州当局的批准。在过去的几个月，他因强奸儿童指控而入狱，但在上周他被释放了。在释放前，他安排了一个保释公司给他交了 15 万美金。㉘根据法院的记录，尽管还有七项待决的重罪指控，他仍然被释放了。

36 Huckabee, a Republican presidential contender in 2008, issued a ㉙ statement（声明）Sunday night mourning the deaths of the Lakewood police officers and saying that if Clemmons is responsible "it will be the result of a series of failures in the criminal justice system in both Arkansas and Washington state."

霍可比是 2008 年共和党总统候选人。他在星期天晚上发表了㉙一个声明，对莱克伍德警官的死亡表示哀悼，同时他还说，如果克莱蒙斯负有责任，"这将是阿肯色州和华盛顿州刑事司法体系一系列失败的结果"。

37 ㉚Huckabee（霍克比）noted that Clemmons' release was approved by the parole board and that prosecutors in Arkansas failed to file additional charges against Clemmons after his parole violation in 2001, which could have extended his time in prison.

㉚霍可比指出，克莱蒙斯的释放是经过假释委员会批准的。2001 年他违反假释后，阿肯色州的检察官未能提出对克莱蒙斯额外的指控，而这能够延长他在监狱的时间。

38 "If I could have known nine years ago and could have looked into the future, would I have acted favorably upon the parole board's recommendation? Of course not," Huckabee told ㉛Fox News（福克斯新闻）Radio on Monday.

"如果我能在九年前就知道这一切并且能预知未来，我会在假释委员会的推荐下顺利行动吗？当然不会。"星期一，霍克比告诉㉛

福克斯新闻广播电台。

39　Tuesday，㉜Huckabee（霍克比）said that some of the criticism he's received for commuting the sentence is "disgusting" and the situation was being used as a political weapon against him.

　　周二，㉜霍克比说他收到的关于减刑的批评都是"令人厌恶的"，而这一局势被用来作为对抗他的政治武器。

40　In an interview on㉝Joe Scarborough's radio show on WABC-AM（乔·斯卡伯勒的广播节目采访）in New York，Huckabee said that the focus should be on the families of the four slain officers.

　　霍克比在纽约㉝WABC-AM 著名主持人乔·斯卡伯勒的广播节目采访中说，人们关注的焦点应该是四位被杀害的警察的家庭。

Arkansas Democrat-Gazette and The Associated Press contributed to this story.

　　《阿肯色州民主党公报》和美联社对本文有贡献。

【2010 年普利策突发新闻奖 7 号文本】

Four days in May set stage for tragedy

五月的四天为悲剧做准备

By：Nick Perry，Maureen O'Hagan，Jonathan Martin and Ken Armstrong，Seattle Times staff reporters

西雅图时报记者尼克·派瑞，莫瑞那·海根，乔纳森·马丁和肯·阿姆斯壮。

December 1，2009

2009 年 12 月 1 日

1　Over four days in May，Maurice Clemmons' behavior and mental state deteriorated. Family members worried he had gone crazy，that he was verging on collapse. His conduct became so erratic—punching a sheriff's deputy，forcing relatives to strip naked，according to①police reports（警方的报告）—that authorities eventually charged him with eight felonies，including one count of child rape.

　　在五月的四天里，莫里斯·克莱蒙斯的行为和精神状态恶化。家人担心他发疯了，他已经濒临崩溃。①根据警方的报告，他的行为变得如此不稳定，他拳打一名警长助理，强迫亲戚脱光衣服。当局最终控告他有八项重罪，包括一项强奸儿童罪。

2　Still，at the end of those four days，Clemmons wound up on the loose-a delusional man with a propensity for violence，who had managed to escape the grip of authorities.

　　尽管这样，在那四天以后，克莱蒙斯还是得到了释放。这个有着暴力倾向的、患有妄想症的男人，设法摆脱了当局的控制。

3　What happened in those four days-and in the months that followed-reflects a system governed by formula and misguided incentives.

　　那四天以及接下来的几个月里发生的事情，反映出一个被规条和误导性动机支配的系统。

4　That legal system，both in Arkansas and Washington，failed to account for the entirety of Clemmons' violence and his disdain for the law. Individual crimes，viewed in isolation，trumped a long and disturbing pattern of warning signs.

　　这一法律体系，无论是在阿肯色州还是华盛顿州，都没有考虑到克莱蒙斯全部暴力行为和他对法律的蔑视。个人的犯罪，孤立地观察，胜过了一个长期的令人不安的警告提示。

5　As a result，Clemmons walked out of jail Nov. 23. A week later，he was on the run again-this time accused of shooting and killing four Lakewood police officers in a Parkland coffee shop，in one of the most horrific crimes in Puget Sound history.

　　克莱蒙斯最终在 11 月 23 号走出监狱。一周后，他再次逃亡，这次他被指控在帕克兰咖啡店射杀了四名莱克伍德警官，这是普吉特历史上最恐怖的犯罪之一。

May 9

五月九号

6　It may have been an argument-precipitated by his wife's discovery that he had a child with another woman that set Clemmons off.

　　这可能是一次争论，是由克莱蒙斯的妻子发现他和别的女人有了孩子而引起的。这让克莱蒙斯大怒。

7 Whatever it was，Clemmons took his rage out on his Parkland neighborhood，throwing rocks at houses，cars and people，according to ② police records（警方记录）.

不管是什么情况，②据警方记录，克莱蒙斯将他的愤怒发泄到帕克兰的居民区，向房子、汽车及他人丢石头。

8 ③A woman who was visiting family（一位当天走访亲友的女性）that day says she was leaving the neighborhood when a man hurled a landscaping brick through the driver-side window of her SUV.

③一位当天走访亲友的女性说道，当她离开社区时，一男子将一块景观砖丢进她越野车驾驶座旁边的窗户里。

9 "I was just in shock," said ④the woman（妇女），who asked not to be identified because Clemmons remains at large. "The look in his eyes is something I will not forget."

"我被吓到了，"由于克莱蒙斯仍在逃，一位不愿意透露姓名的④妇女说，"他的眼神我永远也忘不了。"

10 The woman called 911 only after rounding a corner a safe distance away.

这名女性一转弯到了安全距离，就立刻拨打了911。

11 A Pierce County sheriff's deputy responded to the disturbance at 12：45 p. m. Outside Clemmons 'home，the deputy encountered two of Clemmons' cousins.

皮尔斯县一副警长在12：45的时候对骚扰做出了回应。在克莱蒙斯住宅外，副警长遇到了克莱蒙斯的两个表兄弟。

12 When the deputy tried going into the house in search of Clemmons，one cousin grabbed the deputy's wrist. A struggle followed，during which Clemmons emerged from the house and punched the deputy in the face. Clemmons also assaulted a second deputy who arrived to help，according to ⑤court records（法庭记录）.

当副警长试图进入住宅寻找克莱蒙斯时，其中一个表兄弟抓住了副警长的手腕。随即是一场搏斗，此间克莱蒙斯从住宅中出来并拳击了副警长的面部。⑤根据法庭记录，克莱蒙斯还袭击了前来援助的另一个副手。

13　Ultimately，all three men were arrested and taken to jail. When being booked，Clemmons refused to cooperate and said，"I'll kill all you bitches," according to ⑥ a psychological evaluation obtained by The News Tribune（《新闻论坛报》得到的心理评估）.

　　最终，他们三人均被逮捕并关进了监狱。⑥根据《新闻论坛报》得到的心理评估，在被审问时，克莱蒙斯拒绝合作并说："我要把你们都杀了。"

14　The two cousins pleaded guilty to felony assault and were sentenced to several months in jail.

　　他的两个表兄弟承认犯有袭击的重罪，并被送到监狱关押数月。

15　But the charges against Clemmons would defy such easy resolution.

　　但是对于克莱蒙斯的指控不会像这个判决一样简单。

May 10

5 月 10 号

16　After spending one night in jail，Clemmons caught a break.

　　在监狱待了一晚之后，克莱蒙斯得到一个喘息的机会。

17　May 10 was a Sunday，Mother's Day. Judges rarely work Sundays but bail-bond agents do.

　　5 月 10 号是一个星期天，并且是母亲节。除了保释金经济人外，法官们在星期天是不工作的。

18　Pierce County has devised a system that allows people to post bond without ever facing a judge，if it happens to be a holiday or a weekend.

　　皮尔斯县已经制定了一套系统，如果在假期或者周末人们可以不面见法官提交保释金。

19　Called "booking bail," this system works according to a hard-and-fast formula. Clemmons was booked on four felony charges—two for assault，two for malicious mischief—and，by schedule，his booking bail was set at $ 10,000 per charge, for a total of $ 40,000.

该系统被称为"预订保释金"，它根据一个固定的公式工作。克莱蒙斯被判四项重罪指控，两项是袭击，两项是故意的恶作剧。按规定，他的预定保释为每项 1 万美金，总共为 4 万美金。

20　"If you post booking bail，you can walk out without seeing a judge. And that appears to be exactly what he did，" said ⑦ Pierce County Prosecuting Attorney Mark Lindquist（皮尔斯县检察官马克·林奎斯特）. "When it's booking bail，it doesn't take into account particular details like somebody's history. And that's problematic…it's one of the dangers of booking bail. "

　　"如果你提交了保释金，你可以不用面见法官而直接离开。而这似乎正是他所做的，" ⑦ 皮尔斯县检察官马克·林奎斯特说到，"当保释时，并没有考虑到特定的细节，例如某人的历史。这正是问题所在……而那正是保释的危险之一。"

21　If his history had been taken into account，Clemmons would have fared poorly. He had a criminal record dating to his teen years，with at least five prior felony convictions in Arkansas.

　　如果考虑到他的历史，克莱蒙斯行为不佳。他从青少年时期就有着犯罪记录，在阿肯色州他至少有五项重罪定罪。

22　Aladdin Bail Bonds posted Clemmons' bond on Mother's Day，and Clemmons walked free. Defendants typically pay 10 percent of the bond，with the bonding company on the hook for the rest.

　　在母亲节那天，阿拉丁保释金支付了克莱蒙斯的保释金，然后克莱蒙斯被释放了。被告通常支付 10％的保释金，其余由保释公司承担。

23　⑧ Stephen Kreimer，executive director of the Professional Bail Agents of the United States（斯蒂芬·克瑞姆，美国专业保释代理人执行董事。），said he doesn't think "booking bail" is common nationwide. In most states，he said，defendants must wait until they've seen a magistrate or court representative before being released on bail.

　　作为美国专业保释代理人执行董事，⑧斯蒂芬·克瑞姆认为

"预订保释"在全国并不普遍。他说，在大多数州，被告必须等到见到一名法官或者法庭代表后，才能被保释出来。

May 11

5月11日

24　After his release on May 10，Clemmons' mental state degenerated，with his wife saying he was acting "crazy，" according to ⑨a Pierce County sheriff's report（皮尔斯县治安官的报告）.

　　⑨根据一份皮尔斯县治安官的报告，5月10日克莱蒙斯释放后，他的精神状态恶化，他的妻子说他的行为是"疯狂的"。

25　At about 1 a. m. May 11，Clemmons appeared naked in his living room and demanded that two young female relatives-ages 11 and 12-sit on an ottoman and fondle him，⑩one of the girls（其中一个女孩）later told police. They obeyed，⑪the girl（女孩）said，because they were "scared." The 11-year-old soon fled，and wasn't seen for days.

　　5月11日凌晨1时左右，克莱蒙斯裸体出现在他的起居室，要求两个年轻的女性亲属（一个11岁，一个12岁），坐在无背长椅上抚弄他，⑩一个女孩随后告诉了警察。她们服从了。⑪女孩说，因为她们受到了"惊吓"。这个11岁的女孩很快逃走了，好几天没有被人看到。

26　But Clemmons continued to assault the 12-year-old until she cried herself to sleep，⑫ police records（警方记录）say. Clemmons，still naked，soon woke her and demanded she join him and his wife，Nicole Smith，in their bedroom. Clemmons referred to himself as Jesus and Smith，naked and wrapped in a bedsheet，as Eve. Smith begged her husband to let the girl go，and Clemmons complied，⑬ the girl（女孩）later told police.

　　⑫警方记录显示，克莱蒙斯继续殴打12岁的女孩直到她哭着入睡。克莱蒙斯仍旧赤裸着，很快叫醒女孩，要求她加入他和妻子妮可·史密斯之列，就在他们的卧室。克莱蒙斯把自己当作耶稣，史密斯赤裸身子用床单包裹着，则是夏娃。⑬女孩后来告诉警察，史密斯恳求她丈夫让女孩走，克莱蒙斯照做了。

27 But Clemmons wasn't finished. At about 4 a. m. , he assembled his family back in the living room and demanded they strip naked. ⑭He (他，指的是克莱蒙斯) talked about how "beautiful it was that they were sharing the moment. "

但是克莱蒙斯还没有结束。大约凌晨四点时，他让家人重回到起居室，要求他们赤身裸体。⑭他谈到他们分享这一刻是多么美丽。

28 Pierce County sheriff's deputies arrived at about 5：30 a. m. after a family member called 911. With Clemmons now gone from the house，⑮the family（家庭成员）described his recent erratic behavior，including his statements that the world was coming to an end and he was "going to fly to heaven. "

一名家庭成员打电话给 911 后，皮尔斯县警长的代表在凌晨五点半抵达。在克莱蒙斯离开家后，⑮家人描述他最近的古怪行为，包括他断言地球将灭亡而他将飞向天堂。

29 Acting on a tip from Smith, deputies saw Clemmons nearby, at a second house he was building. But Clemmons ran away before deputies could stop him，and a K-9 unit could not pick up his trail.

在史密斯的提示下，警长代表在克莱蒙斯建造的第二栋房子附近看到他。但是克莱蒙斯在代表阻止他之前逃脱了，即使是一整个 K-9 分队也没能找到他的踪迹。

30 Child Protective Services（CPS），alerted by deputies，also investigated the incident and substantiated the sexual-abuse complaint. ⑯A CPS spokeswoman（儿童保护机构的一位女发言人）said the agency closed the case in October because Smith and the young relative went to counseling and Clemmons was in jail.

在代表的提醒下，儿童保护机构也调查了事件并证实了性虐待投诉。⑯儿童保护机构的一位女发言人说，该机构 10 月份关闭了案子，因为史密斯和年轻的亲属去咨询了，克莱蒙斯也已经入狱。

May 12

5 月 12 日

31 Clemmons was supposed to show up in Pierce County Superior Court

May 12, to be arraigned on charges stemming from the rocks and punches he was accused of throwing three days before.

克莱蒙斯原定于 5 月 12 日在皮尔斯县高等法院出庭，因三天前投掷石块和拳打行为而受到起诉。

32 By now, prosecutors had filed a formal set of charges accusing Clemmons with two counts of assault and five for felony malicious mischief.

到目前为止，检察官已经正式对他提出一系列指控，包括两项袭击和五项恶作剧的罪名。

33 But at 1:30 p. m., when a court official polled the courtroom gallery to see who was there, Clemmons was a no show. Three hours later, at the close of the court's day, he still was nowhere to be found.

但是在下午 1:30，当一位法院官员检查法庭走廊时，却发现克莱蒙斯不见了。三小时后，法庭要休庭时，仍然没有找到他。

34 A judge later issued a bench warrant, calling for Clemmons' arrest for failure to appear.

一位法官随即发出搜捕令，因克莱蒙斯未出现而要逮捕他。

35 Clemmons was on the run with seven felony charges already filed against him and another on the way, given what had happened in his house just one day before.

克莱蒙斯正在逃亡中，鉴于前一天在他家里所发生的一切，已经对他提出了七项重罪指控，目前正在对另一项指控进行起诉。

May 13

5 月 13 日

36 Clemmons wound up being arrested seven weeks later, on July 1, when he showed up in court, in apparent hopes of having the bench warrant thrown out.

克莱蒙斯在七周后的 7 月 1 日被逮捕了。当他现身法庭的时候，很明显有希望将法院的逮捕令否决。

37 The next day, prosecutors charged him with second-degree rape of a child, accusing him of molesting his 12-year-old relative in May.

第二天，检察官指控他对一个孩子有二级的强奸，控告他在 5 月份猥亵一个 12 岁的亲属。

38 Prosecutors also filed a separate charge on July 2—this one accusing Clemmons of being a fugitive from Arkansas. They cited the chain of events involving the alleged assault on the deputies as evidence that Clemmons had violated his parole in Arkansas. If sent back，he faced the prospect of being returned to prison for years.

检察官还在 7 月 2 日提出另一项指控，指控他是阿肯色州的逃犯。他们引述袭击代表的一系列相关的事件作为证据，证明克莱蒙斯在阿肯色违反了假释条例。如果被遣返，他将有可能面临数年的监禁。

39 But July 22，the Arkansas Department of Community Correction notified Pierce County，by letter，that Arkansas had no interest in taking Clemmons back.

但是 7 月 22 日，阿肯色社区惩矫部通过信件通知皮尔斯县，阿肯色无意将克莱蒙斯带回。

40 "Arkansas is releasing its hold on the offender and will not extradite at this time," ⑰the letter（阿肯色社区惩矫部通知皮尔斯县的信）said. "The subject has pending charges in the state of Washington and appropriate action will be taken once the charges have been adjudicated."

"阿肯色州释放了监管的罪犯，目前不会引渡，"⑰信上说，"在华盛顿州，此人有待决的指控，一旦裁决，将采取适当的行动。"

41 Arkansas rescinded its warrant. Had Arkansas not done so，Clemmons would have been held without bail on the alleged parole violation.

阿肯色州撤销了逮捕令。如果阿肯色州没有这么做，克莱蒙斯将被拘留，且没有保释，因为涉嫌违反了假释条件。

42 ⑱Stephen Penner, a deputy prosecuting attorney in Pierce County（斯蒂芬·彭纳，皮尔斯县的一位副检察官），said he sees Arkansas' decision to leave Clemmons to Washington this way: "There's a

built-in incentive to not following through. In a way, the more violent they are, the less you want them in your community."

皮尔斯县的一位副检察官⑱斯蒂芬·彭纳说,他认为阿肯色州的决定让克莱蒙斯以这种方式留在了华盛顿:"有一种内在的动机,就是不跟进。在某种程度上,他们越暴力,你越不想让他们进入你的社区。"

43 Lindquist, Pierce County's chief prosecutor, was asked Monday if he believes Arkansas dumped Clemmons on Washington.

周一,皮尔斯县的首席检察官林奎斯特,被问到他是否认为阿肯色州把克莱蒙斯丢给了华盛顿州。

44 Only Arkansas can answer that question, ⑲Lindquist(林奎斯特)said, but he added:"You could draw that inference."

⑲林奎斯特说只有阿肯色州能够回答这个问题,但他还说:"你可以这么推断。"

45 ⑳A spokeswoman for the Arkansas prison system(阿肯色州监狱体系的一个女发言人)told the Arkansas Democrat-Gazette that the state issued a second warrant in October that would have allowed Clemmons to be held without bail.

⑳阿肯色州监狱体系的一个女发言人告诉《阿肯色州民主党宪报》,阿肯色州在10月份公布了第二个逮捕令,允许在没有保释情况下拘留克莱蒙斯。

46 ㉑Penner(彭纳)said if a second warrant was issued, no one told him.

㉑彭纳说,没有人告诉他发布了第二份逮捕令。

Nov. 23

11月23日

49 In Washington, the courts had to determine bail for the two sets of charges Clemmons faced.

在华盛顿,法庭必须抉择克莱蒙斯要面对的两项指控的保释。

50 ㉒Phil Sorensen, a deputy prosecutor in Pierce County(菲尔·索伦森,皮尔斯县的一位副检察官),said his office asked for $100,000 bail in the assault case—an amount higher than normal for such char-

ges—based on Clemmons' history. The judge, John McCarthy, set the bail at ＄40,000, ㉓Sorensen（索伦森）said.

㉒菲尔·索伦森，皮尔斯县的一位副检察官说，他的办公室基于克莱蒙斯的背景，要求在袭击案件中交纳高于这类案件正常收费的 10 万美元保释金。㉓索伦森说，约翰·麦卡锡法官定保释金为 4 万美元。

51　In the child-rape case, prosecutors wanted ＄200,000 bail, ㉔Lindquist（林奎斯特）said. The judge, Thomas Felnagle, set bail at ＄150,000.

㉔林奎斯特说，在儿童强奸案中，检察官想将保释金定于 20 万美元。托马斯·费格纳法官将保释金定为 15 万美元。

52　㉕Lindquist（林奎斯特）said he thought both judges set bail too low.

㉕林奎斯特说，他认为两位法官设定的保释金都太低了。

53　"As prosecutors, we face an uphill battle walking into court," ㉖he（林奎斯特）said. "We have to show that the defendant is a danger to the community and a flight risk."

"作为检察官，我们在进入法庭时面临着艰巨斗争，" ㉖他说，"我们不许展示被告对于社区存在危险并且有逃跑的风险。"

54　Neither judge could be reached for comment Monday.

星期一，没有任何法官就此事发表评论。

55　In the end, Clemmons needed to come up with ＄190,000 bail.

最终，克莱蒙斯需要拿出 19 万美元的保释金。

56　㉗Penner, the deputy prosecuting attorney（副检察官彭纳），said Clemmons was turned away by two bail-bond agencies, based on his history of failing to appear in court. But then Clemmons found a taker: Jail Sucks Bail Bonds, based in Chehalis.

㉗副检察官彭纳说，基于他有未出席法庭的历史，克莱蒙斯被两家保释机构拒绝，但最终他找到了以奇哈利斯为靠山的监狱吸纳保释金公司。

57　At 8:20 p.m. Nov. 23, bond was posted for Clemmons. That same night he walked out of the Pierce County Jail.

在 11 月 23 日上午 8 点 20 分，克莱蒙斯的债券发布。那天晚上，他走出了皮尔斯县监狱。

【2010 年普利策突发新闻奖 8 号文本】

Clemmons killed by patrolman

克莱蒙斯被巡警击毙

online coverage of breaking news

（在线报道突发新闻）

November 30，2009

2009 年 11 月 30 日

When Maurice Clemmons was killed early Tuesday by a patrolman investigating a stolen vehicle，seattletimes. com posted updates，tweets，video and audio. Our staffers were careful as they posted the information，first that a man matching Clemmons' description had been apprehended，then confirming it was Clemmons，then confirming he'd been shot，and ultimately that he had been killed.

星期二早上，当莫里斯·克莱蒙斯被一名正在调查失窃车辆的巡警击毙时，《西雅图时报》的网站发布了更新：推特、视频和音频。在发布信息时，我们的工作人员非常小心。首先，一个与克莱蒙斯的描述相符的男人已被逮捕，然后确认他是克莱蒙斯，而后确定他已经遭到射击，最终得出结论——克莱蒙斯已被击毙。

【2010 年普利策突发新闻奖 9 号文本】

Uncle：'He was all about money —suddenly，he was all about God'

叔叔："他满嘴都是钱，突然，又全是上帝。"

Clemmons' mental state

克莱蒙斯的心理状态

By：Mike Carter，Seattle Times staff reporter

麦克·卡特，西雅图时报员工

December 2，2009

2009 年 12 月 2 日

Recent jailing, perceived curse sent suspect into tailspin, close relative says

近亲说，近世的监狱，感受到的诅咒将把犯人逼向精神错乱。

1　MARIANNA, Ark. -①An uncle of Maurice Clemmons（莫里斯·克莱蒙斯的一位叔叔）says his nephew had been in a mental tailspin since spring and was withdrawn and "talking crazy about God" when they last saw each other in Washington state.

玛丽安娜，阿肯色州。——①莫里斯·克莱蒙斯的一位叔叔说，从春天开始，他的侄子就变得精神错乱，沉默寡言，当他们叔侄俩在华盛顿州最后一次会面时，克莱蒙斯疯癫地谈论着上帝。

2　②Ray Clemmons（雷·克莱蒙斯）, 39, a lieutenant in the Arkansas Department of Corrections and shift commander in a maximum-security unit, said his nephew was reclusive and withdrawn.

雷·克莱蒙斯，39 岁，是阿肯色州惩教部门的一名中尉，同时也在一个最高安全部门担任轮值指挥员，②他说他的侄子是闭世隐居和精神退缩的。

3　That was a far cry from the hustler who wanted what he had been denied during years of prison and an impoverished childhood in rural Arkansas and the crime-ridden projects of Little Rock.

这和一个被囚禁多年的骗子想要他曾经拒绝的东西一点关系都没有，也和他在阿肯色州乡野穷困潦倒的童年无关，更和小石城（美国阿肯色州首府）犯罪猖獗的事件无关。

4　"Maurice was all about getting, all about having. He was all about money," ③Clemmons（雷·克莱蒙斯）said. "Then, suddenly, he was all about God."

"莫里斯·克莱蒙斯满嘴都是得到，满嘴都是占有，满嘴都是钱，"③克莱蒙斯说，"然而，突然间，他满嘴又是上帝。"

5　Maurice Clemmons, 37, was shot to death by police early Tuesday in South Seattle, ending an intense, two-day manhunt after four Lakewood police officers were shot to death at a coffee shop Sunday.

37 岁的莫里斯·克莱蒙斯，周二早些时候在南西雅图被一名警察击毙，结束了一场激烈的为期两天的追捕行动。这次追捕发生在周日，四名莱克伍德警官在咖啡店被克莱蒙斯射杀之后。

6　④Ray Clemmons（雷·克莱蒙斯）said his nephew "was fine" when he visited his uncle and grandmother in Marianna last spring.

④雷·克莱蒙斯说，去年春天在玛丽安娜，当他的侄子克莱蒙斯来看望他的叔叔和祖母时，看起来相当不错。

7　But when Ray Clemmons and his family later visited his nephew and his wife in their Tacoma home —apparently just before Maurice Clemmons was to be jailed —the man he'd grown up with was hardly recognizable.

但当雷·克莱蒙斯和他的家人后来拜访他的侄子和妻子位于塔科马家的时候，很明显在莫里斯·克莱蒙斯被监禁之前，那个和他一起长大的人已经很难认得出来了。

8　"He stayed off to himself. He was talking about religion and God," ⑤Ray Clemmons（雷·克莱蒙斯）said.

⑤雷·克莱蒙斯说："他远离真实的自己，不停谈论着宗教和上帝。"

9　Ray Clemmons expressed remorse for the families of the slain officers.

雷·克莱蒙斯对被杀害的警察家属深表同情。

10　"This is a bitter pill to swallow," ⑥he（雷·克莱蒙斯）said. "I'm in law enforcement myself. Maurice took away a lot. These families lost everything."

"这是自食苦果，"⑥他说，"我自己就是执法者，莫里斯剥夺了很多，这些家庭失去了一切。"

11　"My family has to live with this, and now some of them are being rounded up. There are a lot of consequences."

"我的家庭不得不生活在这件事的阴影里，并且家里的一些人正在受到困扰。有太多的后果。"

12　⑦He（雷·克莱蒙斯）said he believes two things contributed to his nephew's killing spree.

　　⑦他说他相信有两件事导致了他侄子的滥杀。

13　One involves a bizarre report from Seattle family members that Maurice Clemmons may have believed he'd been cursed by a "devil worshipper." Clemmons supposedly let that man live on a mobile home on his Tacoma property.

　　一件事关涉来自西雅图家庭成员的一份奇怪报告，莫里斯·克莱蒙斯可能相信他被一个"魔鬼的崇拜者"诅咒了。据说，克莱蒙斯让那个人生活在他塔科马港市物业中一间能移动的房子里。

14　⑧Ray Clemmons（雷·克莱蒙斯）said his nephew had gone to the mobile home after reports of a ruckus.

　　⑧雷·克莱蒙斯说，他的侄子在一场骚乱的报道之后去了那间移动的房子。

15　"What I heard was this guy was tearing up the place. There was a fight，and his guy is supposedly chanting things and saying these things to Maurice."

　　"我听到的是这家伙正在摧毁这个地方，那里曾经有一场打斗，据说他的同伙正在聊这件事情并把这些事情说给莫里斯听。"

16　"It did something to him," ⑨Ray Clemmons（雷·克莱蒙斯）said. "After that，he was a terror."

　　"那对他起了作用，"⑨雷·克莱蒙斯说，"在这之后，他变成了一个可怕的人。"

17　The other contributing factor，⑩Ray Clemmons（雷·克莱蒙斯）said，was his nephew's jailing this summer.

　　⑩雷·克莱蒙斯说，另外一个起作用的事情是，他的侄子这个夏天被监禁。

18　Maurice Clemmons was arrested in May on seven counts of assault and malicious mischief after a disturbance during which he allegedly punched a Pierce County sheriff's deputy.

　　莫里斯·克莱蒙斯五月份在一场骚乱后被逮捕，罪名是七项攻击和恶意的恶作剧，他在这场骚乱中据称殴打了皮尔斯县警长的副手。

19　Two days later，he allegedly gathered his wife and younger relatives and forced them to undress，while preaching that he was Jesus and that the world was going to end.

　　两天后，据称他聚集了他的妻子和年轻的亲戚并且强制她们脱掉衣服，同时宣称他是耶稣，而世界末日就要到了。

20　An investigation into that incident led to a second-degree felony charge of child rape in July. Clemmons was in and out of jail through the summer and fall，before his Nov. 23 release after posting bond.

　　一份关于那件事的调查导致了对七月的强奸儿童案的二级重罪指控。在 11 月 23 日交了保释金后他被释放了，但这之前的夏季和秋季他不断地进出监狱。

21　"He was bitter，" ⑪Ray Clemmons（雷·克莱蒙斯）said. "He felt like he'd been mistreated. He did not like police. And he wasn't going to go back to prison."

　　"他心中苦涩，" ⑪雷·克莱蒙斯说，"他觉得他被虐待。他不喜欢警察，而且他不希望再回到监狱里去。"

22　The men were close in age and grew up together in Marianna，85 miles east of Little Rock near the Mississippi border. The tiny town is dilapidated；most buildings on the block-long Main Street have peeling paint and boarded windows.

　　他俩年纪相仿，一起在玛丽安娜长大。玛丽安娜位于靠近密西西比州边界小石城以东 85 英里的地方。这个小镇已破旧不堪，整条主要街道上大多数建筑物油漆剥落，装着木头窗户。

23　Maurice Clemmons lived in a mobile home with his mother and a number of half-siblings. Many aunts，uncles and cousins lived in tar-paper shacks and tiny clapboard houses. The porch door of his grandmother's house—screen ripped and hanging crooked —is tied shut with a shoestring.

　　莫里斯·克莱蒙斯和他的母亲及许多表亲住在一个移动家中。许多阿姨、叔叔和表亲住在焦油纸棚屋和小板屋里。他祖母房子的门廊门裂了口子，被鞋带勉强系着，歪歪扭扭的。

24　"We were poor, but back then, there wasn't the crime," ⑫Ray Clemmons（雷·克莱蒙斯）said. "We spent our days running through the woods, swinging on vines. Doing what kids do."

　　"我们穷，但是回到那时，没有犯罪，"⑫雷·克莱蒙斯说，"我们整天都在林间穿梭，在藤蔓间荡漾。做孩子们所做的事情。"

25　In the mid-1980s, with work hard to find, Ray and Maurice Clemmons moved with their families to the East End Housing Project in Little Rock —just as the first waves of the crack-cocaine epidemic washed over the city.

　　在80年代中期，很难找到工作，雷和莫里斯·克莱蒙斯与家人搬到了小石城的东区住房项目，那时第一波强效可卡因风潮席卷城市。

26　"That was when all the friends started killing each other over money," ⑬Ray Clemmons（雷·克莱蒙斯）said.

　　"就是从那时起所有的朋友们开始因为金钱而互相残杀。"⑬雷·克莱蒙斯说。

27　⑭He（他）said he went to school, the recreational center and home every night. In 1986, he and his family moved back to Marianna. "It was just too dangerous," ⑮he（他）said.

　　⑭他说他每天晚上就是在学校、娱乐中心和家这些地方活动。1986年，他和家人搬回玛丽安娜。"这实在太危险。"⑮他说。

28　Maurice Clemmons stayed in Little Rock. His father, who worked for Chrysler, died in 1987. After that, Maurice Clemmons "got into trouble," ⑯his uncle（他的叔叔）said.

　　莫里斯·克莱蒙斯住在小石城。他的父亲为克莱斯勒工作，死于1987年。从那之后，莫里斯·克莱蒙斯"陷入困境"，⑯他的叔叔说。

29　Maurice Clemmons was convicted of burglary, robbery and other charges in 1989 and 1990, receiving sentences of more than 100 years. Then Gov. Mike Huckabee commuted the sentence in 2000, after 11 years in prison. In 2001, Clemmons was returned to prison in Arkansas for nearly three years.

莫里斯·克莱蒙斯因为在 1989 年和 1990 年的入室盗窃、抢劫以及其他指控而被定罪，被判超过 100 年的有期徒刑。在监狱待了 11 年后，当时的州长迈克·霍克比在 2000 年做出了减刑的判决。2001 年，克莱蒙斯又被送回阿肯色州监狱，待了将近三年。

30 "I think all of this just piled up，" ⑰Ray Clemmons（雷·克莱蒙斯）said. "The rape charge was going to cost him his wife. He was looking at going to prison again, maybe for life. He got taken to the brink, and he snapped."

"我认为所有这一切是在不断累积，" ⑰雷·克莱蒙斯说，"强奸罪将会使他失去妻子。他有可能再次被送进监狱，也许将是终身。他被带进了危险的边缘，他崩溃了。"

【2010 年普利策突发新闻奖 10 号文本】

E-Mail：'Hopefully（he）will not get out on bail'
电子邮件："希望他未获保释。"

By：Jonathan Martin, Jim Brunner and Ken Armstrong, Seattle Times staff reporters
乔纳森·马丁，吉姆·布伦纳和肯·阿姆斯壮，西雅图时报记者
Staff writers Christine Clarridge, Susan Kelleher and Maureen O' Hagan contributed to this report.
其他做出贡献的记者包括：克里斯汀·克拉里奇，苏珊·凯勒赫 和莫琳·奥哈根。

December 2，2009
2009 年 12 月 2 日

1 When Maurice Clemmons, the man suspected of killing four Lakewood police officers, walked free from a Pierce County jail last week, it wasn't for lack of effort on the part of Washington officials to keep him behind bars.

当莫里斯·克莱蒙斯这个被怀疑杀死四名莱克伍德警官的人，上

星期从皮尔斯县监狱自由步出时，不能说华盛顿的部分官员没有为将他留在监狱里做出努力。

2　①Documents（文件）released Tuesday show that a wide variety of state and local officials everyone from prosecutors to sheriff's deputies to corrections officers viewed Clemmons as a dangerous man，and wanted desperately to keep him in custody.

　　①周二发布的文件显示，相当多的州和当地官员，每个人从检察官到州长的副手再到狱警，把克莱蒙斯视为一个危险的男人，竭尽所能想要让他待在监狱里。

3　But Washington officials encountered resistance from an unlikely source—their correctional colleagues in Arkansas. The acrimony has since become so intense，according to ②Pierce County sheriff's spokesman Ed Troyer（皮尔斯县警长发言人艾得·托伊尔），that if the two states were adjacent a "border war" would break out.

　　但是华盛顿的官员遇到了意想不到的阻力，那就是阿肯色州惩教同事。此后的争吵变得如此强烈，②根据皮尔斯县警长发言人艾得·托伊尔的说辞，如果这两个州相邻，一场边境战争将会爆发。

4　The dispute now centers on whether a warrant issued by Arkansas in October would have allowed Washington authorities to prevent Clemmons' release from the Pierce County Jail six days before the shootings occurred. Arkansas says yes. Washington says no.

　　争端现在集中在：阿肯色州在 10 月发布的逮捕令，是否允许华盛顿当局在枪击案发生六天前阻止克莱蒙斯从皮尔斯监狱放出来。阿肯色州说是，华盛顿说不。

5　Clemmons，37，was accused of killing the four police officers Sunday. On Tuesday，a Seattle police officer encountered and killed Clemmons.（这一段是典型的插叙，是新闻文本特有的结构之一，起到提供背景性资料的提示作用）

　　克莱蒙斯，37 岁，被控告星期天杀害了四名警官。在星期二，西雅图警官遇到他并杀死了他。

6　The tension between the two states started in July and is captured in a round of e-mail exchanges that show just how frustrated Washington officials became with their Arkansas counterparts.

两个州之间的张力开始于七月，并且在电子邮件往来中可以捕捉到，显示了华盛顿的官员是如何在阿肯色同僚面前挫败的。

7   Clemmons was arrested in Washington on July 1. The following day he was formally charged with second-degree rape of a child—the eighth felony charge filed against him in Washington this year alone. All eight of those charges traced to a spree of violence in May and were still pending against Clemmons while the two states tangled over how to deal with him.

克莱蒙斯 7 月 1 日在华盛顿被捕。接下来的日子里他正式地被控告，涉及一宗二度强奸儿童罪，这是今年在华盛顿提出的第 8 次重罪指控。所有的这些指控可以追溯到五月的一个暴力狂潮，然而这些指控仍然悬而未决，两个州在如何对付他上纠缠不清。

8   Arkansas had an interest in Clemmons because he remained on parole in that state. Convicted of at least five felony charges, Clemmons served more than 10 years in Arkansas' prison system before being released in 2004 and moving to Washington.

阿肯色州对克莱蒙斯有兴趣，因为他在这个州保留有假释。犯人有至少五项重罪指控。在他 2004 年被释放并搬到华盛顿之前，克莱蒙斯在阿肯色州的监狱体系里服役超过 10 年。

9   When Clemmons landed in trouble in May 2009, Arkansas issued a warrant for violating the conditions of his parole. This warrant, if enforced, would have allowed Washington to keep Clemmons in jail without chance of posting bond.

当克莱蒙斯在 2009 年 5 月陷入困境，阿肯色州颁布了一个逮捕令，因为他违反了假释条件。这个逮捕令如果执行，将允许华盛顿拘留克莱蒙斯，没有任何机会保释。

10   But on July 16, an Arkansas official notified the Washington State Department of Corrections (DOC) that Arkansas was rescinding its warrant.

　　但是 7 月 16 日，一个阿肯色州的官员通知华盛顿惩教部，阿肯色撤销了逮捕令。

11　③Marjorie Owens, a Washington DOC administrator（马乔里·欧文斯。一个华盛顿惩教部的管理人员），wrote a blistering response on July 23, saying Arkansas' decision appeared to violate the Interstate Compact for Adult Offender Supervision（ICAOS），an agreement governing how states treat one another's offenders who are on supervision.

　　一个华盛顿惩教部的管理人员③马乔里·欧文斯，在 7 月 23 日写了积极的回应，说阿肯色州的决定看起来触犯了《州际成年罪犯监督契约》，该契约涉及州际之间一个州如何处理另一个州监督之下的犯罪者。

12　"I'm concerned that you have no problem releasing your offender into our community, based on his behavior," ④ she（她）wrote. "I thought ICAOS was all about community safety."

　　"基于罪犯的行为，我怀疑你释放你的罪犯到我的社区是否有问题，"④她写道，"我想《州际成年罪犯监督契约》关涉的是社区的安全。"

13　⑤Owens（欧文斯）also wrote："Hopefully the offender will not get out on bail."

　　⑤欧文斯还写道："希望嫌犯未获得保释。"

14　On Aug. 5，⑥an Arkansas parole official named Linda Strong（阿肯色的假释官员琳达·斯特朗）sent a terse reply："The warrant was rescinded. When the pending charges are adjudicated we will reconsider the case."

　　8 月 5 日，⑥一个阿肯色的假释官员琳达·斯特朗发了简短的回复："逮捕令撤销了。当待判决的指控完成后，我们将重新考虑此案。"

15　⑦A document（文件）released by Arkansas Tuesday says the warrant "was recalled at the request of［Arkansas Department of Community Correction］director G. David Guntharp after conversations he had with the offender's wife and mother." But⑧Guntharp（冈萨普），

in an interview，said he does not recall discussing the matter with Clemmons' family. Clemmons' mother died years ago.

⑦阿肯色州周二发布的文件说："逮捕令被撤回是应（阿肯色社区惩矫部门）主管官员 G. 大卫·冈萨普与罪犯的妻子和母亲交谈后提出的要求。"但是⑧冈萨普在一个采访中说，他不记得和克莱蒙斯的家人讨论过这些问题，克莱蒙斯的妈妈去世很多年了。

16　⑨Rhonda Sharp（郎达·夏普），a spokeswoman for Guntharp，said Arkansas retracted the warrant because the warrant labeled Clemmons an "absconder" —meaning he had fled or was avoiding supervision. But Arkansas received a letter from Clemmons' defense attorney contradicting that and claiming the Pierce County charges "may be dropped. "

⑨郎达·夏普是冈萨普的女发言人，她说阿肯色州撤回了逮捕令，是因为这个逮捕令将克莱蒙斯定义为逃匿者，意味着他已经逃匿或者避免监督。但是阿肯色州接到了来自克莱蒙斯辩护律师的信，指出矛盾的地方，声称皮尔斯郡指控可能会被撤销。

17　Arkansas' decision baffled Washington officials. Seeking help，they consulted the Washington State Attorney General's Office and the national office that oversees the interstate compact. The latter office said Arkansas "should not have quashed their warrant，" ⑩an internal e-mail（内部邮件）between Washington DOC employees says. ⑪One administrator for the Washington DOC（在华盛顿惩教部的管理人员）called the case a "major malfunction" and suggested ways "to work 'around' Arkansas on this one. "

阿肯色州的决定使华盛顿州的官员困惑，为获得帮助，他们向华盛顿州检察长办公室和监督州际契约的国家办公室请教咨询。⑩一份在华盛顿惩教部雇员间传递的内部邮件说，后一个办公室认为阿肯色州"不应该撤销他们的逮捕令"。⑪一个在华盛顿惩教部的管理人员将此案定为一个"重大事故"，并提出了在阿肯色州"解决"此问题的方法。

18　Washington's alarm could be traced，in part，to concerns about the danger Clemmons posed. ⑫A Pierce County prosecutor（一位皮尔斯县的检察官）worried Clemmons "might continue to make contact" with children he was accused of molesting.

华盛顿的警报可以部分归因于对克莱蒙斯构成的危险的担忧。⑫一位皮尔斯县的检察官担忧克莱蒙斯"可能持续接触"那些他被指控猥亵的儿童。

19　⑬A Pierce County sheriff's detective（一位皮尔斯县治安官的侦探）told a corrections officer "it would not be easy" if DOC officers or sheriff's deputies had to arrest Clemmons again. "She said Mr. Clemmons did not like them，"⑭an e-mail（电子邮件）says.

　　⑬一位皮尔斯县治安官的侦探告诉一个惩戒人员"这并不容易"，如果惩教部的官员或当地治安官的助理不得不再次逮捕克莱蒙斯。"她说克莱蒙斯先生并不喜欢他们。"⑭一份邮件中这样说。

20　⑮The records released Tuesday（周二公布的记录）show that from July until November，Clemmons was in and out of jail. At one point，⑯a DOC employee wrote an e-mail saying（一个惩教部的雇员写了一封电子邮件）："I was going to serve Offender today only to find out he bailed out！"

　　⑮周二公布的记录显示，从 7 月到 11 月，克莱蒙斯出出进进监狱。有一次，⑯一个惩教部的雇员写了一封电子邮件说："我今天将去服务罪犯，但发现他被保释了！"

21　On Tuesday，Washington's top prison official blasted Arkansas.

　　周二，华盛顿最高监狱官员抨击了阿肯色。

22　When the Washington DOC initially asked for and got a nationwide fugitive warrant from Arkansas in May，the Washington DOC closed the case，ending its oversight of Clemmons. The DOC believed Clemmons would now be Arkansas' responsibility.

　　当华盛顿的惩教部最初询问，并在五月从阿肯色得到全国性的逃犯授权令，华盛顿的惩教部关闭了该案件，结束了对克莱蒙斯的监督。惩教部相信现在克莱蒙斯将是阿肯色的责任。

23　"At that point，he's a problem for the state of Arkansas，"⑰Washington DOC Secretary Eldon Vail（华盛顿惩教部的秘书艾登·维尔）said. "If he's picked up, he's going back."

"在那一点上，他是阿肯色的一个问题，"⑰华盛顿惩教部的秘书艾登·维尔说，"如果他被抓住，他将被送还。"

24　But when Arkansas rescinded its warrant, that left DOC temporarily without supervision on a man it considered dangerous. ⑱Vail（维尔）said if the Washington and Arkansas positions were reversed, Washington would have taken Clemmons back. Last year, Washington retook 986 felons from other states, ⑲Vail（维尔）said.

但是当阿肯色撤销了逮捕令，留给惩教部一个被认为是危险的男人，而这个男人暂时没有被监管。⑱维尔说如果华盛顿和阿肯色的位置调换，华盛顿将把克莱蒙斯带回去。⑲维尔说，去年华盛顿从其他州带回 986 名重罪犯。

25　"We do this every day," ⑳he（他，根据上下文指维尔）said.

"我们每天都做这个。"⑳他说。

26　㉑Vail（维尔）said the Clemmons case was his worst experience with another state in his 33 years with the Washington DOC: "［Gov. Chris Gregoire's］question to me about this case is a good one: 'Why would we ever take anyone from Arkansas in the future?' I haven't gotten back to her."

㉑维尔说在华盛顿惩教部工作 33 年来，克莱蒙斯案是他与另一个州交涉经历中最糟糕的案例。（官员克里斯·格雷瓜尔）就这个案子对我发问是一个好例子："为什么未来我们要从阿肯色引渡任何人？"我无法回答。

27　On Oct. 2, after Washington DOC officials pleaded anew with Arkansas, Arkansas issued a second warrant. But the two states differ on whether the warrant could be enforced in Washington state. Arkansas says the second warrant was just as good as the first.

10 月 2 日，华盛顿惩教部官员再次请求阿肯色州，这之后，阿肯色州发布了第二份逮捕令。但是两个州关于这一逮捕令是否在华盛顿执行存在分歧。阿肯色说第二份逮捕令只是与第一份一样。

28 "It is a valid warrant," ㉒Sharp（夏普）said. "It is a warrant that differs little, if at all, from the first."

"这是有效的逮捕令，"㉒夏普说，"和第一个比，这是一个差别不大的逮捕令。"

29 But ㉓Scott Blonien, an in-house attorney for Washington DOC（斯科特·伯卢尼。一个华盛顿惩教部的内部律师。），said two elements show Arkansas did not intend to enforce the Oct. 2 warrant. A cover sheet attached to it left unchecked a box that reads："Warrant issued. Keep us apprised of offender's availability for retaking," a term that means sending an offender home. The May 28 warrant had that box checked.

但是㉓一个华盛顿惩教部的内部律师斯科特·伯卢尼说了两点，显示阿肯色没有想要执行 10 月 2 日的逮捕令。逮捕令的封面上有一个备选框没有被打钩，这个框对应的话是："逮捕令发布，使我们了解罪犯遣返的可能性。"一个术语指的是遣返一个罪犯。5 月 28 日的逮捕令，那个框打了勾。

30 And, unlike the May 28 warrant, the second warrant was not entered into the National Crime Information Center（NCIC），a law-enforcement database. Interstate compact guidelines appear to require that the state issuing a warrant—Arkansas, in this case—must enter the warrant into NCIC in order to make it enforceable.

并且，第二个逮捕令不像 5 月 28 日的逮捕令，并没有输入进国家犯罪信息中心，这是一个执法数据库。州际契约的指导方针显示要求发布逮捕令的州——阿肯色，在这个案件中必须使逮捕令输入进国家犯罪信息中心，以便使其执行。

31 ㉔ Pierce County employees（县里的官员）checked the NCIC twice and found no warrants for Clemmons, a county official said.

㉔县里的官员说，皮尔斯的雇员两次检查了国家犯罪信息中心，并没有发现给克莱蒙斯的逮捕令。

32 Clemmons posted $190,000 bail on Nov. 23 and walked out of the Pierce County Jail.

在 11 月 23 日，克莱蒙斯获得了 19 万美元保释金，然后走出皮尔斯监狱。

附录：克莱蒙斯枪杀四警察案例消息来源分析

序号	消息来源	翻译
文本 2 Person of interest let out of Pierce County jail one week ago		
①	Larry Jegley, prosecuting attorney for Arkansas' Pulaski County	拉里·杰格里，阿肯色州普拉斯基县的检察官
②	a department spokesman	部门发言人
③	the spokesman	发言人
④	court records	法庭记录
⑤	a Pierce County sheriff's report	皮尔斯县警长的报告
⑥	the report	报告
⑦	a sheriff's report	警长的报告
⑧	the report	报告
⑨	Family members	家庭成员
⑩	court records	法庭记录
⑪	news account	新闻报道
⑫	Clemmons	克莱蒙斯
⑬	court records	法庭记录
⑭	a newspaper account	报纸报道
⑮	a story in the Arkansas Democrat-Gazette	阿肯色州民主党公报上的一个故事
⑯	news reports	新闻报道
⑰	a statement	声明
⑱	Huckabee	霍克比
⑲	the Democrat-Gazette	民主党公报
⑳	Clemmons' sister Latanya	克莱蒙斯的妹妹拉塔尼亚
㉑	she	克莱蒙斯的妹妹拉塔尼亚
㉒	she	克莱蒙斯的妹妹拉塔尼亚

续　表

序号	消息来源	翻译
㉓	Clemmons' maternal grandmother, Lela Clemmons, 82, of Marianna, Ark.	克莱蒙斯的外祖母，住在玛丽安娜方舟地区的 82 岁的里拉·克莱蒙斯
㉔	another relative	另一个亲戚
㉕	Maurice Clemmons' grandmother	莫里斯·克莱蒙斯的祖母
㉖	She	莫里斯·克莱蒙斯的祖母
㉗	a probable-cause declaration	可能原因的声明
㉘	the declaration	声明
㉙	the declaration	声明
㉚	court records	法庭记录
㉛	neighbors	邻居
㉜	the declaration	声明
㉝	the declaration	声明
㉞	one neighbor	邻居
㉟	This same neighbor	同一个邻居
㊱	this neighbor	邻居
㊲	Another neighbor, a 70-year-old man	另一位邻居，70 岁的男人
㊳	this neighbor	邻居

文本 3　Huckabee commuted long term		
序号	消息来源	翻译
①	The Associated Press reported in 2007	美联社 2007 年的报道
②	statement	声明
③	Huckabee's statement	霍克比的声明
④	The statement	声明
⑤	Huckabee	霍克比
⑥	he	霍克比
⑦	an Arkansas newspaper, The Leader	阿肯色州的报纸《领袖》
⑧	news accounts	新闻报道
⑨	news accounts	新闻报道

	文本 4	Veteran officers were parents, too
序号	消息来源	翻　译
①	Lakewood Police Chief Bret Farrar	莱克伍德警察局长布雷特·法勒
②	he	莱克伍德警察局长布雷特·法勒
③	he	莱克伍德警察局长布雷特·法勒
④	her former father-in-law, Carroll Kelley of Shelton, Mason County	前岳父梅森县谢尔顿市的卡洛尔·凯利
⑤	Kelley	凯利
⑥	he	凯利
⑦	police and relatives	警察和亲戚们
⑧	public records	公共档案
⑨	Sgt. Scott Eastman, her former supervisor	前任主管斯科特·伊士曼军士
⑩	he	伊士曼
⑪	Eastman	伊士曼
⑫	Eastman	伊士曼
⑬	Eastman	伊士曼
⑭	Eastman	伊士曼
⑮	he	伊士曼
⑯	Eastman	伊士曼
⑰	he	伊士曼
⑱	Lt. Lisa Price, public-information officer for the Kent department	肯特部门公共信息官中尉丽莎·普瑞斯
⑲	Price	普瑞斯
⑳	Price	普瑞斯
㉑	Melanie Burwell, a sister-in-law	嫂子梅勒妮·布鲁威尔
㉒	Burwell	布鲁威尔
㉓	she	布鲁威尔
㉔	a statement published on the Web site of WFMZ-TV	WFMZ-TV 的网站发表的声明
㉕	a statement issued by the Tukwila Police Department	塔克维拉警察局发布的声明

序号	消息来源	翻　译
㉖	According to the program for a state 2008 law-enforcement conference	2008 年州执法会议的计划
㉗	Fisher	费舍尔（雷宁格女儿训练教练）
㉘	Toni Strehlow	托尼·史特瑞劳（房屋中介）
㉙	Strehlow	史特瑞劳.
㉚	Charley Stokes	查利·斯托克斯（邻居）
㉛	he	查利·斯托克斯
㉜	Strehlow and Stokes	史特瑞劳和斯托克斯
㉝	Strehlow	史特瑞劳
㉞	a neighbor，Edie Wintermute	邻居艾迪·温特默特
㉟	she	邻居艾迪·温特默特

文本 6　Persuasive appeal helped Clemmons win clemency

序号	消息来源	翻　译
①	Arkansas court documents and prosecutors	阿肯色州法庭文件和检察官们
②	his appeal	上诉
③	Clemmons	克莱蒙斯
④	application	申请
⑤	Clemmons	克莱蒙斯
⑥	Karen Hodge	凯伦·霍奇
⑦	court records	法庭记录
⑧	his appeal	上诉
⑨	Clemmons	克莱蒙斯
⑩	Mark Fraiser	马克·弗雷泽
⑪	Fraiser	弗雷泽
⑫	Fraiser	弗雷泽
⑬	Humphrey	汉弗莱
⑭	he	汉弗莱

续　表

序号	消息来源	翻　译
⑮	Humphrey	汉弗莱
⑯	a copy of the marriage certificate	结婚证的副本
⑰	Humphrey	汉弗莱
⑱	The proclamation	公告
⑲	corrections officials	惩教官员
⑳	Dina Tyler	迪娜·泰勒
㉑	Tyler	泰勒
㉒	records	记录
㉓	Pulaski County Prosecutor Larry Jegley	普拉斯基县的检察官拉里·杰格里
㉔	Jegley	杰格里
㉕	W. A. McCormick	W. A. 迈克考密克
㉖	Fraiser	弗雷泽
㉗	judge	法官
㉘	court records	法庭记录
㉙	statement	声明
㉚	Huckabee	霍克比
㉛	Fox News	福克斯新闻
㉜	Huckabee	霍克比
㉝	Joe Scarborough's radio show on WABC-AM	乔·斯卡伯勒的广播节目采访

文本 7　Four days in May set stage for tragedy

序号	消息来源	翻　译
①	police reports	警方的报告
②	police records	警方记录
③	A woman who was visiting family	一位当天走访亲友的女性
④	the woman	妇女
⑤	court records	法庭记录

序号	消息来源	翻　译
⑥	a psychological evaluation obtained by The News Tribune	《新闻论坛报》得到的心理评估
⑦	Pierce County Prosecuting Attorney Mark Lindquist	皮尔斯县检察官马克·林奎斯特
⑧	Stephen Kreimer，executive director of the Professional Bail Agents of the United States	斯蒂芬·克瑞姆，美国专业保释代理人执行董事
⑨	a Pierce County sheriff's report	皮尔斯县治安官的报告
⑩	one of the girls	其中一个女孩
⑪	the girl	女孩
⑫	police records	警方记录
⑬	the girl	女孩
⑭	He	克莱蒙斯
⑮	the family	家庭成员
⑯	A CPS spokeswoman	儿童保护机构的一位女发言人
⑰	the letter	阿肯色社区惩矫部通知皮尔斯县的信
⑱	Stephen Penner，a deputy prosecuting attorney in Pierce County	斯蒂芬·彭纳，皮尔斯县的一位副检察官
⑲	Lindquist	林奎斯特
⑳	A spokeswoman for the Arkansas prison system	阿肯色州监狱体系的一个女发言人
㉑	Penner	彭纳
㉒	Phil Sorensen，a deputy prosecutor in Pierce County	菲尔·索伦森，皮尔斯县的一位副检察官
㉓	Sorensen	索伦森
㉔	Lindquist	林奎斯特
㉕	Lindquist	林奎斯特
㉖	he	林奎斯特
㉗	Penner，the deputy prosecuting attorney	副检察彭纳

文本 9　Uncle：'He was all about money—suddenly，he was all about God'

序号	消息来源	翻　译
①	An uncle of Maurice Clemmons	莫里斯·克莱蒙斯的一位叔叔
②	Ray Clemmons	雷·克莱蒙斯
③	Clemmons	雷·克莱蒙斯
④	Ray Clemmons	雷·克莱蒙斯
⑤	Ray Clemmons	雷·克莱蒙斯
⑥	he	雷·克莱蒙斯
⑦	He	雷·克莱蒙斯
⑧	Ray Clemmons	雷·克莱蒙斯
⑨	Ray Clemmons	雷·克莱蒙斯
⑩	Ray Clemmons	雷·克莱蒙斯
⑪	Ray Clemmons	雷·克莱蒙斯
⑫	Ray Clemmons	雷·克莱蒙斯
⑬	Ray Clemmons	雷·克莱蒙斯
⑭	He	他
⑮	he	他
⑯	his uncle	他的叔叔
⑰	Ray Clemmons	雷·克莱蒙斯

文本 10　E-Mail：'Hopefully（he）will not get out on bail'

序号	消息来源	翻　译
①	Documents	文件
②	Pierce County sheriff's spokesman Ed Troyer	皮尔斯县警长发言人艾得·托伊尔
③	Marjorie Owens,a Washington DOC administrator	马乔里·欧文斯，一个华盛顿惩教部的管理人员
④	she	她
⑤	Owens	欧文斯
⑥	an Arkansas parole official named Linda Strong	阿肯色的假释官员琳达·斯特朗
⑦	A document	文件
⑧	Guntharp	冈萨普

续　表

序号	消息来源	翻　译
⑨	Rhonda Sharp	郎达·夏普
⑩	an internal e-mail	内部邮件
⑪	One administrator for the Washington DOC	在华盛顿惩教部的管理人员
⑫	A Pierce County prosecutor	一位皮尔斯县的检察官
⑬	A Pierce County sheriff's detective	一位皮尔斯县治安官的侦探
⑭	an e-mail	电子邮件
⑮	The records released Tuesday	周二公布的记录
⑯	a DOC employee wrote an e-mail saying	一个惩教部的雇员写的一封电子邮件
⑰	Washington DOC Secretary Eldon Vail	华盛顿惩教部的秘书艾登·维尔
⑱	Vail	维尔
⑲	Vail	维尔
⑳	he	维尔
㉑	Vail	维尔
㉒	Sharp	夏普
㉓	Scott Blonien, an in-house attorney for Washington DOC	斯科特·伯卢尼，一个华盛顿惩教部的内部律师
㉔	Pierce County employees	县里的官员

第四章 普利策新闻评论奖案例库及话语分析

第一节 评论要依赖事实讲故事①

重价值判断，轻事实判断，是我国新闻评论写作受到文人论政影响后产生的一种写作惯性。早在都市报新闻评论繁荣时期，有学者就提出了"评论记者"机制②，倡导新闻评论中要有采访，也要重视事实判断。随着纸媒的衰落，新闻评论在向新媒体平台迁徙的过程中，不得不寻找适应互联网的表达方式，"故事化"成为一个有效策略。《楚天都市报》束继泉认为："评论如何做到可读，最根本的一点，就是要在有限的篇幅中，学会讲故事，而且要讲好故事。"③ 然而在走向"故事化"的过程中，却出现了对"事实"的忽略。《刘鑫江歌案：法律可以制裁凶手，但谁来制裁人性?》一文，引发了举国对"江歌案"的关注，然而此文对事实的亵渎也换来了《新京报》的檄文：《杀气腾腾的咪蒙制造了网络暴力的新高潮》。

故事化可以增强新闻评论的亲和力和可读性，易于读者理解和达成共鸣，但是新闻评论需要依赖事实讲故事，离开了事实的故事是虚构，背离了新闻实践的宗旨。

---

①本节部分内容以论文形式发表,发表内容第二作者为王碧云,她承担的主要工作是部分文本的初译和文本首段、人物两个指标的统计。

②成茹,苏蕾.嘉兴时评:评论记者第一时间发表评论[J].军事记者,2007(11):42.

③束继泉.新型评论写作:要采访,还可以讲故事——《楚天都市报》时评创新新探[J].中国记者,2016(6):111.

新闻评论如何依赖事实讲故事？这是当前我国新闻评论实践面临的新问题和新考验。由于受到文人论政典范的深刻影响，我国的时评人擅长逻辑推理和价值判断，他们并不排斥叙事，但是对事实的处理倾向于结构主义的思维方式，喜欢概括、压缩、精简，这就使新闻评论中的叙事缺乏人物、情境、背景、对话、情节、细节、节奏等故事化特征。另一方面，"坐而论道""足不出户"的评论写作模式阻止了"采访"对事实的采集，新闻评论中的事实并非"一手"事实，这就造成叙事缺乏事实性的材料。

既缺乏故事要素的训练，也缺乏事实材料，又受到互联网的冲击，在这种内功不足、外部吃紧的情况下，编故事的怪胎就会出现。

与我国的新闻评论传统不同，普利策奖的新闻评论作品受到非虚构写作和新新闻主义的影响，重视用事实讲故事。2019 年的普利策新闻评论奖颁给了《圣路易斯邮报》的托尼·曼森哲。托尼叙述了 9 个密苏里州的穷人，这些人犯了一些诸如小偷小摸的错误，被起诉后因为付不起保释金就去坐牢，然后产生监狱账单，无力偿还，最终陷入更深的贫困中。托尼在采访中收集事实，用事实讲述社会底层小人物的挣扎人生，揭示了严肃的公共议题：虽然美国宪法保护公民不能因为无力还债而坐监，纳税人也已为此支付账单，但是各县仍会收取服刑穷人的费用。因为这背后是乐于收缴欠款的司法体系、乐于发现罪犯违反缓刑条例的代理公司以及更深层次的种族歧视。

他山之石可以攻玉，在"讲好中国故事，传播好中国声音"[①]的传播格局中，我们深感有必要学习托尼的叙事方式，以拓宽文风和思路。1988 年，Bird 和 Dardenne 开启了"新闻即说故事"的讨论，带动了新闻向叙事学的转向。[②] 故事改变了只传播"信息"带来的坚硬化感觉，故事更能增加沟通、共享情感，促进理解与体谅。[③] 我们在坚守文人论政那独特的优良的评论传统的同时，也需要回应新媒介和新思潮带动的新闻话

①郎竞宁.转变叙事策略 讲好中国故事——从新闻叙事学角度探讨国际传播能力建设[J].传媒论坛,2019(11):100.

②臧国仁,蔡琰.叙事传播:故事/人文观点[M].杭州:浙江大学出版社,2019:5.

③臧国仁,蔡琰.叙事传播:故事/人文观点[M].杭州:浙江大学出版社,2019:38.

语的转型，故事蕴涵着"爱与诗"的理性，辅之以我国新闻评论独特的"逻辑与道德"理性，再加上专业的事实训练，新闻评论在网络化时代一定会绽放出新的光彩。

标题：远离判断，呈现充满事实细节的叙述

标题和首段在新闻评论文本中处于"提神醒脑"的重要地位，历来是编辑选稿的重要依据。例如红网全国大学生"评论之星"选拔赛评委田德政老师就曾指出，无论在《华商报》还是在"红辣椒评论"时期，标题是他选稿的第一看点，而接下来就要看第一段有没有把观点明确表达出来。对新闻事件有提示，对观点明确展示，措辞不老旧、吸引人，是标题和首段引起编辑注意的写作法宝。但是这些法宝在托尼作品中消失了，托尼用充满事实细节的叙述性标题来吸引读者的注意，这种截然不同的处理方式，甚至让人产生"这是新闻评论吗"的疑问。

我国新闻评论"重判断"的特征强调在标题制作上处理一个基本矛盾：表意空间的有限性约束与表意内容的完整性追求之间的矛盾。① 简单讲，就是用尽量少的字表达尽可能完整、重要的信息。

以这组评论标题为例：《九一八纪念日论抗战前途》（张季鸾），《印度独立问题之观察》（储安平），《建立"全民低保"乃扩大内需之基》（鲁宁），《快乐没有那么重要》（马少华）。

解决基本矛盾的迫切性赋予这些标题简练、精确、完整、概括的特征，有的揭示了要评论的问题，有的表达了观点，可以说都实践了用少而精的字表达完整重要信息的功能。读者一看标题，对要评论的问题和观点立刻掌握，这些标题"重判断"的特征，显示了对论题的存在、性质及与其他事物之间的关系肯定或者否定的看法。

托尼的作品则表现出"重叙述"的特点。那么我们凭什么说一个标题是叙述的而不是判断的？Labov 和 Waletzky 两位学者给出了答案：判断一个标题是不是在叙事，只要看它有没有"时间结合点"②。上文提及

---

① 马少华.新闻评论教程[M].北京:高等教育出版社,2012:159.
② 臧国仁,蔡琰.叙事传播:故事/人文观点[M].杭州:浙江大学出版社,2019:24.

的标题都没有明显的"时间结合点",但是托尼的标题,以《释放欠债坐监的密苏里妇女让她过了个好节》为例,"释放"是一个时间点,"过节"又是一个时间点,从"释放"到"过节"产生了时间结合点,也就产生了叙述。

序号	标　题	叙事形式
文本 1	释放欠债坐监的密苏里妇女让她过了个好节	结局、状态
文本 2	各县对穷人的监禁"必须停止",辩护人说	用引语表评价
文本 3	随着选举临近圣弗朗索瓦县检察官再次推迟公义	结局、状态
文本 4	法官试图阻止在登特县参加债务人监狱听证会	复杂行动
文本 5	密苏里州的乡村法院普遍存在"贫困惩罚"	状态
文本 6	是时候彻底关闭债务人的监狱了	解决方式
文本 7	乡村法庭拘捕超速驾驶女子	结局
文本 8	斯托达德县可以教与穷被告人打交道的课了	评价
文本 9	卡姆登县仍在为难那个 2008 年就认罪的女人	结局、状态
文本 10	打破监狱账单和监禁穷人的循环	解决方式

托尼的题目充满了事实细节。这些事实细节包括具体的地点,例如"密苏里""圣弗朗索瓦县""斯托达德县""卡姆登县";包括个体性的特定内涵的人物,例如"密苏里妇女""辩护人""圣弗朗索瓦县检察官""超速驾驶女子""穷欠债人""认罪的女人";包括事件,例如"释放欠债坐监的密苏里妇女""阻止登特县的债务人监狱听证会""拘捕超速驾驶女子";包括时间点,例如"随着""再次""弥漫在""是时候""仍在"。

托尼的作品标题在注重叙述的同时,有没有丧失新闻评论标题提示性和评价性功能呢?答案是没有。因为作为"评论之眼",新闻评论标题不能缺少提示性和评价性功能,这两个功能的发挥是吸引读者注意力的重点。那么问题来了,既然不重判断,重叙述,托尼是怎么做到发挥评论的提示性和评价性功能的? Labov 和 Waletzky 提出叙事的完整形式包括六个基本结构元素:摘要、状态、复杂行动、评价、解决方式、结局。① 这些元素的基本功能有二,正是提示性和评价性功能。以《卡姆登

① 臧国仁,蔡琰.叙事传播:故事/人文观点[M].杭州:浙江大学出版社,2019:24.

县仍在为难那个 2008 年就认罪的女人》为例，标题提示读者故事在何地何时发生，有谁参与，发生了什么事情，同时"仍在""为难""认罪"等词语表达了评价性。因此，叙述性标题并没有丧失新闻评论标题的基本功能，叙述性标题依然会吸引读者。笔者在新闻评论课程上，多次用叙述性标题做测试，测试结果显示叙述性标题并不比判断性标题在吸引力上差。

叙述性标题对文本节奏的影响非常明显。读托尼的题目，感觉时间慢了下来，这些题目缺乏"斩钉截铁"的气质，充满了"娓娓道来"的气息。托尼的题目在表达效率上并不突出，还稍显冗长，随性的就像是从文本中抽出了一句话，既不提示论题，也不宣告观点。也许正因为如此，成为我国新闻评论实践接受叙述性标题的障碍。郭步陶先生完成了我国第一部评论研究著作，他强调好标题就是把最重要的点完全揭出。邵华泽先生则补充说最重要的点就是论点。[①] 这种认识被奉为我国新闻评论标题制作的圭臬。托尼的题目打破了这一原则，给人感觉不精炼、不硬朗、不概括，但是不能说不吸引人。叙述性标题犹如截取了故事的只言片语，吸引读者进入故事中去，不像判断题给人先声夺人之感，叙述性标题在信息冗余的时代更易让人放松和亲近。

悬宕的开头，首段颠覆倒金字塔模式

首段在新闻评论写作中被看得很重，因为按照倒金字塔模式，首段会告诉读者最重要的信息。如张季鸾先生的经典名篇《日本犬养总理遇刺》一文的首段：

> 昨夜东京急电，日相犬养毅氏于昨日午后五时二十分在官邸被暴徒闯入，击中三枪，重伤流血，八时许警士已宣告绝望。同时警察厅中有人掷手榴弹并放枪，受重伤者数人，而内府大臣牧野邸、政友会本部、日本银行皆受手榴弹，幸未伤人。各处行凶者皆得逃逸，途中散传单，请为除君侧之奸，而未几有十八人向宪后仓促自

①马少华.新闻评论教程[M].北京:高等教育出版社,2012:168.

首。在本文撰稿时，所得电讯止此。①

信源、时间、人物、地点、事件的发生、发展、高潮、细节、结果，都集中在这一段展示出来，由于高度概括，作品的节奏也是紧张高效的。然而对比一下托尼的作品《释放欠债坐监的密苏里妇女让她过了个好节》的首段：

It was early Christmas morning and the kids were poised to tear into their gifts. （那是圣诞节的清晨，孩子们正准备拆开他们的礼物。）

我们会发现托尼作品的首段仅仅是为作品开了一个节奏舒缓的头。如果说张季鸾作品的开头重若泰山，那么托尼作品的开头则轻若鸿毛，我们再来体会一下托尼其他作品的首段：

序号	文本首段	功能分析
文本 1	那是圣诞节的清晨，孩子们正准备拆开他们的礼物。	叙事情境
文本 2	丽安·班德曼偷了指甲油。	被述者及事件
文本 3	罗伯·霍普尔是个自由人。	被述者
文本 4	在登特县，贫穷不是偶发事件，而是一个工业。	判断
文本 5	科里·布斯在密苏里州特伦顿的一个雪天遇见了他的妻子。	叙事情节
文本 6	艾米·穆尔挑战了我。	叙事冲突
文本 7	事情发生在 2017 年母亲节的周末。	叙事时间
文本 8	去年 11 个密苏里县通过州巡回法庭作收债人，各收到超过 10 万美金的罚款。	叙事结果
文本 9	阿利辛·拉普在坎登顿大红谷仓阴影那儿被赶下车，那里位于密苏里 5 号和 54 号公路交叉口，有纪念品和 T 恤商店。	叙事细节
文本 10	加里·奥克森汉德勒法官与密苏里州早期立法者想法一致。	叙事关系

"一句话首段"是托尼的风格，并且这句话颠覆了倒金字塔模式，没有按照新闻价值的次序将最重要的信息放置在其中。程之行在《新闻写作》中将这种方法称之为"正金字塔式"，其特点是："不马上揭示高潮，而要把读者的注意力带引着进入高潮，一若小说与戏剧的结构，具有'悬宕'的效果。"②

---

① 张季鸾.张季鸾集[M].上海：东方出版社,2011:189.
② 臧国仁,蔡琰.叙事传播：故事/人文观点[M].杭州：浙江大学出版社,2019:76.

这种"悬宕"的效果揭示出新闻评论的写作可以与一般的叙事作品具有相同的效果,利用一个好的"角度"吊足读者的胃口,而不是像"倒金字塔模式"那样追求快速满足读者的需要。在托尼的十篇作品中,开头的角度各不相同,这些角度包括情境、被述者、事件、情节、细节、冲突、结果、关系。可以看出,作者托尼在寻找一个特别的开头方面是动了脑子的。

倒金字塔模式被认为具有"反叙事"特征,因为他打破了人们了解事物按照"时间序列"进行的方式,而是把最重要的信息放置在最前面,据说这和战地新闻采写有关。然而随着战争的结束和各个领域新事物的涌现,快速高效的报道方式渐渐与具有更加丰富叙事特征的"正写"方式并存。是的,人们既需要"开门见山",也需要"曲径通幽",这两种方式都可以吸引读者的注意力。

正文:反复用事实讲述个人故事

1. 讲述完整的个体故事

托尼迷恋于讲述个体的故事,他没有选择讲述组织、集体、民族的故事。因为个体的故事带有独特的个人生命印痕,这种独特的个人生命印痕为新闻评论增加了揭秘式的阅读感受,也更加有利于读者与故事的人物建立连接。而有效的阅读连接正是促成互联网式的"点赞""转发"的秘密。由此我们就知道,为什么互联网促使我国的媒介话语被迫地转向了"讲故事"的策略,因为我们原本是多么迷恋"讲道理"。

一个叫维多利亚·布兰森的女人给托尼发来了圣诞节的祝福短信,这个女人48岁了,她年轻的时候和丈夫离了婚,有几个月她的孩子被前夫抚养,她却没有支付抚养费,于是遭到了起诉。这件事彻底改变了布兰森的人生轨迹,绵延15年,当初的抚养费加上诉讼费已经累积到5000美元,她无力偿还,因而又面临着监禁,如今虽然她的前夫已选择了自杀,她的儿子已经长大,但是她仿佛跌进了一个泥沼,怎么也爬不出来。这是托尼作品《释放欠债坐监的密苏里妇女让她过了个好节》中讲述的故事。尽管是新闻评论中重要的消息来源,托尼并没有局限于此,他给了这个消息来源人性意义上的关注,不忘记铺设布兰森生命中的独特性,比如她会给反映问题的托尼发"新年快乐"的短信，她会在监狱里帮助推轮椅，她会发出感叹监狱是"我一生去过最糟糕的地方"，她面临着因为坐监经历而难以找到工作的压力。

台湾著名评论家蔡诗萍说："我常常在新闻事件里，看到更多'人的故事'。每一个'人的故事'，于事不关己的他人，是新闻；但，于当事人，或当事人的亲朋好友，却是如此真实的现实，他们如何能事不关己呢？"① 可以说，在新闻评论中用充满人性的笔调讲述个人化的故事，是一种消除"事不关己"阅读感受的大胆尝试，新闻评论越切入故事人物的心灵世界，越能建立读者与故事人物的情感关系，越能增强评论的黏性。

2. 反复讲述相似的故事

托尼一定深深懂得"母题""原型""类型"这些叙事元素的应用，会加深读者对文本的印象，使文本产生主题一致、脉络一致、意义一致的效果。托尼作品的人物都是付不起几百美元保释金的穷人，他们也会犯下偷口红、超速这样的轻微罪行，他们经年累月地陷入听证、服刑、缓刑、欠账、起诉中，他们无法参军、工作，难以结婚、生子。他们的人生犹如一盘断断续续的破录音带，放着令人沮丧的声音。而托尼是那个会反复倾听这些破录音带声音的人。

序号	故事主角	事　情	结　果
文本 1	贫穷的 48 岁的祖母	欠超过 5000 美元抚养费和诉讼费	四年监禁和 3400 美元罚款
文本 2	登特郡一个女人	偷了指甲油	30 天监禁及后续 2160 美元账单
	脑损伤患者	因未支付出租车费被指控偷窃	90 天监禁和服刑账单 1300 美元
文本 3	法明顿一个男性	因不实指控被带上脚铐	6 个月监狱和脚铐费用
文本 4	身世曲折的女子	偷了 8 美元的睫毛膏	入狱一年及超过 15900 美元的账单
文本 5	在家照顾孩子的爸爸	18 岁时偷了一台割草机	11 年间摆脱不了监狱和 7325 美元服刑账单
文本 6	作者本人	忘记偿还一张超速罚单而差点被监禁	支付 80 美元保释金

---

① 臧国仁,蔡琰.叙事传播:故事/人文观点[M].杭州:浙江大学出版社,2019:133.

续　表

序　号	故事主角	事　情	结　果
文本 7	34 岁的女性	因超速和错过开庭日而陷入刑期、罚款、账单中	在短暂服刑期间因迟到问题执行 6 个月刑期
文本 8	小城镇男青年	17 岁时因偷糖果而被判服刑	缓刑被撤销后入狱，得到 2000 美金账单
文本 9	陷入家庭纠纷中的女人	因拖欠诉讼费用缓刑被撤销，又得到刑期和账单	12 年来无法终止和监狱账单的纠缠
文本 10	无	无	无

反复叙述相似的故事，使托尼的作品塑造出原型意义上的故事模型，沉淀下"人们对新闻故事的认知和情感"①。

从认知方面讲，反复叙述为读者准确把握议题提供了安全感，正所谓"不同的故事缔造了文本真实，最后都可以追溯到背后的大故事和价值观"②。这种安全感进而培养了读者识别托尼作品的能力，托尼的作品由此产生"仪式感"。正如 Bird 和 Dardenne 认为新闻功能在报道真相外，也应收集社会事件进行叙事传播，进而产生仪式作用。③

从情感方面讲，"凡动人之叙事皆有传达情感功能"④。而反复叙述动人故事如同古老的歌谣吟颂出对弱者的关怀。弱者关怀一直是普利策和新闻界最为看重的价值，也是新闻评论实践的宗旨之一。文本中的情感流动帮助读者更容易接受议题和观点，毕竟人类易于被故事的"爱与诗性"感动，而不是被劝服。

3. 消息来源、直接引语在故事讲述中的事实担当

消息来源和直接引语是新闻话语的重要特征，彰显了新闻话语的事实本位性。在以"重判断"为特征的新闻评论文本中，消息来源和直接引语从数量上、具名性上都是不被重视的。托尼的作品则利用消息来源、直接引语进行故事讲述。

托尼重视消息来源的数量，十篇作品平均每篇的消息来源在 6.3 个，其中《打破监狱账单和监禁穷人的循环》一文的消息来源达到 11 个。托

---

① 臧国仁，蔡琰. 叙事传播：故事/人文观点[M]. 杭州：浙江大学出版社,2019:82.
② 臧国仁，蔡琰. 叙事传播：故事/人文观点[M]. 杭州：浙江大学出版社,2019:37.
③ 臧国仁，蔡琰. 叙事传播：故事/人文观点[M]. 杭州：浙江大学出版社,2019:5.
④ 臧国仁，蔡琰. 叙事传播：故事/人文观点[M]. 杭州：浙江大学出版社,2019:61.

尼重视消息来源的具名性。在《释放欠债坐监的密苏里妇女让她过了个好节》中，有 7 个消息来源，分别是密苏里的妇女维多利亚·布兰森（出现 5 次）、密苏里最高法院、短信，这 7 个消息来源交代得十分清晰。托尼也重视通过消息来源的对立关系来重构事实。

直接引语在托尼文本中运用十分普遍，每一个个体人物都用引语展露了心灵世界。欠下前夫抚养费的布兰森说监狱是"一生中待过的最糟的地方"；偷了割草机的布斯回忆起第一次入狱的晚上说："我很害怕。"因超速而陷入监狱负债中的琼斯表达了愤怒："他们想榨干我的一切。"因为家庭纠纷而陷入危机中的拉姆说："我正在努力改变我的生活，我希望一切从头开始。"

在"文人论政"框架下思考"用事实讲故事"

1. "文人论政"对中国新闻评论实践的影响

"典范"这个词因为库恩《科学革命的结构》而传播开来。典范用来描述一个圈子的人共享一套话语生产方式。而"典范转移"则反映了后起之秀们对这个典范的突破。我国新闻评论写作受到"文人论政"典范深刻而持久的影响。梁启超作为文人论政最早的践行者，早在 1910 年创办《国风报》时，就提出"造成健全之舆论"，他论述了健全舆论的"五本""八德"。精英分子自身学养修为被拆解为"常识""真诚""直道""公心""节制"，这是保障评论伦理的根本，而评论的操作策略则被概括为"忠告""向导""浸润""强聒""见大""主一""旁通""下逮"。"五本""八德"反映出"文人论政"典范的精髓。文人论政写作主体是精英，其写作的视角是俯视的，其态度情怀是启蒙祛魅的，其表达方式是理性价值论辩的。

文人论政以其写作主体的"大师"特征，以其评论文本的"经典"样貌，不仅创造了难以超越的新闻评论实践典范，而且也潜移默化地影响到新时期时评人的写作取向。然而随着 20 世纪 80 年代以来"叙事转向"的发生，以及媒介网络化的发展，媒介的话语传播更注重人文性、共享性、情感性，故事所包含的好的说服理由，展现了"爱与诗性"①，

---

① 臧国仁,蔡琰.叙事传播:故事/人文观点[M].杭州:浙江大学出版社,2019:11.

这是不逊于理性价值辩论的表达方式，也是叙事传播比肩于信息传播的地方。在这种情况下，我国的新闻评论写作要不要顺应这种趋势，走出对"文人论政"典范过于依赖的思维方式，大胆尝试用事实讲故事的方法，这是来自托尼作品的启示，也是时代赋予我们的思考。

2."用事实讲故事"根源于"非虚构写作"典范

"非虚构写作"典范有三个原则：事实、亲历和诚实。例如，美国著名记者泰德·科诺瓦曾经用"扒火车"的方式写了经典作品《迷踪》。① 科诺瓦完全进入了流浪汉的生活，甚至他的父母都无法认出儿子。非虚构写作对普利策获奖评论的影响是显而易见的。2012 年的普利策奖专栏评论作品《困境中的父亲上了一堂关于给予的课》，作者玛丽·史密琪从亲历的角度讲述了童年与父亲相处的片段。2006 年普利策社论奖作品《孤独的人们》通过搜集事实材料让一个死人"伊娃·约克"讲述了她作为癫痫患者的悲惨故事。托尼也在文本《是时候彻底关闭债务人的监狱了》中，讲述了他自己因为忘记偿还一张超速罚单而差点被监禁，需要支付 80 美元保释金的故事，也是在这一次经历中，他体会到若自己是黑人，是穷人，或者是一个贫穷的白人，可能面临不同的结局，这也使他在面对穆尔"你为什么要写我们这种人的故事"时，有了充足的理由。

大众媒介在早期发展过程中，把"信息"作为传播的根基。② 我国新闻评论实践也符合此规律。然而 20 世纪 80 年代末期开始，整个社会科学领域开始"叙事转向"，特别是进入手机主导的"数位叙事"时代，"以故事为本之传播行动早已成为影响社会大众最为深远的因子"③。臧国仁和蔡琰在最新的著作《叙事传播：故事/人文观点》中把"好故事"视为可以成为人类信仰和行动的准则，故事带来了"良好理性"④。

文人论政典范追求劝服效果的快速实现，"用事实讲故事"看重媒体与受众平等的对话。人是叙事的动物，故事创造了自然、温暖的交流情境，人类的情感、信念都得到了更自然更深刻的传递，故事构筑了共同

---

①罗伯特·博因顿.新新闻主义：美国顶尖非虚构作家写作技巧访谈录[J].刘蒙之,译.北京：北京师范大学出版社,2018:2.

②臧国仁,蔡琰.叙事传播：故事/人文观点[M].杭州：浙江大学出版社,2019:4.

③臧国仁,蔡琰.叙事传播：故事/人文观点[M].杭州：浙江大学出版社,2019:6.

④臧国仁,蔡琰.叙事传播：故事/人文观点[M].杭州：浙江大学出版社,2019:36.

的记忆空间。"用事实讲故事",是新闻话语从枪弹论、劝服论、启蒙论一路走来,走向的新实践。

3. 打破"只评不访",对"评论记者"的再思考

早在 2007 年,正是都市报新闻评论繁荣发展的时期,有学者就提出建立"评论记者"机制,认为长期以来,我国媒体总是将评论与理论联系在一起,建立了"评论理论部",可以尝试考虑建立"新闻评论部",并且推行"评论记者"机制。"评论记者"首先应该是一名记者,在传播观点信息的同时也传播事实信息。① 这样的提法和观点,无疑是对我国新闻评论机制深入思考后得出的倡议。

今天看来,我们还没来得及在都市报评论繁荣时期开启新闻评论工作机制的革新,就被迫开始面对网络媒体。在网络时代,新闻评论的写作遭到了自媒体的挑战,可是在追逐热点,运用网络化写作方式的同时,也丧失了对新闻评论写作规范的坚守,前述以咪蒙作品为代表的事实失信就是典型代表。

托尼的作品打破了"只评不访"的思路,在我们传统思维中新闻评论的事实多是评论员从新闻报道中选择的,评论员对事实不负责鉴别和亲历,这就造成了作者和事实的隔膜。也就是作者和读者一样,对要评价的事实均来自"二手"资料。那么评价只能从经验中来,并不是来自体验后的确知。但是托尼会参与到作品的事实搜集中,他约见他们、倾听他们、和他们保持联系、关注他们的动态、为他们的生命叹息和抱不平,他们也会给他发来祝福的短信,会质问他,会向他展示自己的伤口,会抱怨,也会理解。正是这些经历和思考让托尼展开了对遭遇此类问题的弱势底层小人物的采访。托尼的参与和体验让读者和事实的距离被拉近了,也就增加了信任和真实,更能带动人们反思自己的处境和问题。

第二节　倾听弱者的故事: 63 个消息来源

"我想亲眼看看布鲁克·贝尔根身上会发生什么。"

贝尔根是一个消息来源,出现在 2019 年普利策新闻评论奖作品中。

---

① 成茹,苏蕾.嘉兴时评:评论记者第一时间发表评论[J].军事记者,2007(11):42.

贝尔根身世悲惨，生活坎坷，她从未见过父亲，母亲也在她15岁时去世。为了摆脱被人寄养的命运，贝尔根选择早早结婚，却在三年前失去了一个孩子。她的故事之所以被作者托尼·曼森哲捕捉到，是因为贝尔根偷了一根8美元的睫毛膏，由此开启了她与高额监狱账单纠缠在一起的命运。贝尔根是一个十足的底层人物，出身、犯罪和贫穷让她的生活每天在挣钱和还账中度过，而司法系统通过收取监狱食宿费的做法又使她雪上加霜。托尼把他的笔触伸向贝尔根这样的弱势人群。在获奖作品中和贝尔根相似的弱势消息来源还有6个。

消息来源可以带来事实、观点和背景材料。传统研究只在新闻报道中讨论消息来源。但美国新闻评论发展出评论员记者化的趋势，这使得新闻评论文本同样重视消息来源。《亚特兰大日报》社论撰稿人苏珊·拉赛蒂分享了她的写作经验："我认为，最好的社论撰稿人是那些记者。不是前任记者，而是现任记者。撰写社论——撰写优秀社论——需要细致的调查和挖掘，以确保你获得一个观点。"[1]《冲击力——新闻评论写作教程》的作者康拉德·芬克列举了专栏作家工具箱里的宝贝，其中之一就是渊博而权威的消息来源。[2]

托尼·曼森哲的作品就表现出对消息来源的重视。笔者对托尼的十篇获奖文本进行了消息来源的内容分析。从消息来源的个数、类型、具名性、层级性、对立性、被处理方式等指标入手，深入解读了托尼作品消息来源的使用情况。这项研究，一是可以帮助我们认识到美国新闻评论员记者化对文本的实际影响，拓展我们对新闻评论生产方式的理解。二是可以看到消息来源在新闻评论文本中实际的存在状态和分布，积累对这一文本要素的运用经验。

获奖文本消息来源的总体性描述

我们采集的样本来自2019年普利策新闻评论奖的十篇获奖文本，作

---

① 康拉德·芬克.冲击力——新闻评论写作教程[M].柳珊,顾振凯,郝瑞,译.北京:新华出版社,2002:74.

② 康拉德·芬克.冲击力——新闻评论写作教程[M].柳珊,顾振凯,郝瑞,译.北京:新华出版社,2002:134.

者是托尼·曼森哲。[①] 托尼 1999 年开始担任《哥伦比亚每日论坛》评论员，2008 年加入《圣路易斯邮报》，并在 2012 年成为社论版编辑。托尼的专业性得到美国专业记者协会、美国新编辑协会以及密苏里新闻学院的认可。他在普利策奖之外，还获得过密苏里州新闻奖、美国新闻编辑协会编辑领导奖以及霍华德基金会的写作奖。普利策奖这样描述他的作品："这是一个充满勇气的作家，他的作品揭露了弥漫在密苏里州的重要问题，一些贫穷的人因为犯下一些小罪过，最终陷入一个司法系统构建的罚款和入狱的陷阱中，不仅毁了小人物的生活，也增加了地区的贫困化。"可以说托尼本人的专业性以及普利策获奖的经历保证了采集样本的经典性和代表性。

十篇获奖文本共产生了 63 个消息来源，文本消息来源最多的是 10 号文本，为 11 个；而 4 号文本最少，为 3 个。平均每篇文本 6.3 个消息来源。这 63 个消息来源可以分为人物、机构和证明材料三大类。其中人物消息来源为 54 个，机构为 1 个，证明材料为 8 个。由于本文主要探讨人物消息来源的运用问题，所以去除机构和证明材料消息来源，并且不计算文本内部重复出现的消息来源，还剩下 24 个有效数据。这 24 个消息来源的具名程度非常高，只有 2 个为匿名处理。剩下的 22 个消息来源，对姓名、身份、私人性背景均呈现的消息来源有 8 个，可以知道姓名和身份的为 14 个。例如维多利亚·布兰森这个消息来源，既有姓名，也告知她是一个 48 岁的单亲母亲，还知道她的家庭情况、生命经历以及现实困境。而马修·穆勒这个消息来源，告知了姓名和身份。他是密苏里州公共辩护办公室的高级诉讼律师，主要工作是代表因贫困入狱的穷人提起诉讼，但是文本没有呈现马修的私人性背景。

消息来源的层级性，体现了消息来源在文本中被赋予的话语表达权是有差别的。处于高级别的消息来源通过故事化叙述、话语、细节被呈现。处于低级别层次的消息来源，在信息量上相对较少，在呈现方式上比较公式化，没有私人故事中的建构。高低层次之间是中级别消息来源，他们虽然也没有在故事中呈现，但是话语呈现的数量更多，层次更丰富。在 22 个具名清晰的人物消息来源中，高、中、低的个数分别为：8、11、

①https://www.pulitzer.org/winners/tony-messenger-st-louis-post-dispatch.

3. 值得注意的是，所有弱势人物消息来源都是高阶呈现。

　　消息来源的对立性，是指消息来源与作者观点的关系。如果与作者观点一致，被称为正向消息来源，不一致则被称为负向消息来源。22个具名清晰的人物消息来源都属于正向消息来源。

　　消息来源的被处理程度，是指消息来源在文本中的角色设定，分为受害者、辩护者和加害者。在24个人物消息来源中：受害者有7个，辩护者和守护者有16个，对立者有1个。

偏向研究和弱势消息来源的高阶呈现

　　"偏向"问题是消息来源研究中一个重要议题。王芳在其博士论文《当前我国大众化报纸消息来源偏向研究》中梳理了这一研究的国外学术脉络。从学者 Gans 对电视新闻和杂志消息来源的研究，到学者 Sigal 对《华盛顿邮报》和《纽约时报》头版新闻消息来源的研究；从 Kim 对五个国家报道亚洲金融危机时的消息来源研究，到 Grabe 等人对报纸消息来源性别分布的研究，分别证明了媒介在新闻生产中偏向于使用知名人士、官方人士、专业人士、男性等强势消息来源。王芳本人针对我国大众化报纸的研究，也得出如下结论：新闻报道中更常出现的是政府官员、专家学者、经济精英等强势者，而普通民众作为无权力无权威的消息来源，发言机会很少，且常在被动、单一的情境中说话。强势消息来源是议程设置的主要定义者，而弱势消息来源则无力影响议程，即使成为消息来源，也沦为被他者言说的境地。[①]

　　偏向问题其实质是强势消息来源在文本中被高阶呈现，这首先表现在数量上。王芳发现，在现实生活中，官方阶层占比为2％左右，但是在采集的977篇新闻报道中，官方消息来源占到消息来源总数的42.3％。明显看到，官方消息来源在新闻报道中被放大了。[②] 其次表现在强势消息来源被呈现的方式。他们不仅在各类新闻、不同主题新闻、硬新闻中成为"首要定义者"，而且扮演着评论者、阐释者的角色，甚至成为"一言堂"

---

①王芳.当前我国大众化报纸消息来源偏向研究[D].武汉大学,2007:3.
②王芳.当前我国大众化报纸消息来源偏向研究[D].武汉大学,2007:27.

和"金子塔尖"式的消息来源。

托尼的新闻评论彻底扭转了消息来源偏向问题，弱势消息来源反而被高阶呈现，强势消息来源则成为弱势消息来源的辩护方。这同样表现在数量和呈现方式两个方面。

在数量上，十篇文本的弱势消息来源共有 7 个，他们总的特点是贫穷，穷到偷了一根价值 8 美元的睫毛膏。这种贫穷的命运仿佛是一个诅咒，有人从未见过父亲又早早染上毒瘾，有人被诬告惹上官司，有人身体残疾，有人陷入家庭暴力。当他们因小偷小摸和其他一些轻罪被逮捕后，就会产生一笔监狱食宿费，这笔费用又会加剧他们的贫困，也会让他们陷入司法审查中。这些弱势消息来源在任何一种社会情境中，都是最底层的人物。

在呈现方式上，弱势消息来源被悬宕的开头引入文本，托尼采用一种完整性的叙述视角展现了消息来源的生命故事，也在细节、话语、互动中勾勒出活泛的生命状态。这完全打破了偏向传统中弱势者那种僵化、刻板性呈现。我们以维多利亚·布兰森为例。

布兰森出现在文本 1《释放欠债坐监的密苏里妇女让她过了个好节》中。作者对她的出场勾勒了一个温情和美好的场景。那是个圣诞节的早晨，孩子们正在拆礼物，而托尼享受着美好的音乐和甜蜜的气氛，这时一条短信到来。托尼用期待和惊喜的语气写道：这不是我的父亲，不是我在遥远地方的孩子，不是我的兄弟姐妹发来的，这是维多利亚·布兰森的祝福短信。这种烘托和铺垫显示了托尼对弱势者的情感和尊重。

再来看罗布·霍普的呈现方式。他出现在 3 号文本《随着选举临近圣弗朗索瓦县检察官再次推迟公义》中。托尼首先用故事化方式呈现了他被人诬告陷入牢狱之灾的故事，又通过他的伴侣布朗的话语表达了霍普的态度："他不会为自己没做过的事情辩护。"当霍普脱去囚衣，换上自己的衣服，拥抱了布朗时，这些细节呈现了霍普生活的另一个层面。作者对霍普的高阶呈现，还加入了判断，例如"罗布·霍普是一个自由的人"，让读者感受到托尼对霍普的尊重。在 3 号文本的结尾，托尼又用一种散文诗般的方式赋予霍普一种人格上的美好："在这个清爽的秋日，霍普正忙着享受一切，那洒在他脸上的阳光，也洒在起伏的山丘和落叶上。陪伴他的还有一个始终为他的自由而奋斗的爱人。"

对弱势消息来源的高阶呈现，本质上是托尼新闻观念的彻底胜利，战胜了消息来源偏向问题。被低估被忽视的底层人物在新闻评论文本上被重视，他们不再刻板僵硬，不再无足轻重，每个人都像是一个悲惨命运中的传奇，展示了"疲惫生活中的英雄梦想"。

弱势消息来源在"故事"中被建构

托尼用"故事化"的方式建构弱势消息来源，而对强势消息来源则只保留姓名、职务和话语。正是在这一点上，弱势消息来源显示出了高阶性。

托尼喜欢在评论中为弱势群体搭建一个故事框架，这个故事框架犹如一个保护伞，在温暖的叙述和用心的细节中娓娓道来弱势者的辛酸和坚持。传统的新闻评论倡导一种理性的论证框架，叙述的主要目的是证明论点。在托尼的文章中，叙述是为了讲好一个边缘人物的故事，让弱势者重新站到社会关注的焦点上。故事重复着一个主题，就是这个社会瞧不起穷人，却通过在穷人身上榨取钱财维持着自己的体面。一个是故事框架，一个是说理空间，一个是私人性的故事，一个是公共性的议题，这种叠拼式架构，为文本增添了独特的气质。人类对故事的接纳程度好过说理，故事唤起人类胸腔内的情感共鸣。有趣的是，托尼完全放弃了给任何一个强势消息来源搭建故事框架的机会，强势消息来源被处置得精确和程式化，而弱势消息来源却处置得浪漫、温情、饱满，尽管他们的生活不如意，可是不如意的生活也展示了旺盛的生命力。这就是托尼的思路，他用故事化打通了人们通往坚硬公共议题的路径，借着故事和人物，我们开始关注远离日常生活的悲惨世界。

我们从"下雪"这个细节，可以看出故事化处置的好处。在 5 号文本《密苏里州的乡村法院普遍存在"贫困惩罚"》中，"下雪"被提及了三次。第一次：在一个下雪的日子里，科里·布斯遇到了他的妻子。这里的"下雪"是浪漫回忆中一个记忆深刻的天气细节，展示了布斯浪漫的个性。第二次出现在托尼采访布斯的那天：那是一个下雪的日子，也是布斯每月到法庭报道的日子。这一次的"下雪"对应着布斯生活的无奈和烦恼。第三次出现在文尾：冬季的第一场暴风雪来到了，布斯的孩子生病了，他必须在偿还债务和买药上做一个决定，最后他决定先治病，这样他陷入了又一次违规中。布斯抱怨道："这是拆东墙补西墙的做法，这种做法太疯狂了。"这一次"下雪"对应的是生活的困局和灾难。三次"下雪"，串联起布斯的过去、现在和将来，揭示了他的性格和命运。读者和布斯之间有了深刻的连接，毕竟关于下雪，每个人都有上述的体验。布斯这个弱势消息来源的建构是故事化的，是画面感的，也是具体真实、令人心动的。

反复被托举的弱者故事，情节虽然悲惨，但人性却并不压抑。读者阅读故事，也缓慢走向了公共议题。一位年近半百的祖母，被纠缠在破碎婚姻导致的抚养费诉讼中；一位家世凄惨因穷致偷的女孩；一位因脑损伤忘记支付车费的残疾人；一位少年时偷了割草机的中年父亲；一位热爱自由却被诬告陷入困境的男子；一位遭遇家暴和背叛的女人。每个故事都有独特的叙述视角和故事情节，故事的内核相似，人物却具有独特个性。故事拉近了读者和弱者的距离，引起了读者的同理心、共情力，读者开始思考公共议题与他人和自己的连接点。为了促成这种连接，托尼甚至献出了自己的故事。

托尼作为《圣路易斯邮报》的记者，属于有社会地位和话语权力的强势消息来源，但是托尼甘当管道，实现了双方的深入沟通。6 号文本《是时候彻底关闭债务人的监狱了》，托尼遭遇了采访对象艾米·穆尔的质问："你为什么要这么做？""你为什么要写穷人、瘾君子和重罪犯？你为什么要讲述全州乡村居民的公民权利遭到当地治安官、检察官和法官的践踏这样的故事？"穆尔的发问激发了托尼的耻辱感，因为穆尔质疑了他的动机。这个质疑代表了穆尔作为弱势消息来源个体的不安全感，也可以看作是整个弱势群体对强势群体的怀疑。托尼谦卑自己，敞开了自己的经历。

很多年前，托尼被警察拦下，铐上手铐，起因是他忘记了一张超速罚单，于是警察开了逮捕令。幸好托尼身上有现金可以交保释金。这次经历促使托尼思考：如果他是穷人，而且是黑人，居住在圣路易斯县北部，再如果，他是一个贫穷的白人，住在登特县的乡下，事情可能会变得更糟。如果他在监狱里度过周末，社会服务机构就会带走他的孩子。所以当他听到穆尔的故事，听到贝尔根、班德曼、布斯、艾佛茨的故事，听到人们因轻罪而被监禁，因监禁而无法从债务中脱身，毁了生活，这些故事让他了解到其实穷人和他自己犯的错误是一样的性质，可是结局却如此不同，他被社会的不公平和司法的腐败震撼了，决心写评论揭发这些黑暗面，保护弱势者。

托尼的反思精神和同理心让他的作品获得了悲天悯人的气质，也促进了强势消息来源和弱势消息来源的沟通。托尼无非要表达的是，我作为评论员，是一个管道，也是一个可以体悟到穷人伤痛的媒介。托尼敞开自己的试验性的写作技法，使得评论员记者化这条路走得更远了，也为中国新闻评论提供了深刻的启示。

弱势消息来源在"话语"中被建构

"那是我一生中去过的最可怕的地方。"

托尼借着布兰森的话语说出了弱势消息来源心中对监狱最深的恐惧。与强势消息来源相比，弱势消息来源的话语结构简单，比较直白感性。这与强势消息来源的理性形成了鲜明的对比。在话语中，弱势消息来源的恐惧、纠结、困惑，这些情绪都被传递出来。弱势消息来源不再是被强势消息来源叙述的角色，他们有了自己的话语形象。

科里·布斯是话语表达层次较为丰富的一个弱势消息来源。当他回忆和妻子第一次见面的时候，他说："我想，为什么不和那个漂亮姑娘聊聊呢？"当他谈到第一次坐监狱的时候，他说："我整晚都没睡，我很害怕。"他承认了自己的错误："我把缓刑期搞砸了，是我的错。"坐牢给他的生活态度带来了影响，他说："这让我在很多不同的事情上退缩了。"在选择面前，他说："要么买日用品，要么付钱给法官。"他也表达了对监狱罚款的愤怒："这太疯狂了，他们让缓刑变得如此难以执行，这样他们就可以侵犯你，体制就是问题所在，这是一个恶性循环。太可怕了！"话语也表达了他的困境："我把给法官的钱花在给孩子们买药上了，这是抢劫彼得付钱给保罗的情况，而卡诺伊法官就是保罗。"

整个 9 号文本《卡姆登县仍在为难那个 2008 年就认罪的女人》，都在讲述拉普的故事。拉普的表达能力很强。当她被警察丢在一个陌生地方时，她说："我没有钱，没有车，也没有电话。""我没有办法回到圣路易斯的家，我陷入了困境。"她对监狱账单的荒谬性评价道："这是一个传奇。""不进监狱，给了缓刑，但又撤销了。"拉普还会给卡姆登县巡回法院写信："请求提供服务时间，以代替罚款或者坐牢，以便与我目前的判决同时进行。"她告诉托尼："正在努力改变我的生活，我希望一切像白板一样从头开始。"她也向托尼表达她近乎崩溃的心态："看在上帝的分上，已经 12 年了。""我失去了工作、房子、汽车和孩子。我已经坐够了牢，我已经给他们足够的钱了。这件事一直困扰着我，我永远不可能有一个利落的开始。它什么时候才会停止？"

强势消息来源为弱势者辩护

强势消息来源是社会生活中拥有一定政治、经济、社会地位的人和机构，他们的权威性、可信性和表达性都具有优势，往往受到新闻媒体的青睐，在新闻文本的构建中被赋予更高的话语表达权。

托尼的文章却颠覆了强势消息来源总是处于主要地位的处置方式，在十篇文本中，强势消息来源成为弱势消息来源的辩护方，并且强势消息来源构建了一个为弱势群体辩护的证据链。这个证据链包括了律师、司法官员、众议院、大法官、批评家的话语，分别从法律、政治、舆论方面实现了对弱势者的辩护。

托尼首先赋予了这个证据链以可信性。这些强势消息来源的具名程度很高，例如前法官兼司法部官员、罚款和收费司法中心联合主任丽莎·福斯特，这个消息来源不仅包含名和姓也包括了现任和前任职务，再比如圣查尔斯县检察官、共和党人蒂姆·洛马尔，有名有姓，有党派和职务。精准的具名，增加了文章的可信度。

这个证据链是有层级性的。密苏里州最高法院首席大法官玛丽·罗素是最高级别的强势消息来源，处于证据链的高阶地位。玛丽大法官的话语被引用的最完整，提供了从宏观视野看待公共问题的角度。玛丽首先强调了司法原则："法院的存在是为了帮助人们解决他们的法律纠纷。如果作为市政当局的收入来源，会造成对司法公正性降低的印象。"其次，她强调了法院存在的意义："要确保整个州的市政部门不是由经济驱动，而是由法治下的公平观念驱动的。确保在市法院出庭的人受到公平和尊重的对待。"最后她引用了美国合法性的来源之一——马丁·路德·

金的话语描述密苏里州一个法院的问题是如何成为整个司法系统的问题。她说："我们被困在一个不可避免的相互关系网中，被绑在一件命运的衣服里。任何直接影响到一个人的东西，都会间接影响到所有人。"

玛丽·罗素这个消息来源以下，证据链继续延伸：在文本 10《打破监狱账单和监禁穷人的循环》中，对证据链完整性和相关性的体现最为充分。首先是前两个消息来源，它们分别是布恩县巡回法院法官奥克森汉德勒，检察官、共和党人蒂姆·洛马尔，这两个消息来源提供了重要事实：布恩县、圣查尔斯县没有收取监狱账单。既然这些地方可以做到不向穷人收取费用，那么其他县的做法就没有了逃避的借口。其次是众议员德格鲁特、彻斯特菲尔德、艾尔布兰特，李波特提出并发起第 192 号法案，旨在制止无力支付费用的被告月复一月地出现在法庭上，以往在某些案件中如果这些被告错过听证会，将面临藐视法庭的指控和更长的监禁时间。最外围的消息来源就是智囊人员，如布伦南司法中心的律师和研究员劳伦·布鲁克·艾森，他通过撰写大量各县收取监禁费过程的文章来揭露问题，保护穷人。

律师作为强势消息来源层级谱系中一个较为下级的存在，它与弱势消息来源的关系最近。所以，这个层级更多地表达了对弱势消息来源的了解和同情。例如吉姆·鲁斯特律师代理了麦克纳布的案子，所以他就这样评价："这孩子不是罪犯。""他是一个试图摆脱困境的小镇子上的人。"乔安娜·韦斯律师则表达了对问题普遍性的担忧："在密苏里州的许多农村县，贫困惩罚依然存在。"法明顿律师沃恩·卡拉克为那些声称受到司法系统伤害的人服务。她倾听人们抱怨马胡林和马丁内斯。她提出阳光法案，寻求预算，出席圣弗朗索瓦郡委员会会议，提出质疑。她和许多同她交谈过的人在脸书上发表了批评意见，引用了关于马胡林的具体案例和公众投诉。仅圣弗朗索瓦县的政治网页就邀请到 2900 多名成员。卡拉克这个消息来源，充分展示了与弱势消息来源的连接和参与感。

托尼也借着强势消息来源，表达他的观点。马修·穆勒是一个中级消息来源，在 2 号文本中展示了他很多话语。第一，描述了公共议题的普遍性："这种事情正在全州范围内发生。"第二，分析了公共议题的起因："实际情况是，人们是因贫困而被捕。""他们对此无能为力。只能蹲在监狱里，看着账单越堆越高。"第三，揭示了公共议题的本质：问题不仅仅在于农村各县因穷人入狱而向他们收费，而是他们会将监狱债务视为"罚款"，在人们无力支付罚款时使用郡政府的逮捕权。第四，表达对公共议题的态度："这种做法是非法的，必须停止。""这些都不符合宪法。""发生的事情真的很可怕。""这是无限期的承诺。这些人完全无助。这必须停止。"

第三节　案例库：密苏里州穷人被监禁罚款案[①]

1. 评奖标准

奖励杰出的评论，这些评论可以使用任何可用的新闻工具，奖金是一万五千美元。

2.2019 年普利策评论奖作者简介

托尼·曼森哲是《圣路易斯邮报》的专栏作家，从 2016 年 9 月开始，他每周写 4 篇专栏。他从 2012 年 7 月起担任社论版编辑，直到成为专栏作家。他于 2008 年加入《圣路易斯邮报》，在杰斐逊城做财经记者和政治专栏作家。

他在科罗拉多州的一家小周报开始了职业生涯，他在那里出生并长大。他曾在科罗拉多州、亚利桑那州、内布拉斯加州、南达科他州和密苏里州的周刊、日报和杂志工作。

2016 年，托尼被授予密苏里荣誉勋章，这是密苏里大学新闻学院授予的最高奖项。当年，我国著名报人张季鸾先生也获得过此殊荣。同年，他凭借社论写作获得了国家头条新闻奖（National Headliner）。2015 年，托尼因社论写作入围了普利策奖，也在这一年获得了职业记者协会颁发的年度最佳社论奖。2014 年，他获得了美国新闻编辑协会颁发的伯尔·奥斯本编辑领导力奖，以及斯克里普斯-霍华德基金会颁发的沃克·斯通

---

①该案例库英文文本版权属于原作者和首发媒体,本书作者通过电子邮件等形式联系原作者 Tony Messenger ,但均未收到关于版权的回复。本书作者最终决定在书中收录英文文本,一是方便读者感受英文新闻评论的特色,二是在文本中标注了大量话语分析符号和记录文字,供读者学习使用。本书作者会继续保持和原作者的沟通联系,并承诺保护原作者的版权权益。

编辑写作奖。他的写作已经赢得了其他许多州和地区的荣誉。[①]

3. 获奖作品颁奖词、发表时间和中英文标题

颁奖词：这是一个有勇气的专栏，这些文章暴露了渎职和不公正的行为，即迫使犯下轻罪的农村穷人支付无法承受的罚款或入狱的行为。

获奖作品 WINNING WORK		
发表时间	英文标题	中文标题
2018/1/4	Release from debtor's prison raises holiday spirit of Missouri woman	释放欠债坐监的密苏里妇女让她过了个好节
2018/10/9	Counties' jailing of the poor 'has got to stop,' defender says	各县对穷人的监禁"必须停止"，辩护人说
2018/10/25	St. Francois County prosecutor delays justice again as vote nears	随着选举临近圣弗朗索瓦县检察官再次推迟公义
2018/11/4	Judge tries to block access to debtors prison hearings in Dent county	法官试图阻止在登特县参加债务人监狱听证会
2018/11/17	'Poverty penalty' pervades rural courts in Missouri	密苏里州的乡村法院普遍存在"贫困惩罚"
2018/11/22	Time to close debtor's prison for good	是时候彻底关闭债务人的监狱了
2018/11/24	Rural court traps woman with ticket for speeding	乡村法庭拘捕超速驾驶女子
2018/11/29	Stoddard County can teach a lesson about dealing with poor defendants	斯托达德县可以教与穷被告人打交道的课了
2018/12/4	Camden County still bedevils woman after 2008 guilty plea	卡姆登县仍在为难那个 2008 年就认罪的女人
2018/12/8	Breaking the cycle of board bills, jailing the poor	打破监狱账单和监禁穷人的循环

4. 决赛入围者

《大西洋》的凯特琳·弗拉纳根（Caitlin Flanagan）。作品用个性的、敏锐的分析和专业性探索了性别与政治的交汇点。

《堪萨斯城之星》的梅琳达·亨内伯格（Melinda Henneberger）。作品以空灵而勇敢的风格探讨了她的家乡 NFL 小组，她的前州长办公室和天主教堂内，制度上的性别歧视和厌女症。

[①] https://www. pulitzer. org/winners/tony-messenger-st-louis-post-dispatch.

5. 评审团

凯蒂·格雷（Katti Gray 主席）

自由记者，纽约州蒙蒂塞洛/方舟小石城。

迈克·范宁（Mike Fannin）

《堪萨斯城之星》副总裁/编辑；麦克拉奇中央区域编辑

卡洛斯·洛萨达（Carlos Lozada）

副编辑/非小说类书评家，《华盛顿邮报》

莱尔·穆勒（Lyle Muller）

艾奥瓦州公共事务新闻中心执行主任/编辑

雷内·桑切斯（Rene Sanchez）

明尼阿波利斯（Minneapolis）《星论坛报》编辑

戴维·冯·德勒（David Von Drehle）

《华盛顿邮报》专栏作家

阿曼达·萨莫拉（Amanda Zamora）

《得克萨斯论坛报》首席官

【2019 年普利策评论奖 1 号文本】

Release from debtor's prison raises holiday spirit of Missouri woman
释放欠债坐监的密苏里妇女让她过了个好节

1　It was early Christmas morning and the kids were poised to tear into their gifts.

又是一个圣诞节的清晨，孩子们兴致勃勃地准备拆礼物。

2　I sat in my favorite chair, coffee in hand. It had a little extra shot of holiday cheer. Nat King Cole was singing in the background when the first "Merry Christmas" text popped up on my phone.

我坐在心爱的椅子里，端着咖啡，蛮有节日气氛。房间里飘着纳·金·高尔①那柔和的男中音，这时候，第一条"圣诞快乐"的短信跳了出来。

---

①纳·金·高尔是一位美国的音乐家，以出色的爵士钢琴演奏而闻名。他是柔和的男中音。

3　It wasn't from one of my grown children in a faraway state——not my dad, nor any of my siblings.

　　这短信不是我成年的孩子从其他遥远的州发来的，也不是我父亲，更不是我的兄弟姐妹。

4　No, the two-word holiday greeting came from Victoria Branson.

　　这简短的节日问候来自维多利亚·布兰森。

5　Just a couple of months earlier, the 48-year-old grandmother had been in a Missouri prison, facing a four-year sentence for the audacious crime of being too poor.

　　几个月前，这位 48 岁的祖母还在密苏里州的一所监狱里服刑，因为实在太穷犯下的"胆大包天"罪让她面临着四年的监禁。

6　She's in Desloge, Mo. , now, living with her 15-year-old son, checking in with her parole officer, hoping never to go back to the prison she should not have been sent to in the first place.

　　布兰森现在和她 15 岁的儿子住在密苏里州的德斯洛格，她需要经常向假释官报到，她希望自己永远不要回到当初本不应该被送进的监狱。

7　"That was the most terrible place I've ever been in my life," ①Branson（布兰森。她是本文的主要叙述者，也是本文最重要的消息来源。）says of the state women's prison in Vandalia.

　　"那是我一生中去过的最可怕的地方。"①布兰森在谈到位于万达利亚州女子监狱时说。

8　I wrote about Branson's plight in August.

　　我八月份报道过布兰森的困境。

9　She had been hauled before St. Francois County Circuit Judge Sandra Martinez on a decade-old child support case that Branson thought was long ago resolved. At the time, nearly 15 years ago, she was behind a few hundred bucks on support for her then-teen son who had left for a few months to live with his father. The father later killed himself, and the son moved back with Branson. He's 30 now and lives on his own. Over the years, the costs of the old child support combined with court costs climbed to more than ＄5, 000.

布兰森曾被圣弗朗索瓦县巡视法官桑德拉·马丁内斯传唤，为的是一个布兰森认为早已解决的十年前的儿童抚养案。那时是大约15年前，她十来岁的儿子有几个月和他父亲住在一起，布兰森因此欠下了几百块钱的抚养费。他儿子的父亲后来自杀了，然后儿子搬回来和布兰森一起住。儿子现在30岁了，一个人住。多年来，赡养费和诉讼费加在一起已经超过了5000美元。

10　Martinez revoked Branson's probation on the case because those costs hadn't been paid. Twice in the past couple of years, the Missouri Supreme Court had over turned similar sentences handed out by the judge because it's unconstitutional to send poor people to jail simply because they can't afford to pay fines and court fees.

因为没有支付上述费用，马丁内斯撤销了布兰森的缓刑。在过去的几年里，密苏里州最高法院曾两次驳回法官做出的类似判决，因为仅仅因为穷人付不起罚款和诉讼费就把他们送进监狱是违宪的。

11　"So, in this case we are left with a system in which all Missouri taxpayers have to pay for the salaries of judges, clerks, prosecutors, public defenders and probation officers to collect money from a grandmother on disability supporting her grandchildren in order to operate the St. Francois County jail," ②the court（法院，根据上文可以判断为密苏里最高法院。这是一个机构消息来源。）wrote in overturning Martinez on a case similar to Branson's. "The amount of resources devoted to this task is astonishing. "

"所以，在这个案子中，我们只剩下一个体系，所有密苏里州纳税人要为法官、职员、检察官、公共辩护人和缓刑监督官支付薪水，而这些人却从一个抚养她孙子的残疾祖母那里收钱，来运作圣弗朗索瓦县监狱，"当它推翻了马丁内斯另一个类似布兰森的案子时，②法院写下了这段话。"投入到这项事务上的资源惊人。"

12　The issue of rising court costs and its effect on poverty is a longstanding problem in American courts. In 2014, protests in Ferguson helped shine the light on that harsh reality in many urban municipalities in north St. Louis County. Poverty is poverty, whether it affects poor, black residents in big cities or poor white ones such as Branson in rural areas.

不断上涨的法院费用及其对贫困的影响是美国法院长期存在的问题。2014 年，弗格森的抗议活动，帮助人们认清了圣路易斯县北部许多城市的残酷现实。对于大城市的黑人贫民，或是像布兰森一样的农村地区的白人贫民，贫穷就是贫穷。

13 That's why in March 2016, the U. S. Justice Department sent a letter of guidance to all judges and court clerks in the country, reminding them of constitutional protections that are as old as the nation.

这就是为什么 2016 年 3 月，美国司法部向全国所有法官和法院工作人员发出了一封倡议书，提醒他们宪法的保护是这个国家存在时就建立的。

14 In December, just a few days before Branson wished me a Merry Christmas, Attorney General Jeff Sessions revoked that guidance, part of President Donald Trump's obsessive effort to erase the legacy of President Barack Obama.

12 月，就在布兰森发给我圣诞祝福的前几天，资深大法官杰夫·塞申斯无视这一倡导，这也可以看作是唐纳德·特朗普总统抹杀巴拉克·奥巴马总统影响的一种执拗努力了。

15 Rescinding the letter doesn't change the Constitution. It doesn't suddenly make debtors prisons legal again. But it sends a message to judges such as Martinez that it's OK to put people like Branson in prison just because they can.

撤销这封信并不能改变宪法。它不会突然使债务人监狱再次合法化。但它向马丁内斯这样的法官传递了一个信息，那就是把布兰森这样的人关进监狱是可以的，因为他们可以这么做。

16 While she was in Vandalia, Branson was "a pusher."

然而布兰森在万达利亚的时候是个"推动者"。

17 She helped other prisoners who were in wheelchairs by volunteering to push them around the prison yard, to and from the infirmary,

wherever they needed to go. A couple of months into her four-year sentence, not long after I wrote about her, she got called into the warden's office.

她帮助其他坐在轮椅上的囚犯，志愿推着他们在监狱院子里转来转去，来去医务室，或者他们需要去的任何地方。在她被判四年徒刑的几个月后，在我写了关于她的文章后不久，她被叫进了监狱长的办公室。

18 "They called me in on the first of October and asked if I knew you," ③Branson（布兰森）says.

　　③布兰森说："他们在 10 月 1 日给我打电话，问我是否认识你。"

19 Ten days later, she was a free woman, released on parole without even a hearing. "If you didn't raise awareness, I'd still be in there," ④she（她。根据上下文判断是布兰森）says.

　　十天后，她成了一名自由的女性，获得假释，甚至没有举行听证会。④她说："如果你不提高人们的意识，我还会在那里。"

20 Maybe. Or perhaps the Department of Corrections simply realized a nonviolent prisoner such as Branson simply didn't belong in the state's overcrowded prison system. Either way, they cut her loose.

　　也许吧，或者可能惩教署只是意识到像布兰森这样的非暴力囚犯根本不属于这个州过于拥挤的监狱系统。不管怎样，他们把她放了。

21 On the last day of December, Branson sent me another text.

　　12 月的最后一天，布兰森又给我发了一条短信。

22 "Happy New Year's," ⑤it（短信）said.

　　"新年快乐。"⑤短信上写着。

23 Branson's year isn't starting out so great. She was working for a while as a medical technician at a nursing home, but in December she got laid off. Now she's looking for work so she can pay down the $3,400 she still owes the court. A lot of doors get slammed in her face. "All they hear is the word prison," ⑥she（她。根据上下文指布兰森）says. "I'm labeled for life now."

　　布兰森的这一年开局并不好。她曾在一家疗养院当过一段时间的医务技师，但 12 月她被解雇了。现在她正在找工作，这样她就能还清她欠法院的 3400 美元。很多门在她面前砰的一声关上了。"他们听到的都是'监狱'这个词，"⑥她说，"我这一辈子都被打上标签。"

24　If she can't pay down her debt, she's afraid she'll end up before Martinez again.

　　　如果她不能还清债务，她担心自己又会栽在马丁内斯面前。

25　"She can't keep doing this to people," ⑦Branson（布兰森）says of the judge. "This cannot continue."

　　　⑦布兰森谈到法官时说："她不能一直对人们这样做，这个不能继续了。"

26　The attorney general of the United States suggests it can.

　　　而美国司法部长表示可以。

【作品鉴赏】

我们需要特别注意 1 号文本的开头。

　　又是一个圣诞节的清晨，孩子们兴致勃勃地准备拆礼物。

　　我坐在心爱的椅子里，端着咖啡，蛮有节日气氛。房间里飘着纳·金·高尔那柔和的男中音，这时候，第一条"圣诞快乐"的短信跳了出来。

　　这短信不是我成年的孩子从其他遥远的州发来的，也不是我父亲，更不是我的兄弟姐妹。

　　这简短的节日问候来自维多利亚·布兰森。

这个开头完全颠覆了我们对新闻评论开头的认知。我国的新闻评论开头严格遵循着三个特点：第一是时效性，第二是概括性，第三是倒金字塔结构。但是 1 号文本的开头描绘了一个情境，这是一个圣诞节的早晨，温馨、快乐，直到维多利亚·布兰森的短信打破了这种家庭气氛。这种"悬宕"效果的开头是美国新闻评论的一种特征，它追求的是用故事情境吸引人们阅读。

维多利亚是这篇文本中最重要的消息来源，也是叙述的中心人物。我国的新闻评论也包含叙述，但是人物在叙述中会被处理成一个概括性的符号。但是在 1 号文本中，关于维多利亚过去、现在、未来的经历，维多利亚的话语和情感表达，作者都给予大量笔墨，这种处理方式让我们对维多利亚有更多的了解，也拉近了读者和维多利亚的情感距离。

维多利亚是一个贫穷的罪犯，但在新闻评论中被处理成具有话语表达权的人物，这也颠覆了新闻话语消息来源倚重权势、权威人物的偏向问题，体现了媒介对底层和边缘人物话语表达的重视。作者和维多利亚之间构建的关系进一步加深了对底层人物的重视和同情。布兰森会第一个给托尼发来圣诞快乐的短信。在传统的中国新闻评论认知中，作者是肩负教导和劝服责任的，这种责任使其拉开了与叙述对象的距离。

与布兰森处于对立地位的两个人物分别是马丁内斯和大法官杰夫·塞申斯。马丁内斯是圣弗朗索瓦县巡回法院法官，她撤销了对布兰森的缓刑。杰夫撤销了美国司法部给的建议，也是支持让穷人坐牢的。马丁内斯和杰斯都没有在文本中被赋予话语表达机会。

【2019 普利策评论奖 2 号文本】

Counties' jailing of the poor 'has got to stop', defender says
各县对穷人的监禁"必须停止"，辩护人说

Messenger: Jailed for being poor is a Missouri epidemic
曼森哲：因贫穷而入狱是密苏里州的流行病

1　Leanne Banderman stole nail polish.

　　莉安·班德曼偷了指甲油。

2　It was two years ago in Dent County.

　　那是两年前在登特郡的时候。

3　Banderman pleaded guilty to a misdemeanor for shoplifting the $24.29 product at a Walmart. Judge Brandi Baird sentenced her to 30 days in the county jail.

　　班德曼承认她在沃尔玛商店偷了价值 24.29 美元的货物，这是个轻罪。布兰迪·贝尔德法官判处她 30 天县监狱监禁。

4　Then Baird sent Banderman a bill for $1,400.

　　然后贝尔德寄给班德曼一张 1400 美元的账单。

5　This is the reality in rural Missouri if you're poor and find yourself crossways with the law. First you do time in jail because you can't afford bail, even on minor offenses. In many Missouri counties, more than 60 percent of people in prison are there on nonviolent offenses. Then you get a bill for your jail time.

如果你身在密苏里州很穷又犯了法，那这就是你要面对的现实了。首先你坐牢是因为你付不起保释金，即使你犯了小罪过。在密苏里州的许多县里，超过 60% 的囚犯是因非暴力犯罪入狱的。然后你还会得到一张服刑的账单。

6　Then things really get tough.

然后事情就会变得很艰难。

7　Banderman couldn't afford the "board bill" for her jail time.

班德曼无力支付她服刑期间的"伙食费"。

8　So Baird put her in jail again.

所以贝尔德又把她关进监狱了。

9　This time the bill was ＄2,160.

这次账单是 2,160 美元。

10　For the past couple of years, I've been writing about this problem in St. Francois County, where Judge Sandra Martinez has been overturned twice by the Missouri Supreme Court for similar offenses. But the problem is much bigger than one county.

在过去的几年里，我一直在圣弗朗索瓦县写这方面的文章。在那里，桑德拉·马丁内斯法官因为类似的案件被密苏里州最高法院推翻了两次，但是问题远不止一个县。

11　It's happening all over the state, says①Matthew Mueller（马修·穆勒。他是密苏里州公共辩护办公室的高级债券诉讼律师，主要工作是代表因贫困而入狱的穷人提起诉讼）. He's the senior bond litigation counsel for the Missouri Public Defender's Office, and his primary job these days is filing lawsuits on behalf of poor people like Banderman who end up in jail because they're poor, and then the judicial system buries them in poverty even deeper than they imagined.

①马修·穆勒说，这种事情正在全州范围内发生。他是密苏里

州公共辩护办公室的高级债券诉讼律师，目前主要工作是代表像班德曼这样因贫困而入狱的穷人提起诉讼，然而司法系统让他们陷入超出想象的更深的贫困之中。

12　"The practical reality is that people are being arrested for being poor," ②Mueller（穆勒）says. "And there's nothing they can do about it. They just sit in jail and the bill keeps getting higher."

　　　②据穆勒所言："实际情况是，人们是因贫困而被捕。""他们对此无能为力，只能蹲在监狱里，看着账单越堆越高。"

13　On Wednesday, Mueller will be in Kansas City to ask the Western District of the Missouri Court of Appeals to find this practice unlawful.

　　　周三，穆勒将在堪萨斯城要求密苏里上诉法院西区裁定这种做法非法。

14　The problem, ③Mueller（穆勒）says, isn't just that the rural counties are charging poor people for being in jail. It's that they're then treating that jail debt as a "fine" and using the county's arrest power when people can't afford to pay the fine.

　　　③穆勒说，问题不仅仅在于农村各县因穷人入狱而向他们收费，而是他们会将监狱债务视为"罚款"，在人们无力支付罚款时使用郡政府的逮捕权。

15　Take John Wright, of Higginsville, Mueller's client in the Wednesday appeal.

　　　以约翰·莱特为例，他来自希金斯维尔，是穆勒周三上诉中的客户。

16　Wright, who suffered a traumatic brain injury when he was 19, was charged with stealing for failing to pay for a taxi ride in 2016. He was sentenced to 90 days in jail.

　　　莱特19岁时受了创伤性脑损伤，因2016年未支付出租车费而被指控偷窃，他当时被判处90天监禁。

17　Upon being released, Wright was served with a $1,300 bill for his jail time. Every month thereafter, if the bill wasn't fully paid, the judge would schedule a show-cause hearing on the debt. If Wright didn't show up, a warrant would be issued for his arrest. The court never determined whether he had the ability to pay. Wright is indigent and was represented by the public defender.

莱特获释后，被判服刑账单 1300 美元。此后的每个月，如果账单没有全部付清，法官就会安排一次关于债务的诉讼听证会。如果莱特没有出现，就会对他发出逮捕令。法院从未判定他是否有支付能力。莱特很穷，由公设辩护人代理。

18　It's a long-standing constitutional protection in U. S. courts that people can't be jailed for failure to pay debt. But whether it's municipal courts in St. Louis County stacking up traffic tickets, or rural counties issuing bills for jail time, the practice is still common in Missouri.

在美国法院，人们不能因不还债而被监禁，这是一项长期的宪法保护。但是，无论是圣路易斯县的市政法院堆积交通罚单，还是农村各县签发入狱票据，这种做法在密苏里州仍然很普遍。

19　"This entire practice is unlawful and must cease," ④Mueller（穆勒）writes.

④穆勒写道："这种做法是非法的，必须停止。"

20　At some point, state lawmakers might want to pay attention to what's happening in the circuit courts in their jurisdictions. That's because in many of them, the counties are billing poor people for money they've already collected from the state.

在某种程度上，州立法者可能想关注他们管辖范围内巡回法院发生的事情。那是因为在其中许多州，县政府向穷人收取已经从州政府收取的钱。

21　Under ⑤state law（州法律），if a person is held in the county jail for a state felony, Missouri taxpayers end up paying about $ 22 a day of that bill. State law actually allows for more than twice that amount of payment, but the Legislature never provides full funding. Among the biggest recipients of that county money are those rural counties also known for taking extrajudicial steps to keep poor people in jail while they rack up higher costs.

　　⑤根据州法律，如果一个人因州重罪被关在县监狱里，密苏里州的纳税人最终每天要为此支付大约 22 美元。州法律实际上允许支付两倍以上的数额，但立法机关从未提供全额资金。那些农村县是该县资金的最大接受者之一，这些县也因采取法外措施将穷人关在监狱里，同时抬高成本而闻名。

22　In 2017，for instance, St. Francois County was reimbursed nearly ＄155，000 from the state for "board bill" costs. Franklin County took in ＄162，000；Caldwell collected ＄149，000；Camden and Laclede counties both topped ＄200，000. And in most of those counties，the people in jail were billed even after the state paid.

　　例如，2017 年，圣弗朗索瓦县从该州报销了近 15.5 万美元的"董事会议案"费用。富兰克林县收入 16.2 万美元，考德威尔收集了 14.9 万美元，卡姆登县和拉克莱德县都超过了 20 万美元。在这些县中的大多数，监狱里的人甚至在政府付费后也要付费。

23　None of this is constitutional，⑥Mueller（穆勒）says. He now has cases before all three appeals courts in the state seeking a determination that would put an end to this practice. The American Civil Liberties Union has filed briefs supporting Mueller's clients in all three cases.

　　⑥穆勒说，这些都不符合宪法。他现在在该州所有三个上诉法院都有案件，寻求结束这种做法的裁定。美国公民自由联盟在这三起案件中都提交了支持穆勒客户的辩护状。

24　"It's really scary what's going on，" ⑦Mueller（穆勒）says. "It's indefinite commitment. These people are totally helpless. This has got to stop. "

　　"发生的事情真的很可怕，" ⑦穆勒说，"这是无限期的承诺。这些人完全无助。这必须停止。"

【作品鉴赏】

　　2 号文本讲述了莉安·班德曼和约翰·莱特的经历。莉安承认她在沃尔玛商店偷了价值 24.29 美元的货物，这让她进了监狱。文本分析道：

如果你身在密苏里州很穷又犯了法，那这就是你要面对的现实了。首先你坐牢是因为你付不起保释金，即使你犯了小罪过。在密苏里州的许多县里，超过 60% 的囚犯是因非暴力犯罪入狱的。然后你还会得到一张服刑的账单。

故事结合着分析，使得美国新闻评论充满了娓娓道来的气质，文本不会充满直接下判断带来的坚硬和强势感。

善于数据修辞，也是文本用事实来说服读者的策略。

2017 年，圣弗朗索瓦县从该州报销了近 15.5 万美元的"董事会议案"费用。富兰克林县收入 16.2 万美元，考德威尔收集了 14.9 万美元，卡姆登县和拉克莱德县都超过了 20 万美元。在这些县中的大多数，监狱里的人甚至在政府付费后也要付费。

马修·穆勒，作为一个律师，他代表班德曼这样因贫困而入狱的穷人提起诉讼。文本引用了穆勒的很多话语，这些话语表达了意见和看法。

【2019 年普利策评论奖 3 号文本】

St. Francois County prosecutor delays justice again as election approaches
随着选举临近圣弗朗索瓦县检察官再次推迟公义

1 FARMINGTON, Mo. Rob Hopple is a free man. （定义式的开头）

（密苏里州法明顿）罗布·霍普是一个自由的人。

2 Well, he has an ankle bracelet. He still faces a December felony trial. He's tethered to the judicial system that has, in his longtime mate's words, destroyed his life.

然而，他脚踝上还戴着脚铐。他将面临 12 月份的重罪审判。用他长期伴侣的话来说，他已经被司法系统束缚住了，那毁掉了他的生活。

3 But on Wednesday, he breathed clean air. He shed a jail jumpsuit for his own clothes. He hugged his domestic partner, Kristin Brown.

但是在周三，他呼吸到了新鲜的空气。他脱去监狱的囚衣，换上自己的衣服，拥抱了他的伴侣克里斯汀·布朗。

4　He was supposed to be in court，defending himself against an allegation that three years ago he exposed himself to an 11-year-old girl who was spending the night with Hopple's daughter. He and Brown，who was home at the time，vehemently deny he did that. A state Child and Neglect Review Board agreed，dismissing the allegation.

他本应该在法庭上为自己辩护，三年前有人控告他对一个 11 岁女孩裸露身体，那女孩那天夜里正和霍普的女儿在一起。他和当时在家的布朗，都强烈否认他做了那件事。经一个州儿童和疏忽审查委员会同意，驳回了这一指控。

5　But St. Francois County Prosecuting Attorney Jerrod Mahurin sought，and obtained，a grand jury indictment.

但是圣弗朗索瓦县检察官杰罗德·马胡林寻求并获得了大陪审团的起诉书。

6　That was in November 2016. Since then，the wheels of justice have turned slowly.

那是在 2016 年的 11 月。从那以后，正义的车轮缓慢转动。

7　That's the way things seem to be in St. Francois County，where a growing chorus of ①critics（批评家。这是一个不具名的消息来源）believe Mahurin and Circuit Judge Sandra Martinez unnecessarily keep mostly low-income defendants in jail for months. Unable to make bail，some of these defendants eventually agree to a plea bargain to get out of jail.

圣弗朗索瓦县的情况似乎一直就是这样，越来越多的①批评家认为，马胡林和巡回法官桑德拉·马丁内斯没必要将大部分低收入被告关在监狱里几个月。由于无法保释，其中一些被告最终同意辩诉交易出狱。

8　Hopple had been in jail since May after falling behind on payments on an ankle bracelet. Court dates kept coming and going，with Mahurin seeking continuances and Martinez granting them.

霍普自从五月份拖欠脚铐的付款后就一直在监狱里。庭审日期不断变来变去，马胡林一直寻求延期并得到马丁内斯的应允。

9　That's what happened Tuesday. It was the fifth trial date pushed back since April，all at Mahurin's request.

　　这种事在周二刚发生。这是自 4 月以来第五次推迟审判日期。这些都是在马胡林的要求下才推迟的。

10　This time，Mahurin blamed me for the delay.

　　这一次，马胡林把延误归咎于我。

11　In a court motion he cited my September column about Hopple as an attempt "to poison the jury panel against the victim…" ②Mahurin said in the motion（马胡林在议案中说。这里的消息来源实际上是议案）that he just found out about the column，even though I emailed and called him for comment about a month ago，when the column ran. He didn't return my calls.

　　在一项法庭议案中，他引用了 9 月份我关于霍普的专栏文章，称其试图"毒害陪审团对受害者的看法……"②马胡林在议案中说，他刚刚发现了这个专栏。尽管大约一个月前，这个专栏在运行的时候，我就给他发了电子邮件并打电话征求意见，他没有回我电话。

12　Now ③he says in that court motion（法庭议案）that he wants to talk to me before the trial goes forward.

　　现在③他在法庭议案中说，他想在审判进行之前和我谈谈。

13　As Hopple was being set free，I was interviewing Farmington attorney Vonne Carraker，at her office about a block south of the courthouse.

　　霍普被释放的时候，我在法院南边一个街区，在法明顿律师沃恩·卡拉克的办公室里采访她。

14　She practices elder law but has become a clearinghouse of sorts for people who claim to have been harmed by the judicial system. They come to her to complain about Mahurin and Martinez. She files Sunshine Law requests，asks for budgets，and shows up to St. Francois County Commission meetings to ask questions. She and many of the people she talks to post on a Facebook page with criticisms，citing specific cases and public complaints that have been made about

Mahurin. The invite-only St. Francois County politics page has more than 2，900 members.

　　她（本来）从事老年法律工作，但现已变成了票据交换中心，为那些声称受到司法系统伤害的人服务。他们来找她抱怨马胡林和马丁内斯。她提出阳光法案的要求，寻求预算，出席圣弗朗索瓦郡委员会会议并提出质疑。她和许多同她交谈过的人在脸书上发表了批评意见，引用了关于马胡林的具体案例和公众投诉，仅圣弗朗索瓦县的政治网页就邀请到 2900 多名成员。

15　Hopple's case，④she（她，法明顿律师沃恩·卡拉克，主要工作是帮助受到司法系统伤害的人服务）says，is endemic of what is happening in St. Francois County.

　　④她说，霍普的案例是圣弗朗索瓦县正在发生的流行病。

16　Many of Mahurin's cases，⑤she（她，指沃恩·卡拉克）says，end up as settlements，often after defendants have served months in jail.

　　⑤她说，马胡林的许多案件最终都以和解告终，通常是在被告服刑数月之后。

17　"He's bankrupting people and forcing them to plead guilty,"⑥Carraker（沃恩·卡拉克）says.

　　"他让人们破产，迫使他们认罪。"⑥卡拉克说。

18　Hopple was offered a plea for time served but turned it down.

　　霍普被要求社工时间服务，但又被拒绝了。

19　"He's not going to plead to something he didn't do,"⑦Brown（布朗，霍普的妻子）says of Hopple.

　　⑦布朗谈到霍普时说："他不会为自己没做过的事情辩护。"

20　For now，his fate might lie in the Nov. 6 election.

　　现在，他的命运可能就看 11 月 6 日的选举了。

21　For the first time，Mahurin has a serious opponent. A Democrat，he faces Republican Melissa Gilliam. If Mahurin loses，Hopple hopes he'll be able to shed the ankle bracelet and get back to work and life by January. If Mahurin wins，Hopple expects more hearings，more delays，and，of course，the bill he hasn't yet received for his jail time.

马胡林第一次有了一个严肃的对手。作为民主党人，他与共和党人梅丽莎·吉利姆正面交锋。如果马胡林输了，霍普希望自己能在一月前脱掉脚铐，回归到正常工作和生活中。如果马胡林赢了，那霍普估计会有更多的听证会，更多的延误，当然还有他至今还没收到的服刑账单。

22　This is how the judicial system in some parts of rural Missouri works to keep people poor. Hopple has spent nearly six months in jail for a charge a state investigation found no evidence to support. He faces monthly fees for the ankle bracelet, and if he is ever convicted or a-grees to plea to a lower charge, Martinez will send him a bill for his jail time that will likely be several thousand dollars. Like many others in St. Francois County, in Dent and Crawford counties, and in other counties in rural Missouri, he'll face a trip to debtor's prison if he falls behind on those payments.

密苏里州乡村的一些司法系统就是这样让人们陷入贫困的。霍普因一项经州调查发现无证据支持的指控，在监狱里待了近六个月。他承担着脚铐的每月费用，如果他被判有罪或者以较低的费用请罪，马丁内斯将会给他一张可能是几千美元的刑期账单。像圣弗朗索瓦县、登特县和克劳福德县以及密苏里州乡村的其他县的许多人一样，如果他拖欠还款，他将去债务人监狱蹲大牢。

23　But that's all a fight for another day.

但这都是为了新的一天而战。

24　On this crisp, fall day, Hopple is enjoying the splash of sun on his face, the rolling hills and falling leaves, and the love of a woman who has been fighting to set him free.

在这个清爽的秋日，霍普现在正忙着享受一切。洒在他的脸上、起伏的山丘和落叶上的阳光，还有一个始终为他的自由而奋斗的女人的爱。

25　It's a good day.

真是美好的一天。

26　Justice will come later

　　正义终将到来。

【2019 年普利策评论奖 4 号文本】

Judge tries to block access to debtors' prison hearings in Dent County

法官试图阻止在登特县参加债务人监狱听证会

1　SALEM，MO. In Dent County, poverty isn't an accident. It's an industry.

　　（密苏里州塞勒姆）在登特县，贫困不是偶然的，而是一个行业。

2　Perhaps that's why Associate Circuit Court Judge Brandi Baird didn't want me in her courtroom on Thursday.

　　也许，这就是巡回法院助理法官布兰迪·贝尔德不希望我周四出现在她的法庭上的原因。

3　It was payment review hearing day，which is to say Baird was asking about 50 poor people who have already completed their sentences to come in and offer an explanation as to why their court costs—from a few hundred bucks to several thousand—hadn't been paid off.

　　这是支付审查听证会日，这意味着贝尔德要求大约 50 名已经服完刑期的穷人过来解释他们从几百美元到几千美元的诉讼费为什么还没有付清。

4　Baird is a collection agent，and her chief henchman is Lisa Blackwell，who works for the private probation company MPPS. Together, they use the judicial system in one of the poorest counties in Missouri to make sure folks who are down on their luck have little chance to climb out from their debts.

　　贝尔德是一名收款代理人，她的主要随从是在私人缓刑公司 MPPS 工作的丽莎·布莱克威尔。她们一起利用密苏里州里一个最贫穷的县的司法系统，来让那些运气不好的人几乎没有机会从债务中脱身。

5　I was there on Thursday to see what happened to Brooke Bergen.

　　周四我去了那里，想（亲眼）看看在布鲁克·贝尔根身上会发生什么。

6　You might remember her. She's the woman I wrote about last month who got arrested for shoplifting an $8 mascara tube from the local Walmart. Bergen has the sort of back story that would inspire one of the movies or television episodes based in the Ozarks that seem to be all the rage these days. She's fought opioid addiction. Her mother died when she was 15. She never met her father. She got married early to get out of the foster care system. She lost a baby three years ago.

你可能还记得她，就是我上个月写的那个女人，因为在当地沃尔玛商店偷了一根价值 8 美元的睫毛膏而被捕。贝尔根是个有故事的人，这些故事甚至能激发奥扎克去拍个现在似乎很流行的电影或电视剧。她曾与吸食鸦片做斗争。母亲在她 15 岁时去世，她从未见过父亲。她为了摆脱寄养制度结婚很早。她三年前还失去了一个孩子。

7　Despite all of that trauma, she's determined. She's strong. She's brave.

尽管有这些创伤，她还是下定了决心。她很强壮，也很勇敢。

8　But all of that is back story. This is a story about shoplifting.

这都是后话了，我要说的是关于她入店行窃的事。

9　Bergen, 30, pleaded guilty and got a suspended sentence of a year in jail. As long as she fulfilled the conditions of her bond, she would spend little time behind bars.

30 岁的贝尔根认罪，并被判缓刑一年。只要她满足了债券条件，她就不会在监狱里待太久。

10　This is where Blackwell comes in. Everybody who appears before Baird and bonds out of jail or pleads guilty ends up on a form of probation with the privately operated MPPS. Blackwell isn't elected, but she has her own chair in Baird's courtroom, right next to the prosecutor.

轮到布莱克威尔上场了。通过私人公司 MPPS 的操作，每个出现在贝尔德面前的人，那些深陷牢狱之灾或者认罪的人，最终都会得到某种缓刑。布莱克威尔没有当选，但她在贝尔德的法庭有自己的位置，就在检察官旁边。

11　During payment review hearings—which aren't defined in statute and don't exist in Missouri's urban court circuits—Blackwell stands up when the defendant's name is called and tells Baird whether they've met their conditions. Those conditions often include twice weekly drug tests at a cost of $30 a week, even if the offense has nothing to do with drugs. Blackwell sometimes orders random drug tests. Miss her call? Arrive late to an appointment?

　　　　在缴费审查听证会上（其实法规中没有规定，在密苏里州的城市法院巡回法庭上也不存在），在叫到被告名字时，布莱克威尔站起来，告诉贝尔德他们是否符合条件。这些情况通常包括每周两次药物测试，费用为每周30美元，即使犯罪行为与药物无关。布莱克威尔有时会随机进行药物测试。此外，还有错过电话和迟到的问题。

12　You're going to jail.

　　　　你会进监狱的。

13　That's what happened to Bergen. She did more than a year in jail on the shoplifting charge because she didn't answer one of Blackwell's calls. This is not an uncommon experience in Dent County.

　　　　这就是贝尔根所面临的。因为没有接到布莱克威尔的电话，她因入店行窃受到指控，在监狱待了一年多。这在登特县时有发生。

14　After her time in jail, Bergen got the bill: more than $15,900. It is what many Missouri counties call a "board bill." Get convicted of a crime and you pay about $50 a day for your confinement, regardless of the charge. Meanwhile, in some cases, the county also bills the state.

　　　　账单随着入狱而来：超过15,900美元。这就是密苏里州许多县号称的"伙食费"。无论是什么指控，只要被定罪，每天就要支付50美元的监禁费用。此外，在某些情况下，县还从州里拿钱。

15　Don't have the money? Baird schedules you for a payment review hearing, and another, and another, all the while threatening you with more jail if you don't pay.

没钱？贝尔德会安排一个缴费审查听证会，一个接着一个，如果不付款，更多的监狱时光就等待着你。

16 The underfunded Missouri State Public Defender's office is trying to stop this practice, pushing cases in all three appeals courts in the state, arguing the practice is akin to the state operating illegal debtors prisons.

资金不足的密苏里州公设辩护人办公室，正试图阻止这种做法，在该州的所有三个上诉法院都推进案件，辩称这种做法类似于该州运营的非法债务人监狱。

17 The day before her hearing, Bergen had $60 in her pocket. She rented a room for a week in Rolla, not sure where she'd be after her day in court.

在听证会的前一天，贝尔根口袋里有 60 美元。她在罗拉租了一个星期的房子，不知道出庭后该去哪里。

18 "Judge Baird threatened me with jail if I didn't make a substantial payment," ①she（贝尔根，在当地沃尔玛商店偷了一根价值 8 美元的睫毛膏而被捕。）told me. She planned to spend the rest of the day trying to borrow some more money, to be able to make a $100 payment. "Three figures seems more substantial to me. I'm freaking out. I really am afraid she's going to put me back in jail."

①她告诉我："贝尔德法官威胁我，如果不付一大笔钱，就会被关进监狱。"她打算用这天剩下的时间尽力借更多的钱，以便支付 100 美元的款项。"三位数对我来说似乎更为重要。我……我吓坏了。我真的很担心她会把我送回监狱。"

19 Bergen came up with the extra $40. But I almost didn't get to see the relief on her face when she told Baird that she had made a payment. When I got to court, where dozens upon dozens of defendants line up and are allowed in one at a time as they check in, the head bailiff said he needed to speak with me. He asked for my identification. He went back to speak to the judge. Then he took me into a small room, shut the door, and told me I couldn't attend court.

贝尔根凑齐了剩下的 40 美元。但是当她告诉贝尔德她已经付了钱时，我几乎没有看到她脸上的如释重负。当我到达法庭时，首席执行官说他需要和我谈谈。法庭几十个被告排成一排，每次只允许一个人登记进入，他要求我出示证件，又回去和法官谈话。然后他把我带进一个小房间，关上门，告诉我，我不能出庭。

20　The judge said for me to be there I would have to follow a Supreme Court rule that requires the media to request access，②the bailiff（法警）told me. That rule only applies to requesting audio and video recording，③I（我，指作者托尼·曼森哲）responded. You can't keep a reporter—or any citizen—out of a public court hearing with no cause. I asked to speak with the judge.

　　②法警对我说，法官说了，如果我要出庭，我必须遵守最高法院的规定，即媒体必须被同意进入才可以进入。③我回答说，这条规则只适用于要求录音和录像。你不能在没有任何理由的情况下阻止一名记者或任何公民出席公开的法庭听证会。我要求和法官谈谈。

21　Though he had just returned from her chambers for a conversation, he told me she wasn't there. It was five minutes before court was to begin.

　　司法人员明明刚从法官的房间谈话回来，但他告诉我法官不在那里。这时离开庭还有五分钟。

22　A few minutes later，the bailiff waved me in.

　　几分钟后，司法人员挥手示意我进去。

23　Bergen didn't go to jail. Nobody else did either. Not on this day. They came one by one and explained how hard they were working，at a job or community service，to try to make payments. One man handed Blackwell a wad of cash to be in compliance. She said she'd get him a receipt later. Baird complimented some of them for their efforts. But Blackwell stood and told the judge several times that some people were out of compliance.

　　贝尔根没有进监狱，其他人也没有，今天什么也没发生。他们一个接一个进来，解释他们是如何努力工作，做着社区服务，努力还钱。一名男子递给布莱克威尔一叠现金以示服从规定，贝尔德说稍后会给他一张收据。贝尔德称赞了他们中的一些人的努力，但是布莱克威尔站起来好几次告诉法官，有些人违反了规定。

24 Those folks will be back in a month or two for a probation violation hearing. The cash bail will be high. The others will be back in January, taking half a day off of a minimum wage job hoping a $60 payment keeps them from being locked up.

这些人一两个月后就会回来参加缓刑违规听证会，现金保释金会很高。其他人将在一月份回来，从一份最低工资的工作中休息半天，希望 60 美元的工资能让他们免于牢狱之灾。

25 In Dent County, if you're poor and you stand before the judge, jail is never far away.

在登特县，如果你是穷人，要是站在法官面前，你离监狱就不远了。

【2019 年普利策评论奖 5 号文本】

'Poverty penalty' pervades rural courts in Missouri
密苏里州的乡村法院普遍存在"贫困惩罚"

Missouri teen stole a lawnmower in high school—11 years later he's still going to court
密苏里州的一名少年在高中时偷了割草机——11 年后，他仍然要去法庭

1 BRECKENRIDGE, Mo. Cory Booth met his wife on a snowy day in Trenton, Mo.

（密苏里州布雷肯里奇）在密苏里州特伦顿一个下雪的日子里，科里·布斯遇到了他的妻子。

2 Then 18, he was at drug rehab, and on furlough from a misdemeanor jail sentence for theft. It was visiting day, and Booth's mother couldn't make the trip.

18 岁时，他正在戒毒，因盗窃被判轻罪正在服刑中。那天是探监日，布斯的妈妈没能去看他。

3　In walked Shaelee Moore. She was there to see her dad.

　　谢莉·摩尔走了进来。她是去见她爸爸的。

4　"I figured，why not talk to the pretty girl?" ①Booth（布斯）remembers.

　　"我想，为什么不和那个漂亮姑娘聊聊呢?" ①布斯记得。

5　They've been married 10 years now. They live in Breckenridge，a tiny Caldwell County town of about 300 people in northwest Missouri. They have four children. She works at a local hotel. He takes care of the kids. They've done the math. It makes more sense than him getting a low-paying job and spending a majority of their income on day care.

　　他们已经结婚十年了，住在一个名叫布雷肯里奇的小镇。小镇位于密苏里州西北部，住着 300 来人，属于考德威尔县。他们有四个孩子，妻子在当地的一家旅馆工作，他照顾孩子们。他们已经盘算过了，这样比他找一份低收入的工作再把大部分收入花在日托上更划算。（细节展示贫苦。）

6　On the day we talked，it was snowing again，and Booth was heading to court. He is scheduled to go there，and appear before Caldwell County Associate Circuit Court Judge Jason Kanoy，once a month. Why?

　　我们谈话的那天，又下雪了，布斯正要去法庭。他计划每月去那里一次，出现在考德威尔县联合巡回法院法官贾森·卡诺伊面前。为什么?

7　Because 11 years ago，when he was in high school，he stole a lawn mower.

　　那是因为 11 年前，他还在上高中的时候，偷了一台割草机。

8　It was the summer of 2007，and Booth was a self-described knuckle-head. He dabbled in marijuana. He got into trouble. A friend fingered him for the lawn mower theft，and he spent two nights in the Caldwell County Jail. It was his first time in jail. His cellmate was in on a federal warrant for bank robbery.

那是 2007 年的夏天，布斯自称是个傻瓜。他染上了大麻并遇到了麻烦。一个朋友指认他偷了割草机，之后他在考德威尔县监狱待了两个晚上。这是他第一次入狱，他的狱友因抢劫银行被联邦逮捕。

9 "I stayed awake all night," ②Booth（布斯）says. "I was scared."

　　"我整晚都没睡，"②布斯说，"我很害怕。"

10 He pleaded guilty and Kanoy gave him a year in jail but suspended the sentence. He was placed on probation for two years with a private probation service that could drug test him anytime, at his cost. By November, he had violated his probation. He did seven days in jail and received a bill for his time there. In January 2008, he violated probation conditions again. Kanoy sentenced him to 10 days in jail, and told him he could serve his time on weekends.

　　他认罪，卡诺伊判他入狱一年，但缓期执行。他通过一家私人缓刑服务获得缓刑两年，该服务可以随时对他进行药物测试，费用他自己承担。到了 11 月，他违反了缓刑规定。于是又在监狱里待了七天，并收到了一张关押期间的账单。2008 年 1 月，他再次违反缓刑条件。卡诺伊判处他 10 天监禁，并告诉他可以在周末服刑。

11 In November 2008 he was arrested again on a probation violation. He was held in jail on ＄5,000 cash-only bail. Kanoy told him he had to serve a year in jail.

　　到 2008 年 11 月，他因违反缓刑条例再次被捕。他必需缴纳5000 美元现金作为保释金才能从监狱中出来。卡诺伊告诉他，他必须在监狱服刑一年。

12 Booth doesn't blame the judge for his problems. In fact, he likes Kanoy. Over the past 11 years they've talked often. He believes the judge has given him second chances, and some good advice. （比较客观）

　　布斯不会因为自己的问题而责怪法官。事实上，他喜欢卡诺伊。在过去的 11 年里，他们经常交谈。他相信法官给了他第二次机会和一些好的建议。

13 "I messed up on probation," ③he（他，指布斯）says. "It was my

fault."

　　"我把缓刑期搞砸了,"③他说,"是我的错"。

14　Still，he doesn't think it makes sense that he's still hauled to court once a month with the threat of jail time if he doesn't show up or doesn't pay.

　　然而他还是认为,如果他不出现或者不付款,每个月就会被拖上法庭,被威胁要坐牢,这是没有道理的。

15　His jail bill started small enough，$80 for his first two-night stay.

　　他的监狱账单一开始很少,第一次两个晚上需要80美元。

16　"Thank you for your business，" the bill says.（这里的"账单"只是一种修辞,并不是消息来源。）

　　该账单说:"感谢你的业务。"

17　Then came the $400 bill，and $2,791，and $3,531.

　　然后就是400美元、2791美元和3531美元的账单。

18　By July 2009，when his probation should have been over and his connection to the court system severed，Booth owed $7,325.

　　到2009年7月,他的缓刑期应该结束了,与法院系统的联系中断了,布斯欠了7325美元。

19　He thinks the bill is down to about $5，000 now，and every month he tries to make a $50 payment. When he doesn't have it，he has to go to Kanoy's courtroom and explain.

　　他认为现在账单已经减少到5000美元了,每个月他都努力还上50美元。当他没钱的时候,就不得不去卡诺伊的法庭解释。

20　It has been that way now for 11 years.

　　这种情况已经持续了11年。

21　"It's held me back from a lot of different things，"④Booth（布斯）says.

　　"这让我在很多不同的事情上退缩了。"④布斯说。

22　At one point he planned to enlist in the Army. Kanoy told him he wouldn't be able to do that if he didn't first pay his board bill.

　　一度计划应征入伍。但卡诺伊告诉他,如果他不先支付法庭账单，他就不能这样做。

23 So every month he makes a decision.

所以每个月他都需要做一个决定。

24 It's groceries or pay the judge," ⑤he（他，指布斯）says.

"要么买日用品，要么付钱给法官。"⑤他说。

25 This is the reality for a lot of poor Missourians in rural parts of the state who end up on the wrong side of the law. Long after they've served their time and paid their fines, they end up tethered to the court system by private probation companies that have built-in financial incentives to find probation violations，and judges who are all too willing to serve as debt collectors. Pay the bill，or debtors prison awaits.

这是密苏里州许多农村地区穷人的现实，他们最终都与法律相悖。他们服完了刑也支付了罚金，很长时间之后，还是被私人缓刑公司拴在法庭系统中，这些公司有内在的经济动机来发现他们违反缓刑规定的行为，而法官们都非常愿意充当收债人。付账单或者债务人监狱都等着他们。

26 It is a problem that threatens the independence of the judiciary，says ⑥Lisa Foster，a former judge and Department of Justice official（丽莎·福斯特。前法官兼司法部官员、罚款和收费司法中心联合主任）who is a co-director of the Fines and Fees Justice Center.

⑥前法官兼司法部官员、罚款和收费司法中心联合主任丽莎·福斯特说，这是一个威胁到司法独立性的问题。

27 "The idea that you pay for the privilege to be in jail is absurd," ⑦Foster（福斯特）says. "There should never be a charge for jail."

⑦福斯特说："要为坐牢的特权买单的想法是荒谬的。""监狱永远不应该收费。"

28 But what her co-director ⑧Joanna Weiss（合作主任乔安娜·韦斯，律师兼教育家，曾在美国律师协会特别工作组任职）calls the "poverty penalty" is alive and well in many rural Missouri counties. Weiss，an attorney and educator，served on the American Bar Asso-

ciation task force that in August passed a resolution aimed at ending the sort of practices that have Booth still answering to a judge and facing the possibility of jail time on an 11-year-old charge.

⑧她的合作主任乔安娜·韦斯说，但是在密苏里州的许多农村县，"贫困惩罚"依然存在。律师兼教育家韦斯曾在美国律师协会特别工作组任职，该工作组于 8 月份通过了一项决议，旨在结束这类做法，像是布斯在一个 11 年之久的指控后，仍需要回答和面对法官，并面临着可能入狱的事情。

29 "It's crazy," ⑨Booth（布斯）says. "They make probation so hard so they can violate you. The system is the problem. It's a vicious circle. It's horrible."

"这太疯狂了，"⑨布斯说，"他们让缓刑变得如此难以执行，这样他们就可以侵犯你，体制就是问题所在，这是一个恶性循环。太可怕了!"

30 This week, his kids are sick. The first winter storm of the season will do that to a family. Booth showed up to court and explained his predicament. Now he has to come back and appear before Kanoy again before the end of the month.

这周，他的孩子生病了，冬季的第一场暴风雪会对一个家庭造成这种影响。布斯在出庭中解释了他的困境。现在他必须在月底之前再次回到卡诺伊面前。

31 "I spent my judge money on medicine for the kids," ⑩Booth（布斯）says. "It's a rob Peter to pay Paul situation, and Judge Kanoy is Paul."

"我把给法官的钱花在给孩子们买药上了，"⑩布斯说，"这是抢劫彼得付钱给保罗的情况，而卡诺伊法官就是保罗。"

【2019 年普利策评论奖 6 号文本】
Time to close debtor's prison for good
是时候彻底关闭债务人的监狱了

Messenger：Time for Missouri's leaders to put the debtors' prison band back together

曼森哲：密苏里州的领导人是时候让债务人监狱重新组织起来了

1   SALEM，Mo. Amy Murr turned the tables on me.

    （密苏里州塞勒姆）艾米·穆尔挑战了我。

2   We were sitting at J. B. Malone's, a restaurant at the T intersection where Missouri Highway 72 heading southeast from Rolla runs into Highway 32. It's a crossroads of sorts，which is where Murr's life has been after several interactions with the law. Murr owns her bad decisions，but like many others in Dent County，she seems to be treated differently by a judicial system that looks down on those who are poor，or who have been caught up in the area's rampant drug culture. Murr has been both of those things.

    我们坐在 J. B. 马龙家的餐厅，餐厅位于 T 形交叉路口，是在密苏里州 72 号高速公路从罗拉向东南方进入 32 号高速公路的地方。这个十字路口像极了穆尔在与法律多次交锋之后的生活。穆尔承认自己做出了错误的决定，但和登特县的许多人一样，她似乎受到了司法系统的不同对待。司法系统瞧不起那些穷人，或者那些被卷入该地区猖獗的毒品文化的人。穆尔两个都占。

3   "Why are you doing this?" ①she（艾米·穆尔）asks me. Why are you writing about poor people, drug addicts and felons? Why are you telling stories about folks in rural towns all over the state who are having their civil rights trampled upon by local sheriffs and prosecutors and judges?

    "你为什么要这么做?" ①她问我。你为什么要写穷人、瘾君子和重罪犯? 你为什么要讲述 "全州乡村居民的公民权利遭到当地治安官、检察官和法官的践踏" 这样的故事?

4   It's the simple indignity of it all, ②I（我，指作者托尼）said.

    ②我回答道，这简直就是一种侮辱。

5   Then I told her a story.

    然后我给她讲了一个故事。

6　Many years ago, I got pulled over by police in the city where my daughter is now a cop. My tags were expired. The officer seemed to be taking a long time running my name and driver's license through the computer. Another police car showed up. The officer took the slow walk back to my car. She asked me to get out of the vehicle. She cuffed me, put her hand on my head and lowered me into the back seat of her police cruiser.

很多年前，我在我女儿现在当警察的城市被警察拦下。我的标签过期了。警官似乎花了很长时间在电脑上查我的名字和驾驶执照。之后另一辆警车出现了，那个警察慢悠悠地走到我的车旁，让我下车，给我戴上手铐，把她的手放我头上，然后把我押到警车的后座上。

7　It turns out I had forgotten about a speeding ticket from about a year before.

原来我忘了大约一年之前的一张超速罚单。

8　There was a warrant out for my arrest.

就有了一张要逮捕我的逮捕令。

9　The officer asked if I had any cash for bail. It was the day after payday, and I had about $80. So that's where she set my bail.

警官问我有没有现金可以保释。那天正好是发工资的第二天，我身上有大约 80 美元。那就是她为我保释的地方。

10　She took me to the police station, fingerprinted me, took my cash and let me go.

她把我带到警察局，录了指纹，拿走现金，然后放我走了。

11　On that day, my kids were home alone, being watched by their oldest sibling.

那天，我的孩子们独自在家，他们中最大的兄弟姐妹照看着其他小的。

12　Were I poor, and black and in north St. Louis County, things could have turned out so much worse.

如果我是个穷人，而且是个黑人，居住在圣路易斯县北部，事情可能会变得更糟。

13 Were I poor, and white and in rural Dent County, things could have turned out so much worse.

再如果，我是一个贫穷的白人，住在登特县的乡下，事情也可能会变得更糟。

14 I didn't spend the weekend in jail. Social services didn't show up and take my children.

我没有在监狱里度过周末。社会服务机构没有出现并带走我的孩子。

15 I paid for my mistake and moved on.

我为自己的错误付出了代价，继续过我的日子。

16 When I hear the stories of Murr, of Brooke Bergen and Leann Banderman, of Cory Booth and William Everts, of people who are jailed for minor offenses and forced by the courts to suffer consequences far worse than many of us would for the same mistakes, I think to myself: "There but by the grace of God go I."

当我听到穆尔的故事，听到布鲁克·贝尔根、莉安·班德曼、科里·布斯 、威廉·艾佛茨的故事，听到人们因为轻微的犯罪而被监禁，他们犯了和许多人一样的错误，却被法庭强迫承受更严重的后果时，就想到自己："若非上帝恩典，我也会如此。"

17 Three years ago, the governor, the Missouri Supreme Court and the Missouri Legislature realized that this sort of disparate treatment in the judicial system was a problem. As protesters and journalists and attorneys and law professors brought to light the abuses of municipal courts in St. Louis County, where poor defendants were, in effect, being jailed for an inability to afford traffic fines, the leaders in all three branches of Missouri government acted.

三年前，州长、密苏里州最高法院和密苏里州立法机构意识到，司法系统中的这种不同待遇是一个问题。当抗议者、记者、律师和法学教授揭露圣路易斯县市政法院的虐待时，那里贫穷的被告因为无力支付交通罚款而坐监狱，密苏里州政府里三个部门的领导行动了。

18 In her annual speech to the Legislature, Mary Russell, then chief

justice of the Missouri Supreme Court，set the stage for what would be a year of reform：

密苏里州最高法院首席大法官玛丽·罗素对立法机构发表了年度演讲，这为今年的改革奠定了基础。

19　"From a local municipal division to the state Supreme Court，Missouri's courts should be open and accessible to all. Courts should primarily exist to help people resolve their legal disputes. If they serve，instead，as revenue generators for the municipality that selects and pays the court staff and judges—this creates at least a perception，if not a reality，of diminished judicial impartiality，" ③Russell（罗素，密苏里州最高法院首席大法官。）said. "It is important to ensure that municipal divisions throughout the state are driven not by economics，but by notions of fairness under the rule of law. The Supreme Court is ready to work with you to ensure that people who appear in municipal courts are treated fairly and with respect."

③罗素说："从地方市政部门到州最高法院，密苏里州的法院应该向所有人开放。法院的存在首先是为了帮助人们解决他们的法律纠纷。相反，如果他们只是作为市政当局的收入来源，选择和支付法务人员和法官的薪酬，倘若不是现实的话，也至少会造成对司法公正性降低的印象。""重要的是，要确保整个州的市政部门不是由经济驱动，而是由法治下的公平观念驱动的。最高法院愿意与你们合作，确保在市法院出庭的人受到公平和尊重的对待。"

20　The court adopted new rules setting out parameters for municipal judges to operate more professionally and to take into account a defendant's inability to pay. The Legislature passed a law reducing how much revenue cities could take in from court fines.

法院采纳了新规，为市政法官设定了一些参数，使之可以更专业地开展工作并考虑到被告无力支付的情况。立法机关通过了一项法律，减少城市从法院罚款中的所得。

21　All along，unbeknownst to many，a similar problem—maybe worse in some cases—lurked in circuit courts throughout rural Missouri.

There, in places like Dent and Crawford and St. Francois and Caldwell and Lafayette and many other counties, defendants are jailed with high cash bail that poor people can't afford. They're given a bill for those stays in jail, and they're often jailed over and over on alleged violations of pretrial release conditions set by private probation companies that have an incentive to send their clients back behind bars.

一直以来，密苏里州乡村地区的巡回法院都潜伏着一个许多人不知道的类似问题——在某些案件中可能更严重。在那里，在登特、克劳福德、圣弗朗索瓦、考德威尔、拉斐特和许多其他县，被告被判入狱，保释金很高，穷人负担不起。坐牢的会收到一份账单，而且他们经常会因为违反私人缓刑公司设定的预审释放条件而一次又一次地被关进监狱，这些私人缓刑公司有把当事人送回监狱的动机。

22 Years after pleading guilty to relatively minor offenses, they still face penalties of jail, without legal representation, as judges bring them back each month to try to collect their debts.

在承认较轻罪行后数年，他们仍然面临没有法律代理而被监禁的惩罚，因为法官每个月都会把他们带回来，试图收回他们的债务。

23 A system that is still threatening a man with jail 11 years after he served his time for stealing a lawn mower at 17 isn't just. A system that seeks $15,000 from a woman for her year-long jail sentence that was imposed after she stole an $8 tube of mascara is the very definition of a modern day debtors' prison.

这个系统是不公正的，它威胁着一个在 17 岁时偷了一台割草机而服刑 11 年的人。这个系统从一名女子身上搜刮 15,000 美元，这个女子因为偷了一支 8 美元的睫毛膏而被判处一年监禁，这就是现代债务人监狱的恰当定义。

24 When Russell spoke at the opening of the 2015 legislative session, ④ she（玛丽·罗素）quoted Martin Luther King Jr. in describing how a problem with one court in Missouri was a problem for the entire judicial system: "We are caught in an inescapable network of mutuality, tied in a single garment of destiny. Whatever affects one direct-

ly，affects all indirectly."

④罗素在 2015 年立法会议的开幕式上发言时，引用了马丁·路德·金的话来描述密苏里州一个法院的问题是如何成为整个司法系统的问题："我们被困在一个不可避免的相互关系网中，被绑在一件命运的衣服里。任何直接影响到一个人的东西，都会间接影响到所有人。"

25　The garment of justice in Missouri is still terribly torn.

　　在密苏里州，正义的外衣仍然撕裂得很厉害。

26　Who will fix it?

　　谁来修复它？

【2019 年普利策评论奖 7 号文本】

Rural court traps woman with ticket for speeding

乡村法庭拘捕超速驾驶女子

Messenger：St. Louis woman did 20 days in jail for speeding；now rural Missouri judge wants her for 6 more months

曼森哲：圣路易斯的一名妇女因超速行驶入狱 20 天；现在，密苏里州乡村的法官要求她再服刑 6 个月

1　It was Mother's Day weekend in 2017.

　　那是 2017 年的母亲节，是一个周末。

2　Precious Jones was in a hurry to get to her sister's house in Kansas City.

　　普瑞斯·琼斯急着去在堪萨斯城的姐姐家。

3　Too much of a hurry.

　　太急了。

4　Jones，34，lives in the Baden neighborhood in north St. Louis. Headed west on Interstate 70，she got pulled over by the Missouri Highway Patrol for going 120 miles per hour. She was given a ticket and sent on her way.

　　34 岁的琼斯住在圣路易斯北部的巴登社区。在 70 号州际公路向

西行驶时，她因时速 120 英里被密苏里高速公路巡警拦下。她被开了罚单，然后就放走了。

5　She missed her August court date in Lafayette County.

　　她错过了八月在拉斐特县的开庭日期。

6　"It slipped my mind," ① she（她，指普瑞斯·琼斯。）says.

　　①她说："我忘记了。"

7　Jones straightened it out. She turned herself in to local police, paid the bond on her outstanding warrant, and called the court to set up a new court date. She took driver education classes and did community service. She hired a local attorney. He told her that if she agreed to pay a higher fine, the points on the speeding ticket wouldn't be assessed against her driver's license.

　　琼斯捋顺了这件事。她到当地警方那里，支付了未付的逮捕证的保证金，请求法院设定新的开庭日期。之后她参加了驾驶教育课程还做了社区服务。她雇了一名当地律师。律师告诉她，如果她同意支付更高的罚款，超速罚单上的积分将不会根据她的驾照进行评估。

8　In May, Jones pleaded guilty to the Class B misdemeanor of speeding at least 26 mph over the speed limit. She didn't expect what came next.

　　五月，琼斯承认了 B 级轻罪，即至少超速 26 英里。她没想到接下来会发生什么。

9　Associate Circuit Court Judge Kelly Rose gave her a six—month jail sentence and two years probation. The jail sentence would be suspended if Jones did 20 days "shock time" in jail, on consecutive weekends.

　　联邦巡回法院法官凯利·罗斯判处她六个月监禁和两年缓刑。如果琼斯在连续的周末在狱中进行 20 天的"休克时间"，监禁将被暂停。

10　"She just threw the book at me," ②Jones（琼斯）says. "I could have gotten this deal myself. Why did I pay＄300 for a lawyer?"

　　"她只是把书扔给了我，" ②琼斯说，"我本来可以达成这个交易。为什么要花 300 美元请律师？"

11　Because of the conviction, Jones'driver's license was suspended, and would stay that way until she paid all her court fines and did her time. She asked the judge if she could do her weekends in jail in St. Louis. The judge said no.

由于这次定罪，琼斯的驾照被吊销了，除非她支付了所有的法庭罚款并付上时间。她问法官是否能在圣路易斯监狱服刑，法官拒绝了。

12 So，this summer，she begged for rides，and every Friday for 10 weeks was dropped off at the Lafayette County Jail. On one day in May，she was an hour late to jail. Jones had gotten a job working for the United Way in St. Louis. She works until 6 p. m. Making it to Lafayette County by 10 p. m. was no easy task.

所以，今年夏天，她开始求搭车，连续 10 个星期，每周五她被捎到拉法叶县监狱。五月的一天，她到监狱迟了一个小时。琼斯在圣路易斯的联合之路找到了一份工作，每天工作到下午 6 点，所以要在晚上 10 点前赶到拉法叶县可不是件容易事。

13 In June，on one of the days she was supposed to be in jail，her car broke down.

六月份，在她本该待在监狱的那一天，车抛锚了。

14 Jones called the jail，which documented the call. The next day she made it to Lafayette County. The jail kept her for her full two days.

琼斯给监狱打了电话，监狱记录了这通电话。但是等第二天她来到拉法叶县，监狱还是把她关了整整两天。

15 By July，Jones figured she had paid her debt. She did all of her time，and she paid all of her fines，including a bill for her jail time. In September，she got a notice from Lafayette County in the mail.

到了七月，琼斯认为她已经还清了债务。她服完了所有的刑期，缴纳了所有的罚款，包括一张监禁账单。不料九月份，她还是收到了来自拉法叶县的邮件通知。

16 There was a warrant out for her arrest.

邮件里有对她的逮捕令。

17 Because she had been late to jail，even though she stayed and did her

full time, prosecutor Kristen Hilbrenner was seeking to revoke her probation.

检察官克里斯汀·希尔布伦纳寻求撤销她的缓刑。就因为琼斯去监狱时迟到了，即使她到了监狱做了全时间的工作。

18 The attorney in her case, James Worthington, of Higginsville, withdrew, saying he wasn't retained to work on a probation violation case. So now, Jones has a warrant out for her arrest, with a ＄2, 500 bond attached to it, and she's facing a six—month jail sentence.

来自希金斯维尔的律师詹姆斯·沃星顿退出了，他说自己没有被留下来去处理一个违反缓刑的案子。所以现在，琼斯收到了逮捕令，上面附有 2500 美元的保释金，她将面临 6 个月的监禁。

19 For a speeding ticket.

就因为一张超速罚单。

20 "I don't know what I'm going to do," ③Jones（琼斯）says. "They are just not going to let me go."

"我不知道我该做什么，" ③琼斯说，"他们就是不让我走。"

21 Jones is an example of a widespread problem in Missouri's rural courts, in which in too many situations, especially when the defendant is poor, the system seems to look for reasons to cite probation violations in misdemeanor cases, and tie people to the court system for years, in an effort to increase local revenue. If Jones ends up doing more jail time in Lafayette County, she'll be billed for that time, and could end up owing thousands of dollars. And if she can't afford to pay it, she'll be summoned by the judge across the state every month to explain herself.

琼斯的遭遇是密苏里州乡村法院普遍存在问题的一个例子，在大多数情况下，尤其是当被告很穷的时候，这个系统似乎会寻找在轻罪案件中引用缓刑违规的理由，由此来将人们与法院系统捆绑多年，以努力增加地方收入。如果琼斯最终在拉法叶县服刑更长时间，她将为此付账，并最终可能欠下数千美元。如果她支付不起，全州的法官每个月都会传唤她来为自己辩解。

22 For Jones，that will be quite a hardship at the moment.

对琼斯来说，那将是一个相当艰难的时刻。

23 Despite the promise from her attorney and the court，as outlined in court records，that the speeding ticket wouldn't carry points against her license，nobody told the Department of Revenue. So Jones' license has been suspended.

尽管她的律师和法庭承诺，正如法庭记录所概述的那样，超速罚单不会对她的驾照扣分，但没有人通知税务局，所以琼斯的驾照还是被吊销了。

24 She gets rides or takes the bus to get to work or wherever she needs to go. She's called the NAACP and the American Civil Liberties Union，in hope that somebody will help get her out of a new jail sentence that she can't believe is even an option.

她搭乘或乘坐公共汽车去上班或她需要去的任何地方。她打电话给全国有色人种协进会（1909 在纽约建立）和美国公民自由联盟（1920 建立），希望有人能帮助她摆脱新的监禁。她甚至不相信这是一个选择。

25 "I'm losing everything，" ④Jones（琼斯）tells me. "They keep coming back for more. They're trying to milk me for all I've got."

"我正在失去一切，" ④琼斯告诉我，"他们不断回头要求更多，他们想榨干我的一切。"

【2019 年普利策评论奖 8 号文本】

Stoddard County can teach a lesson about dealing with poor defendants

斯托达德县可以教与穷被告人打交道的课了

Messenger：A tale of two counties on opposite ends of Missouri's debtors' prison cycle

曼森哲：一个两个县完全相反做法的故事终结了密苏里州债务人监狱循环

1 Eleven Missouri counties last year took in more than ＄100，000 each by using the state's circuit courts as a debt collector.

185

去年，密苏里州的十一个县通过利用该州巡回法院作为收债人，每个县收入超过 10 万美元。

2 In some cases，that's enough money to pay a judge's salary，or a prosecutor's，or hire a few jailers.

在某些情况下，这些钱足够支付法官或检察官的工资，或者雇佣一些监狱看守。

3 The money came from inmates in the county jail，many of them poor people.

而这些钱来自县监狱的囚犯，这些囚犯很多都是穷人。

4 Every week in Missouri，a judge somewhere holds a crowded docket to collect room and board from people who were recently in jail. The judges call them payment review dockets，or show cause dockets，because calling them what they really are—debtors prison dockets—hurts too much.

每周在密苏里州，会有法官在某地拿着一份布满待审案件的清单，收缴最近刚入狱人的食宿费。法官们称之为支付审查清单，或者称之为原因陈明清单，因为如果称呼它真正的名字——债务人监狱清单，太难听了。

5 For the elected officials who work in most of Missouri's historic courthouses that sit on small—town squares near empty storefronts，show cause day is pay day.

挨着空铺子的小镇广场，有法院的老建筑，那里工作着密苏里州的民选官员，那些陈明原因的日子就是发薪日。

6 Two counties that border the Lake of the Ozarks took in the most money from "board bills" in 2017. Laclede County collected more than ＄261，000；neighboring Camden County took in just ＄20，000 less.

2017 年，与奥扎克斯湖接壤的两个县从"监狱账单"中获得的钱最多。拉克莱德县收入超过 26.1 万美元，而邻近的卡姆登县比它只少收入 2 万美元。

7 In southeast Missouri，Scott County took in ＄143,000 and Cape Girardeau County collected ＄124,000. North of there，St. Francois

County pocketed nearly ＄155,000. Some of the collar counties around St. Louis played the game，too. Franklin County added ＄162,000 to its coffers and Warren County took in ＄125,000. Near Kansas City, Lafayette County collected ＄100,000.

在密苏里州东南部，斯科特县收入 143，000 美元，开普吉拉多县收入 124，000 美元。再往北，圣弗朗索瓦县集团获得了近 155,000 美元。圣路易斯周围的一些邻县也玩这个游戏。富兰克林县增加了 162,000 美元的收入；沃伦县增加了 125,000 美元。在堪萨斯城附近，拉法叶县筹集了 100,000 美元。

8 The biggest winner on a per capita basis was tiny Caldwell County in northwest Missouri，which used its circuit court judges to help pull in ＄149,877，or ＄16.47 for each of the 9,100 people who live in the county. There，Associate Circuit Judge Jason Kanoy has become the poster child for how to turn the judicial branch of government into a tax—collecting subsidiary of the executive branch.

按人均计算，最大的赢家是位于密苏里州西北部的小考德威尔县，它利用巡回法院法官帮助该县 9100 人每人赚取 16.47 美元，即 149,877 美元。在那里，副巡回法官杰森·卡诺伊已经成为如何将政府的司法部门变成行政部门的征税附属机构的典范。

9 Once a month he schedules his debtors on the docket. If they pay，they don't have to show up. If they don't，he issues a warrant for their arrest. Many of them are like Nicholas T. McNab，men or women who long ago served their time. Now they're paying for it.

他每月一次把债务人列在日程表上。如果他们付了钱就不用出现了，但如果他们不付钱，他就会签发逮捕令。他们中的许多人都像尼古拉斯·T. 麦克纳布一样，是很久以前服过刑的男人或女人。现在他们要付钱。

10 In May 2008，McNab stole some candy. Then 17，he and some buddies broke into a concession stand in the city of Polo. They took candy bars，taffy and beef jerky. He was arrested and put in jail with a ＄10,000 cash—only bond.

在 2008 年 5 月，麦克纳布偷了一些糖果。17 岁的时候，他和几个朋友闯进了波罗市的一家小卖部。他们拿走了棒棒糖、太妃糖和牛肉干。之后他便被捕入狱，保释金为 10,000 美元。

11 He pleaded guilty to misdemeanor stealing and was given time served for the eight days he already spent in jail. McNab was put on probation for two years, and a 60—day jail sentence was suspended.

他承认犯有盗窃行为的轻罪，并已在监狱待了八天。麦可纳布又被判处缓刑两年，缓期 60 天执行。

12 Almost two years later, right before his probation was to have ended, he tested positive for marijuana. His probation was revoked and he went to jail.

差不多两年后，就在他的缓刑期即将结束之前，他的大麻检测呈阳性。他的缓刑被撤销，进了监狱。

13 By the time he was released, McNab's board bill was more than $2,000.

到麦克纳布被释放的时候，他的服刑账单已经超过了 2000 美元。

14 So the payment hearings started. Miss one. Get arrested. Go to jail. The cycle would repeat itself year after year. Each time, his bill would rise, $45 for one visit, $270 for another, then $900, and $945.

于是支付听证会开始了。错过一个？抓起来，坐牢吧。年年来一遍。每次，他的账单都会上涨，一次 45 美元，另一次 270 美元，然后是 900 美元和 945 美元。

15 His latest hearing was Thursday.

他最近一次听证会是在星期四。

16 Attorney Jim Rust doesn't get it. He represents McNab in a misdemeanor marijuana possession case in another county.

吉姆·鲁斯特律师不明白。他在另一个县为麦克纳布代理一起持有大麻的轻罪案件。

17 "This kid is not a criminal," ①Rust（鲁斯特，律师）says of McNab. "He's a small town guy trying to get by."

"这孩子不是罪犯，"①鲁斯特这样评价麦克纳布，"他是一个试图摆脱困境的小镇子上的人。"

18　But here he is, 10 years after doing his time, still tied to Kanoy's court because he owes the county money. Rust calls it a form of double jeopardy, with poor defendants punished over and over for the same crime.

但是在他服刑10年后，他仍然和卡诺伊的法庭牵扯在一起，因为他欠了县里的钱。鲁斯特称之为双重伤害，可怜的被告因为同样的罪行而一次又一次地受到惩罚。

19　"This kind of thing happens a lot around here,"② Rust（鲁斯特）says. "It's not just Judge Kanoy. This stuff has got to stop."

"这种事在这里经常发生，"②鲁斯特说，"不仅仅是卡诺伊法官，这种事情必须停止。"

20　In one small Missouri county, it has. Or maybe it never started in the first place.

在密苏里州的一个小县，它曾发生过，又或许这个县从一开始就没有发生过。

21　Almost 400 miles southeast of the Caldwell County Courthouse is the one in Stoddard County. It's across the street from the funeral home owned by Greg Mathis, who doubles as the presiding commissioner. For 16 years, Mathis has led Stoddard County, and during that time, the county has never collected a board bill from people who stay in its jail.

离考德威尔县法院东南近400英里的地方是斯托达德县一处地方。它就在格雷格·马西斯拥有的殡仪馆的街对面，马西斯也是首席专员。16年来，马西斯一直领导着斯托达德县，在此期间，该县从来没有向监狱服刑人员收过膳食费。

22　"We have never, ever charged room and board for our inmates,"③ Mathis（马西斯，斯托达德县的领导者）says. "It's never been brought up."

"我们从没向囚犯收取过食宿费，"③马西斯说，"从来没提起过。"

23 Southeast Missouri is among the poorest parts of the state. Like many areas of rural Missouri, it is struggling with opioid and meth use. Its jail, built for about 40 people, is crowded. Taxpayers approved a bond issue recently to build a new jail.

  密苏里州东南部是该州最贫穷的地区之一。像密苏里州的许多乡村地区一样，它也在与阿片类药物和毒品的使用做斗争。这座可容纳 40 人的监狱拥挤不堪，所以纳税人最近批准发行债券建造一座新监狱。

24 But Stoddard County is one of only two rural counties in Missouri—McDonald County in the southwest part of the state is the other—to not charge board bills. None of the state's primarily urban counties charge them, including Boone County, home of the University of Missouri.

  但是，斯托达德县是密苏里州仅有的两个免收伙食费的乡村县之一，该州西南部的麦当劳县是另一个。这个州主要的县没有对他们收费，包括布恩县。布恩县是密苏里大学的所在地。

25 Missouri lawmakers who want to address the state's debtors' prison problem can hold up tiny Stoddard County as a place that does it right.

  想要解决该州债务人监狱问题，密苏里州立法者可以把小小的斯托达德县作为一个样板。

26 "Why would I want to overcrowd our jail with people who would be there just because they couldn't pay their jail bill?" ④Mathis（马西斯）says. "It's just a never—ending vicious cycle that targets poor people."

  "为什么要让监狱挤满那些只是因为付不起监狱账单就被关在那里的人？"④马西斯说，"这只是一个针对穷人的永无休止的恶性循环。"

【2019 年普利策评论奖 9 号文本】
Camden County still bedevils woman after 2008 guilty plea
卡姆登县仍在为难那个 2008 年就认罪的女人

Messenger：St. Louis woman had a bad break up in 2006. Camden County still keeps putting her in jail because of it.

曼森哲：圣路易斯的一个女人在 2006 年经历了一次糟糕的分手，但卡姆登县仍然因此把她关进监狱。

1　Alicyn Rapp was dropped off in the shadow of the big red barn in Camdenton，the one that houses a souvenir and T—shirt shop at the intersection of Missouri Highways 5 and 54.

　　阿利辛•拉普是在坎登顿红色大谷仓的阴影下车的，那地方位于密苏里州 5 号和 54 号高速公路交叉路口，有一个纪念品和 T 恤商店。

2　"I had no money，no car and no phone，"①Rapp（拉普）remembers. "I had no way to get back home to St. Louis. I was stranded. "

　　"我没有钱，没有车，也没有电话，"①拉普回忆道，"我没有办法回到圣路易斯的家，我陷入了困境。"

3　A stranger bought her a hot dog at Sonic and let her use her phone. Her dad would be able to come get her in a couple of days. She found a cheap motel and the good Samaritan paid for her room.

　　一个陌生人在索尼克给它买了个热狗，还借手机给她。她爸爸过几天就能来接她了。她找到一家便宜的汽车旅馆，好心的撒玛利亚人帮她付了房钱。

4　That was in July.

　　那时是七月。

5　Rapp，36，had just been let out of Camden County Jail. She had been picked up on a warrant from a case for which she long ago served her time. Her troubles stemmed from a bad breakup.

　　36 岁的拉普刚从卡姆登县监狱释放。她是因很早以前就服刑的一个案子的逮捕令而被捕的。她的麻烦源于一次糟糕的分手。

6　In 2006.

　　发生在 2006 年。

7　Rapp believes she might have the oldest ongoing case in Camden County. She met a guy that summer at Lake of the Ozarks. Things moved fast. She moved in with him in the loft above his window—tinting business. They drank a lot. They fought. Then he cheated on her. That's what ②the police report（警方报告）says. It also says she hit him and trashed his loft. Rapp says he hit her first. Police charged her with domestic violence and property damage，both misdemeanors.

拉普认为她的案子可能是卡姆登县正在进行中的案子里年头最久的那一个。那年夏天，她在奥扎克斯湖畔遇到了一个男人，他们发展得很快，不久就一起搬进了他窗饰店楼上的阁楼里。（后来有一天）他们喝了很多酒然后打了起来，然后他骗了她。②警方报告上是这么说的。上面还说她打了他，还砸了他的阁楼。虽然拉普说是男人先打她的。警方指控她犯有家庭暴力和致人财产损失两项轻罪。

8 A warrant was issued for her arrest，but Rapp had already moved back to St. Louis，where she grew up.

警方发出了逮捕令，但拉普已经搬回了她成长的圣路易斯。

9 She's a south city Catholic girl. There was St. Gabriel's for elementary and middle school，followed by Bishop DuBourg for high school.

她是南方城市的天主教女孩。那里有圣加布里埃尔小学和中学，然后在杜布尔格主教上高中。

10 By the age of 14，she was fighting addiction，mostly alcohol and meth. In 2004，she caught her first drug possession case and went to prison. Since then，she's done three stints in prison—all for drug possession—and has found herself in nine different county jails.

14 岁的时候，她开始与毒瘾做斗争，主要是酒精和冰毒。2004年，她涉嫌人生中第一个持有毒品的案子，进了监狱。从那时起，她已经在监狱里待过三段时间——全都是因为持有毒品——她发现自己被关在九个不同的县监狱里。

11 Only one case remains on her record. Camden County.

只有一个案子留在她的档案里，卡姆登县。

12 She was arrested in 2007，went through a couple of attorneys and by 2008 pleaded guilty. Her sentence was one year in jail，but it was suspended. She received two years of probation and a bill for the nine

days she spent in jail. Altogether, her court costs came to about $1,200.

她 2007 年被捕，经手了几个律师，在 2008 年认罪。她被判入狱一年，但缓期执行。她获得两年的缓刑和一张在监狱待了九天的账单。总之，她的诉讼费用约为 1200 美元。

13 By 2009, Rapp was behind in her payments and the court revoked her probation. She did a couple of days in jail and her cash bond of $400 was applied to her costs. Then again in 2010. Revocation. Jail. Another bill for jail time. And 2012.

到 2009 年，拉普拖欠了款项，于是法院撤销了她的缓刑。她在监狱里待了几天，并用 400 美元现金保证金支付监狱账单。2010 年也是如此。撤销、入狱，又一笔关于监禁的账单。2012 年继续。

14 This is the pattern that creates de facto debtors prisons in rural Missouri. Poor people who can't afford to pay their costs—even after doing their time on misdemeanor charges—end up with even larger bills by spending more time in jail on probation revocation or contempt of court for missing hearings. Camden County collects more in so—called "board bills" than any county in the state except for neighboring Laclede County. The practice has earned the lake area jail there a motto often repeated by its inmates.

这就是在密苏里农村地区建立事实上的债务人监狱的模式。那些支付不起诉讼费用的穷人，即使他们因轻罪服刑，也会因为缓刑撤销或错过听证会这种藐视行为而在监狱里待更长的时间，然后又得到更大的账单。卡姆登县收集的所谓"膳食费"比其他县更多，除了邻近的拉克莱德县。这种做法为湖区监狱赢得了被狱友们反复诟病的主题。

15 "It's legendary," says ③Rapp（拉普）. "Come on vacation, leave on probation, come back on revocation."

"这是一个传奇，"③拉普说，"不进监狱，给了缓刑，但又撤销了。"

16 Since 2006, this has been Rapp's life.

从 2006 年开始，这就是拉普的生活。

17 In 2013, she tried to put an end to the cycle. She was in the Chillico-the Correctional Center, doing 120 days for possession of meth, and she was trying to turn her life around. Her record has been clean since then, though she knows her battle with addiction will last a life time.

2013 年，她试图结束这种循环。她在奇利科西惩教中心，因私藏冰毒而服刑 120 天。她试图改变自己的生活，尽管知道以后与毒瘾的斗争将会持续一生，但从那以后她的纪录一直很干净。

18 "I am writing you requesting time served in lieu of fines and/or jail time to run concurrent with my current sentence..." ④ Rapp（拉普）wrote the Camden County Circuit Court. "I am trying to change my life and I would like a clean slate to start over."

④拉普在给卡姆登县巡回法院的信中写道："我写信给你，请求你提供服务时间，以代替罚款或者坐牢，以便与我目前的判决同时进行。""我正在努力改变我的生活，我希望一切像白板一样从头开始。"

19 The prosecutor in Camden County was willing to grant the request. The judge said no, not unless Rapp also paid the $1,639. 70 in outstanding bills.

卡姆登县的检察官愿意同意这一请求。法官说不，除非拉普付了那 1639. 70 美元的账单。

20 So when Rapp walked out of prison, she was picked up by Camden County deputies, who drove her back to the county jail, and then added a bill for mileage to her ever increasing jail costs.

所以当拉普走出监狱时，她被卡姆登县的副警长接走了，把她送回了县监狱，然后在她不断增加的监狱费用上增加了里程数的账单。

21 In 2015, still behind in payments, she got picked up again.

2015 年，她仍然拖欠费用，她又被接走了。

22 "I sat in Camden County Jail for 18 days, waiting to go to court just for them to release me with a new payment schedule," ⑤ she（她，拉普）says. "It's ridiculous."

"我在卡姆登县监狱蹲了 18 天，等着上法庭，只是为了让他们给我一个新的付款时间表，"⑤她说，"这太荒谬了。"

23　On Monday，she had a court date again to discuss her payments with the judge，the fifth one to handle her case since it began in 2006. She didn't go.

周一，她又有了一个开庭日期，与法官讨论她的赔偿问题，这是自 2006 年开庭以来第五次处理她的案子，她没有去。

24　She is living with her husband in Woodson Terrace these days. Her car doesn't work. Next week she starts training for a job with Jack in the Box. The idea of scraping together the money to find a way to make it to Camden County just to tell the judge she can't afford a payment makes no sense to her.

她最近和丈夫一起住在伍德森露台，她的车坏了。下周，她就要开始进行一项工作培训，准备和杰克一起工作。凑钱去卡姆登县，只是为了告诉法官她付不起赔偿金，这种想法对她来说毫无意义。

25　"It's been 12 years，for God's sake，"⑥Rapp（拉普）says. "I've lost jobs，my house，cars，my children. I've done enough time. I've paid them enough money. With this hanging over my head，I'm never going to get a clean start. When is it going to stop?"

"看在上帝的分上，已经 12 年了，"⑥拉普说，"我失去了工作、房子、汽车和孩子。我已经坐够了牢，我已经给他们足够的钱了。这件事一直困扰着我，我永远不可能有一个利落的开始。它什么时候才会停止?"

【2019 年普利策评论奖 10 号文本】
Breaking the cycle of board bills，jailing the poor
打破监狱账单和监禁穷人的循环
Messenger：St. Charles County points the way as lawmakers seek to end debtors prisons in Missouri
曼森哲：圣查尔斯县指明了一条路：立法者寻求结束密苏里州债务人监狱

1　Judge Gary Oxenhandler shares an affinity with Missouri's early lawmakers.

加里·奥克森汉德勒法官与密苏里州的早期立法者有着密切的关系。

2　The founders of the Show-Me state recognized that the courts shouldn't be used to exacerbate poverty. The sentiment shows up loud and clear in the state's constitutional prohibition against jailing a person because of debt. It even shows up in the early versions of a law that allows counties to charge defendants room and board for staying in jail.

"求证之州"（这是一个传统说法）的创始人认识到，法院不应该被用来加剧贫困。这种情绪在该州宪法禁止因债务而监禁人的禁令中表现得淋漓尽致，它甚至出现在一项法律的早期版本中。该法律允许各县对被告在监狱中的食宿收费。

3　①The 1909 version of the law（1909 年版的法律），for instance，said that "insolvent prisoners" could be discharged from their debts—and jail—if they had no property nor other means to satisfy their court costs. That year's version of the law also allowed prisoners to bring food and bedding from home to make them more comfortable and reduce costs.

①例如 1909 年版的法律规定，如果"资不抵债的犯人"没有财产或其他手段来支付诉讼费用，他们就可以免除债务——也可以免除监禁。当年的法律还允许囚犯从家里带食物和被褥，以使他们更舒适并降低成本。

4　Such provisions have been erased from Missouri law，and these days，it's not uncommon for poor people to be jailed in Missouri because they can't afford to pay their jail bill.

这些规定在密苏里州的法律中已被删除，而现在，在密苏里州，穷人因为付不起监狱账单而被监禁的情况并不少见。

5　"It's horrible，" says ②Oxenhandler（奥克森汉德勒，前布恩县巡回法院法官），who two years ago retired as a circuit court judge in Boone County，one of the few places in the state that doesn't bill defendants for their jail stays.

"这太可怕了。"②奥克森汉德勒说。他两年前从布恩县巡回法院法官的职位上退休了。布恩县是该州为数不多的不向被告收取监禁费用的地方之一。

6　In almost every rural county in Missouri, people who do time in jail, both before trial and after conviction, are charged "board bills" for room and board. The charges are generally around $50 a day, and when people don't pay, they are often hauled before judges who try to collect. In many cases, ③the Post-Dispatch（《圣路易斯邮报》）has found, defendants are still dealing with their cases, even misdemeanors, years after they've served their time. They are scheduled to appear at payment review hearings every month, even more than a decade after they have pleaded guilty and spent time in jail.

在密苏里州的几乎每个乡村县，在监狱服刑的人，无论是在审判前还是定罪后，都要支付"食宿费"。这些费用通常在一天50美元左右，如果人们不付钱，通常就会被拖到要收钱的法官面前。③《圣路易斯邮报》发现，在许多案件中，被告在服刑多年后仍在处理案件，即使是轻罪。他们被安排每月出席支付审查听证会，甚至在他们认罪并入狱十多年之后。

7　In Caldwell County, Dent County, Camden County and St. Francois County, this is the norm.

在考德威尔县、登特县、卡姆登县和圣弗朗索瓦县，这是很正常的。

8　Cory Booth stole a lawn mower when he was 17 and 10 years later is still going to court month after month to pay his board bill.

科里·布斯在17岁时偷了一台割草机。10年后，他仍然一个月又一个月上法庭以支付他的膳食账单。

9　Nicholas McNab broke into a concession stand to steal candy; a decade later, he's in more debt than when he did his jail time.

尼古拉斯·麦克纳布闯进一个小卖部偷糖果。十年后，他的债务比坐牢的时候还多。

10　Brooke Bergen stole an $8 mascara tube and now she owes $15,000 on a board bill.

布鲁克·贝尔根偷了一支 8 美元的睫毛膏管，现在她欠了一张 15,000 美元的食宿费。

11 The results can be devastating: increased poverty, long jail sentences, lost kids, cars, houses and jobs. There are stories like this in nearly every county in rural Missouri.

这些结果可能是毁灭性的：贫困增加，长期监禁，失去孩子、汽车、房子和工作。在密苏里州的乡村地区，几乎每个县都有这样的故事。

12 But there are exceptions.

但也有例外。

13 Boone County is one. So are all the most urban counties in the state: both the city and county of St. Louis, Clay and Platte counties in Kansas City. Also, two tiny counties, Stoddard in the southeast and McDonald in the southwest. None charge board bills.

布恩县就是其中之一。该州所有城市化程度最高的县也是如此：包括圣路易斯市和圣路易斯县，以及堪萨斯城的克莱和普拉特县。还有两个小县，东南部的斯托达德和西南部的麦当劳，这些地方的监狱不收账单。

14 "It's just not right," ④Oxenhandler（奥克森汉德勒）says, to force defendants, the vast majority of whom live in poverty, to pay for their time in jail, and then put them back behind bars when they can't afford to pay.

"这本身就是不对的，"④奥克森汉德勒说，"强迫绝大多数生活在贫困中的被告为他们在监狱里的时间付钱，然后在他们付不起钱的时候再把他们送回监狱。"

15 In St. Charles County, a place that straddles urban and rural sensibilities, elected officials have found a balance that might serve as a guide as Missouri lawmakers consider addressing the state's debtor prison problem.

在圣查尔斯县这个城乡交错的地方，民选官员找到了一个平衡点，可以作为密苏里州立法者考虑解决该州债务人监狱问题的指南。

16　There，defendants who have some financial means will be sent a board bill by the sheriff for county jail sentences，but not for any time they spent in jail before trial. If they pay within 30 days，the rate is cut significantly. If they don't pay，it goes to civil collection.

　　在那里，有一些经济能力的被告在被判刑的时候，治安官会送一份食宿账单，但不包括他们在审判前的任何监禁时间。如果他们在 30 天内付款，利率就会大幅降低。如果他们不付钱，这笔钱就归民事征收。

17　But poor people are never charged in St. Charles County. The county，with the agreement of its top elected officials，doesn't use its judicial system as a debt collector. "Our general rule of thumb is if the person is indigent—which is about 80 percent of our defendants—we don't try to collect it," says ⑤St. Charles County Prosecuting Attorney Tim Lohmar，a Republican（圣查尔斯县检察官、共和党人蒂姆·洛马尔）. Last year the county collected a mere ＄45,000 in board bill charges，none of it through the court system. It expects to collect less than that this year.

　　但是在圣查尔斯县，穷人从来不会被起诉。这个县，在其最高民选官员的同意下，不把其司法系统当作收债人。⑤圣查尔斯县检察官、共和党人蒂姆·洛马尔表示："我们的一般经验法则是，如果被告是穷人——在我们的被告中占到 80%——我们就不会去收钱。"去年，该县仅仅收取了 45,000 美元的伙食费，没有一项是通过法院系统收取的，预期今年的收入还将低于这一水平。

18　Laclede County，with about a tenth of the population of St. Charles County，led the state in board bill collections obtained through its circuit courts，with ＄261,000 in revenue last year.

　　拉克莱德县的人口约占圣查尔斯县人口的十分之一，通过巡回法院收取伙食的账单年收入达 261,000 美元，在该州居首位。

19　Lohmar，who is president of the Missouri Association of Prosecuting Attorneys，might find himself explaining how St. Charles County deals with board bills during the 2019 session of the Missouri Legislature. That's because at least two lawmakers have already filed bills to try to address the situation throughout the state.

洛马尔是密苏里州检察官协会主席，他可能发现自己需要在 2019 年密苏里州立法会议期间，解释圣查尔斯县是如何处理食宿账单的。这是因为至少有两名立法者已经提交了法案，试图解决整个州的情况。

20　One of them, House Bill 192, filed by Rep. Bruce DeGroot, R-Chesterfield, and cosponsored by Rep. Mark Ellebracht, D-Liberty, seeks to stop the practice of many rural judges requiring defendants who can't afford to pay their court costs to show up in court month after month, for years in some cases, and face contempt of court charges and more jail time if they miss a hearing.

其中之一，众议院第 192 号法案，由众议员布鲁斯·德格鲁特，彻斯特菲尔德提出，并由众议员马克·艾尔布兰特、李波特共同发起，旨在制止许多农村法官要求无力支付法庭费用的被告月复一月地出现在法庭上，在某些案件中持续数年，如果他们错过听证会，将面临藐视法庭的指控和更长的监禁时间。

21　Instead, DeGroot's bill would have the rest of the state mimic practices in St. Charles County, allowing for civil collection of past-due amounts but no more show-cause hearings and warrants issued for arrest. The state public defender's office is also challenging this practice in several court cases.

取而代之的是，德格鲁特的法案将允许其他州效仿圣查尔斯郡的做法，允许民事征收逾期款项，但不再举行显示原因的听证会和发出逮捕令。国家公设辩护人办公室也在几起法庭案件中挑战这种做法。

22　"The practice of jailing people who cannot afford to pay for their costs while incarcerated is very close to debtors prison," ⑥DeGroot（德格鲁特，众议员）says. "As a state we must end this practice. We are better than this."

"监禁无力支付费用的人的做法非常接近债务人的监狱，"⑥德格鲁特说，"作为一个州，我们必须结束这种做法，我们做得应该比这更好。"

23　Indeed，the practice is "disturbing," says ⑦Lauren-Brooke Eisen，a lawyer and researcher at the Brennan Center for Justice（布伦南司法中心的律师和研究员劳伦-布鲁克·艾森）. Eisen has written extensively on the process of counties charging for jail time，and it's not just a Missouri phenomenon. Nearly every state has some similar charge in either county or state courts，but its application differs depending on the jurisdiction.

　　　⑦布伦南司法中心的律师和研究员劳伦-布鲁克·艾森说，的确，这种做法"令人不安"。艾森写了大量各县收取监禁费过程的文章，这不仅仅是一个密苏里州现象。几乎每个州在县法院或州法院都有一些类似的指控，但根据管辖权的不同，其适用也有所不同。

24　"It creates a never-ending cycle of debt," ⑧Eisen（艾森）says. "It is criminalizing poverty. That's what we're doing. It's a tax on the poor."

　　　"这造成了一个无休止的债务循环，"⑧艾森表示，"这将贫困定为犯罪。这就是我们正在做的。这是向穷人征税。"

25　In 2009，the Minnesota Supreme Court struck down a "pay-to-stay" program that was operating in that state，but lawmakers there made changes to allow it to continue.

　　　2009年，明尼苏达最高法院否决了一项在该州实施的"付费入狱"计划，但该州的立法者做出了改变以使其继续实施。

26　Ellebracht and DeGroot hope the Missouri Legislature goes in the opposite direction. Besides working together on a bill to address Missouri's law，the two lawyers are in the process of setting up a nonprofit to help people across Missouri who are stuck with old board bills and can't escape the court system because of it. "There is no room for debate on this," ⑨Ellebracht（艾尔布兰特，众议员）says. "This is not a partisan issue."

　　　艾尔布兰特和德格鲁特希望密苏里州的立法机构走向相反的方向。除了共同致力于一项针对密苏里州法律的法案，这两位律师还正在建立一个非营利组织，以帮助密苏里州那些陷入旧账单而无法逃脱法院制度的人们。"在这个问题上没有讨论的余地，"⑨艾尔布兰特说，"这不是党派问题。"

27 State Rep. Justin Hill, R-Lake Saint Louis, has also filed a bill, House Bill 80, to deal with the issue. He hopes to stop the practice of drug testing defendants who are awaiting trial on cases that have nothing to do with drugs or alcohol.

州众议员贾斯汀·希尔，雷克·圣·路易斯也提交了一份众议院第 80 号法案来处理这个问题。他希望停止毒品测试被告的做法，这些被告正在等待与毒品或酒精无关的案件的审判。

28 That practice leads to defendants often being jailed on probation or bond-condition violations and increasing the board bills they owed the county by hundreds or thousands of dollars.

这种做法导致被告常常因缓刑或违反保释条件而入狱，并使得他们欠县上的账单增加了数百或数千美元。

29 Hill's bill also would create earned compliance in misdemeanor cases, which would reduce probation by a month for every month a defendant serves probation without a violation. The same process already exists in felony cases overseen by state probation officers.

希尔的法案还将在轻罪案件中建立必须遵守的条款，这将使被告在没违规的情况下每服缓刑一个月，减少一个月的缓刑。同样的程序已经存在于由州缓刑监督官监督的重罪案件中。

30 ⑩Hill（州众议员贾斯汀·希尔）says he's glad his home county isn't contributing to the state's debtors' prison problem, and hopes it becomes a model for others to follow.

⑩希尔说，他很高兴他的家乡没有加剧州债务人的监狱问题，并希望它成为其他人效仿的榜样。

31 Lohmar, the St. Charles County prosecutor, agrees. He's not sure when or why St. Charles County started doing things the way they do them. Neither are the leaders of the other counties who buck the Missouri debtors prison trend. "I'm glad we don't try to collect board

bills on poor defendants，"⑪Lohmar（洛马尔）says. "It's just a bad practice. "

圣查尔斯县检察官洛马尔对此表示赞同。他不确定圣查尔斯郡是什么时候或者为什么开始按照他们的方式做事的。反对密苏里债务人监狱趋势的其他县的领导人不确定。"我很高兴我们没有试图向可怜的被告收取伙食账单，"⑪洛马尔说，"这本身就是一种糟糕的做法。"

表：2019 普利策评论奖文本消息来源出现次数统计分析表

文本 1	Release from debtor's prison raises holiday spirit of Missouri woman	
编号	英　文	中　文
①	Branson	布兰森
②	the court	法院，根据上文可以判断为密苏里最高法院
③	Branson	布兰森
④	she	她，根据上下文判断是布兰森
⑤	it	短信
⑥	she	她，根据上下文指布兰森
⑦	Branson	布兰森
文本 2	Counties' jailing of the poor 'has got to stop'，defender says	
①	Matthew Mueller	马修·穆勒，他是密苏里州公共辩护办公室的高级债券诉讼律师，主要工作是代表因贫困而入狱的穷人提起诉讼
②	Mueller	穆勒
③	Mueller	穆勒
④	Mueller	穆勒
⑤	state law	州法律
⑥	Mueller	穆勒
⑦	Mueller	穆勒
文本 3	St. Francois County prosecutor delays justice again as election approaches	
①	critics	批评家，这是一个不具名的消息来源
②	Mahurin said in the motion	马胡林在议案中说。这里的消息来源实际上是议案
③	he says in that court motion	法庭议案

④	she	她，法明顿律师沃恩·卡拉克，主要工作是帮助受到司法系统伤害的人服务
⑤	she	她，指沃恩·卡拉克
⑥	Carraker	沃恩·卡拉克
⑦	Brown	布朗，霍普的妻子

文本 4　Judge tries to block access to debtors' prison hearings in Dent County

①	she	贝尔根，在当地沃尔玛商店偷了一根价值 8 美元的睫毛膏而被捕
②	the bailiff	法警
③	I	我，指作者托尼

文本 5　'Poverty penalty' pervades rural courts in Missouri

①	Booth	布斯
②	Booth	布斯
③	he	他，指布斯
④	Booth	布斯
⑤	he	他，指布斯
⑥	Lisa Foster, a former judge and Department of Justice official	丽莎·福斯特，前法官兼司法部官员、罚款和收费司法中心联合主任
⑦	Foster	福斯特
⑧	Joanna Weiss	合作主任乔安娜·韦斯，韦斯是律师兼教育家，曾在美国律师协会特别工作组任职
⑨	Booth	布斯
⑩	Booth	布斯

文本 6　Time to close debtor's prison for good

①	she	艾米·穆尔
②	I	我，指作者托尼
③	Russell	罗素，密苏里州最高法院首席大法官
④	she	玛丽·罗素

文本 7　Rural court traps woman with ticket for speeding

①	she	她，指普瑞斯·琼斯
②	Jones	琼斯

③	Jones	琼斯
④	Jones	琼斯

文本 8　Stoddard County can teach a lesson about dealing with poor defendants

①	Rust	鲁斯特，律师
②	Rust	鲁斯特
③	Mathis	马西斯，斯托达德县的领导者
④	Mathis	马西斯

文本 9　Camden County still bedevils woman after 2008 guilty plea

①	Rapp	拉普
②	the police report	警方报告
③	Rapp	拉普
④	Rapp	拉普
⑤	she	她，拉普
⑥	Rapp	拉普

文本 10　Breaking the cycle of board bills，jailing the poor

①	The 1909 version of the law	1909 年版的法律
②	Oxenhandler	奥克森汉德勒，前布恩县巡回法院法官
③	the Post-Dispatch	《圣路易斯邮报》
④	Oxenhandler	奥克森汉德勒
⑤	St. Charles County Prosecuting Attorney Tim Lohmar，a Republican	圣查尔斯县检察官、共和党人蒂姆·洛马尔
⑥	DeGroot	德格鲁特，众议员
⑦	Lauren-Brooke Eisen，a lawyer and researcher at the Brennan Center for Justice	布伦南司法中心的律师和研究员劳伦-布鲁克·艾森.
⑧	Eisen	艾森
⑨	Ellebracht	艾尔布兰特，众议员
⑩	Hill	州众议员贾斯汀·希尔
⑪	Lohmar	洛马尔

附录：2019 年普利策评论奖全文本人物消息来源使用分析图表

文本	数目	消息来源	消息来源类型	消息来源具名性	消息来源话语呈现	消息来源故事建构	消息来源被处理方式
文本 1	1	布兰森	弱势人物	清晰	有	有	受害者
文本 2	2	马修·穆勒	强势人物	清晰	有	无	守护者
文本 3	3	批评家	强势人物	匿名	无	无	辩护方
	4	卡拉克律师	强势人物	清晰	有	无	守护者
	5	克里斯汀·布朗	弱势人物	清晰	有	有	受害者
文本 4	6	贝尔根	弱势人物	清晰	有	有	受害者
	7	法警	强势人物	匿名	无	无	对立方
	8	我	强势人物	清晰	无	无	守护者
文本 5	9	科里·布斯	弱势人物	清晰	有	有	受害者
	10	丽莎·福斯特	强势人物	清晰	无	无	守护者
	11	乔安娜·韦斯	强势人物	清晰	无	无	守护者
文本 6	12	艾米·穆尔	弱势人物	清晰	有	有	受害者
	13	我	强势人物	清晰	有	无	守护者
	14	玛丽·罗素	强势人物	清晰	有	无	守护者
文本 7	15	普瑞斯·琼斯	弱势人物	清晰	有	有	受害者
文本 8	16	吉姆·鲁斯特	强势人物	清晰	有	无	守护者
	17	格雷格·马西斯	强势人物	清晰	有	无	守护者
文本 9	18	阿利辛·拉普	弱势人物	清晰	有	有	受害者
文本 10	19	前布恩县法官奥克森汉德勒	强势人物	清晰	有	无	守护者
	20	圣查尔斯县检察官、共和党人蒂姆·洛马尔	强势人物	清晰	有	无	守护者
	21	众议员布鲁斯·德格鲁特	强势人物	清晰	有	无	守护者
	22	布伦南司法中心的律师和研究员劳伦-布鲁克·艾森	强势人物	清晰	有	无	守护者
	23	众议员马克·艾尔布兰特	强势人物	清晰	有	无	守护者
	24	众议员贾斯汀·希尔	强势人物	清晰	无	无	守护者

后　记

20世纪80年代，伴随着改革开放，国人也开启了对普利策新闻奖的关注。相比国际上众多的新闻奖项，普利策新闻奖在我国受关注程度颇高，每年4月，中国媒体都要报道关于最新一届普利策奖的获奖情况。在学界，对普利策奖的研究也构成了一种"情结"，40年来，从未中断。

普利策奖的创立者为该奖项设计的严格的评审标准和制度，被保留和发展，因而获奖作品能够具备相对稳定的专业水准，特别在文本新闻格局要素的周全和完备方面堪为"经典"。例如在对普利策突发新闻奖获奖作品消息来源的采集中发现，消息来源的数目、类别、层级性等指标都有较为突出的表现。而在对新闻评论文本的分析中发现，获奖作品也注重采访，注重消息来源的使用。

本书建立了两个全文本案例库。一个是2010年普利策突发新闻奖：克莱蒙斯枪杀四警察案；一个是2019年普利策新闻评论奖：密苏里州穷人被监禁罚款案。对这两个案例库的二十篇文本，该书进行了翻译和消息来源的标识、统计和分析。此外围绕着这两个案例库展开的危机传播与话语分析、突发新闻框架基模、中外新闻评论事实表达的差异等研究也逐步产生。

这本书的出版是国内关于普利策新闻奖获奖作品理论研究和话语分析的一次突破。感谢长春出版社出版《普利策新闻奖案例库及话语分析》，感谢编辑孙振波先生为此书出版付出的智慧和辛劳！

本书得到长安大学2020年研究生教育教学改革项目《普利策新闻奖文本案例库和话语分析》（300103101160）的资助。